Juveniles at Risk

Juveniles at Risk
A Plea for Preventive Justice

Christopher Slobogin and Mark R. Fondacaro

OXFORD
UNIVERSITY PRESS

OXFORD
UNIVERSITY PRESS

Oxford University Press, Inc., publishes works that further
Oxford University's objective of excellence
in research, scholarship, and education.

Oxford New York
Auckland Cape Town Dar es Salaam Hong Kong Karachi
Kuala Lumpur Madrid Melbourne Mexico City Nairobi
New Delhi Shanghai Taipei Toronto

With offices in
Argentina Austria Brazil Chile Czech Republic France Greece
Guatemala Hungary Italy Japan Poland Portugal Singapore
South Korea Switzerland Thailand Turkey Ukraine Vietnam

Published by Oxford University Press, Inc.
198 Madison Avenue, New York, New York 10016
www.oup.com

Oxford is a registered trademark of Oxford University Press

Library of Congress Cataloging-in-Publication Data

Slobogin, Christopher, 1951-
Juveniles at risk : a plea for preventive justice / Christopher Slobogin, Mark R. Fondacaro.
p. cm. — (American psychology-law society series)
Includes bibliographical references.
1. Juvenile delinquency. 2. Juvenile justice, Administration of. 3. Juvenile delinquents—Rehabilitation.
I. Fondacaro, Mark R., 1957- II. Title. III. Series.
HV9069.S64 2011
364.36—dc22 2010054223
ISBN: 978-0-19-977835-5

To my two favorite (grown-up) juveniles, Leslie and Lauren

-Christopher Slobogin

This book is inspired by Sal and Willie and dedicated to my loving wife, Sabrina.

-Mark R. Fondacaro

Series Foreword

This book series is sponsored by the American Psychology-Law Society (APLS). APLS is an interdisciplinary organization devoted to scholarship, practice, and public service in psychology and law. Its goals include advancing the contributions of psychology to the understanding of law and legal institutions through basic and applied research; promoting the education of psychologists in matters of law and the education of legal personnel in matters of psychology; and informing the psychological and legal communities and the general public of current research, educational, and service activities in the field of psychology and law. APLS membership includes psychologists from the academic, research, and clinical practice communities as well as members of the legal community. Research and practice is represented in both the civil and criminal legal arenas. APLS has chosen Oxford University Press as a strategic partner because of its commitment to scholarship, quality, and the international dissemination of ideas. These strengths will help APLS reach its goal of educating the psychology and legal professions and the general public about important developments in psychology and law. The focus of the book series reflects the diversity of the field of psychology and law, as we will publish books on a broad range of topics.

In the latest book in the series, *Juveniles at Risk: A Plea for Preventive Justice*, Christopher Slobogin and Mark R. Fondacaro propose a new conception of the juvenile court, based on risk management and prevention. This fresh approach reinvigorates the juvenile court's rehabilitative roots without succumbing to the paternalism that has led American courts to mandate adult-type procedures and legislatures to impose adult-type punishments in juvenile court. In addition, the focus on prevention dismisses the notion that culpability be the linchpin of the juvenile justice system.

Slobogin and Fondacaro begin by recounting the history of the juvenile court and describing four possible models of juvenile justice: rehabilitative, adult retribution, diminished retribution, and individual prevention. They then summarize the research on what is known about the causes of juvenile crime, how those causes might differ from those associated with adult crime, and the methods for reducing juvenile recidivism in an attempt to answer a number of important questions: Why do so many juveniles engage in bad behavior? What distinguishes juveniles who engage in such behavior from those who do not? Why do most juveniles who engage in antisocial behavior desist once they become adults? Why do some of these juveniles continue their wayward path even after the age of eighteen? Are there interventions that can reduce juvenile crime and the likelihood of crime in adulthood? The answers to these questions and conclusions drawn from this research provide the basis for the individual prevention model of juvenile justice presented in this book and justified from both theoretical and pragmatic perspectives.

Juveniles at Risk presents a detailed description of the individual prevention model and includes case studies that allow for comparison and contrast between this model and the rehabilitative and retributive regimes. Both the substantive aspects of juvenile justice as well as the procedural framework are described. Slobogin and Fondacaro discuss the implications of the available research and propose that due process in juvenile justice be reconceptualized in a way that allows empirical research and a performance-based management system to identify those procedures that might best promote fairness, accuracy, and efficiency. Concrete proposals are made with respect to competency requirements, the right to remain silent, the right to a jury trial, and various other components of the pretrial and trial process.

Scholars, policy makers, and practitioners will undoubtedly find that this book will shape the future of juvenile justice. The application of criminal law jurisprudence to juveniles and the connections made between the jurisprudence and social science findings about adolescents will appeal to scholars; the information on treatment efficacy and cost, the specific suggestions on how to implement substantive and procedural changes to the system, and the way in which the general theme of prevention can be used rhetorically to achieve real reform in the juvenile justice system will appeal to policy makers and those who advise them; and the wealth of advocacy data presented throughout will appeal to both legal and clinical practitioners. *Juveniles at Risk* is sure to revolutionize legal thinking about juvenile justice.

Patricia A. Zapf
Series Editor

Preface

Between 15 percent and 20 percent of all crime in the United States is committed by people younger than eighteen. Each year, one out of every eight juveniles between the ages of fourteen and eighteen is arrested for a criminal offense, and by age seventeen well over 20 percent of youths (and well over 40 percent of male youths) engage in at least one serious assault, drug crime, or theft.* This book is about these youthful offenders. It proposes a new way of thinking about how the legal system should treat them and maps out a fairly detailed plan of implementation.

Since the beginning of the last century, the American legal system has been extremely ambivalent about how to handle juvenile offenders. Should they be treated like adults, children, or some mixture of the two? Should they be punished severely, receive treatment, or be subjected to a hybrid approach? To what extent should the courts provide them with adult procedural protections?

We wrote this book because we believe the current approach to the juvenile crime problem is insufficiently conceptualized and too beholden to myths about youth, the crimes they commit, and effective means of responding to their problems. The currently dominant punitive approach to juvenile justice, modeled on the adult criminal justice system, either ignores or misapplies current knowledge about the causes of juvenile crime and the means of reducing it. We argue that,

* Bureau of Justice Statistics, 2007 National Report, Criminal Offenders, Table 32, available at www.ojjdp.ncjrs.org/ojstatbb/nr2006/downloads/chapter3.pdf; 2006 National Report, Juvenile Offenders 70, available at www.fbi.gov/ucr/cius2007/data/table_32.html.

with some significant adjustments that take this new knowledge into account, the legal system should continue to maintain a separate juvenile court, but one that is preventive in orientation, with a new emphasis on both rehabilitation and flexible procedures. The view that culpability should be the linchpin of juvenile justice (touted by liberals as well as conservatives) is misguided, not only because it leads to unnecessarily harsh punishment but also because it deemphasizes crime-reducing interventions and undermines the case for handling adolescent offenders through a system that is independent of the culpability-based adult system. The currently popular view that adult-type procedures should govern the juvenile process is also open to serious doubt, given social science research that questions the extent to which such procedures promote accuracy and fairness.

We hope the proposals made in this book will provide policy makers, judges, lawyers, and interested citizens grounds for questioning and improving current juvenile court practice. For their feedback and assistance during this project, we would like to thank Lois Weithorn, the late Charles Whitebread, Barbara Woodhouse, and members of workshops and conferences at the 2010 Law and Society Conference, Brooklyn Law School, John Jay College of Criminal Justice, Ohio State Law School, San Diego Law School, the University of Florida Levin College of Law, Vanderbilt University Law School, Wayne State Law School, and Washington University School of Law. We also want to acknowledge that parts of this book are based on work one or both of us previously authored, which has been adapted with permission from the relevant editors. In the approximate order in which they influence this book, they are Christopher Slobogin, Four Visions of Juvenile Justice, in *Children as Victims, Witnesses and Offenders: Psychological Science and the Law* (Bette L. Bottoms, Gail S. Goodman, & Cynthia J. Jajdowski, eds., 2009); Mark R. Fondacaro and Lauren G. Fasig, Judging Juvenile Responsibility: A Social Ecological Perspective, in *Handbook of Children, Culture, and Violence* 355–373 (Nancy E. Dowd, Dorothy G. Singer, & Robin Fretwell Wilson, eds., 2006); Christopher Slobogin and Mark Fondacaro, Juvenile Justice: The Fourth Option, 95 *Iowa Law Review* 1 (2009); Christopher Slobogin, Treating Kids Right: Deconstructing and Reconstructing the Amenability to Treatment Concept, 10 *Journal of Contemporary Legal Issues* 299 (1999); Christopher Slobogin, Mark R. Fondacaro, and Jennifer Woolard, A Prevention Model of Juvenile Justice: The Promise of Kansas v. Hendricks for Children, 1999 *Wisconsin Law Review* 185; Mark Fondacaro, Christopher Slobogin, and Tricia Cross, Reconceptualizing Due Process in Juvenile Justice: Contributions from Law and Social Science, 57 *Hastings Law Journal* 955 (2006).

Christopher Slobogin
Milton Underwood Professor of Law
Vanderbilt University Law School

Mark R. Fondacaro
Professor of Psychology
John Jay College of Criminal Justice
City University of New York

Contents

Juveniles at Risk

1

Juvenile Justice in Flux

C.D. grew up in the projects of Baltimore. As he reached adolescence, he came to believe that, as he put it, "there was more going on in the street corner than in the classroom." In order to earn the respect of his peers, C.D. actually tried to get *into* prison, because "you gained 'rep' by being tough." He eventually was involved in a knife fight and convicted of manslaughter. In prison he punched a guard during a riot. He spent over thirteen years incarcerated, including a long stint in solitary confinement.

When he was sixteen, R.D.B. took a car away from its owner at gunpoint and went on a joyride with a friend. He later said, "I did it for all kinds of reasons I can't clearly reason out. At that moment I wanted to do it, and I had no idea that it would define me for the rest of my life." He spent his remaining teenage years in prison, trying to maintain his "sanity," living in a prison environment ruled by violence.

From the time he was seven L.R. stole things. By the time he was eleven, he was a member of a Los Angeles gang. As a teenager, "I was destructive and self-destructive. I was willing to shoot, stab and even kill for the gang—and I was willing to die for the gang as well." By age fifteen he had been arrested several times for theft and assault, become addicted to drugs, and been expelled from school and from home. At seventeen, he engaged in a revenge shooting and was convicted of assault with intent to commit murder. That offense carried a maximum sentence of six years, although he ended up serving a much shorter sentence in county jail.

Despite their tough beginnings, all three of these individuals became productive citizens. C.D., or Charles Dutton, developed into a respected actor and director and received two Tony Award nominations and an Emmy Award. R.D.B., or R. Dwayne Betts, is now a well-known poet, who has won numerous writing contests and scholarships. L.R., or Luis Rodriguez, is also an acclaimed writer and poet who has published fourteen books.[1] Perhaps prison scared the first two "straight" while the more lenient treatment of Rodriguez enabled him to get his act together. Perhaps these individuals would have succeeded regardless of their contact with the court system. There is no way to know for sure. But we do know that thousands of juveniles like them end up with long criminal records and that many do not desist from crime until much later in life.

These facts are made disturbingly clear in two books published in the 1990s about adolescent offenders, one focusing on Los Angeles and the other on Chicago. In the Pulitzer prize-winning book *No Matter How Loud I Shout*, Edward Humes paints a picture of a completely dysfunctional Los Angeles juvenile justice system where "each side in the process—the prosecutors, the defenders, the judges, cops and probation officers, the crime victims, the kids on trial . . . and their families—sees itself as being on the one and only losing side."[2] According to Humes, adolescent offenders who could be "saved" are routinely sent to detention or adult prison and forgotten, while adolescents who may be unsalvageable are sometimes released because an overburdened system cannot accommodate them. The result is that while over half of the juveniles arrested for crime are never arrested again, roughly a quarter become recidivists who continue criminal activity through adolescence, and the remainder (over 15%) become chronic offenders, committing offenses ranging between theft and murder.[3] In *A Kind and Just Parent*, William Ayers tells an equally powerful and depressing story about a Chicago juvenile court system whose extremely high caseloads, caused in part by the inundation of the system with "minor problems," tends to overlook juvenile offenders who commit more serious crime.[4] The latter offenders usually spend considerable time in detention which, according to Ayers, "teaches youngsters to temper their commitments, to check their emotions, to avoid intimacy, to live inside themselves," and makes life with a gang much more likely as "the culture and distrust and loneliness inside the joint strengthens formal organization affiliations that boys bring with them."[5]

Do adolescent offenders, often immature and heedless, "deserve" their sentences? Should they instead be offered or forced to undergo treatment programs? Is the best approach some mix of punishment and rehabilitation?

Perhaps most important, whatever disposition is chosen, should it be meted out by a justice system separate from the adult system or administered through the criminal justice system? Every state in this country has established a court system for juvenile offenders that is independent of the adult criminal system. This book explores whether this separate juvenile justice system should continue to exist and, if so, in what form. We will not offer a magic bullet solution for the types of problems outlined above. What we do propose is a reimagination of the legal basis for the juvenile court that facilitates its use as a way of ensuring that juvenile offenders end up on the right track rather than in prison. Conceived of as a crime prevention mechanism rather than as simply a vehicle for punishment or treatment, a separate juvenile court makes eminent sense and can be assured a promising future.

* * *

Four Visions of Juvenile Justice

The juvenile justice system is a relatively modern innovation. The first juvenile court did not come into being in this country until the turn of the last century, and the concept was not universally embraced in the United States until the 1930s.[6] The jurisdiction of the juvenile court has varied considerably over time, with respect to both the types of acts that trigger jurisdiction and the circumstances under which that jurisdiction is surrendered to adult court through the process known as "transfer" or "waiver of juvenile court jurisdiction." The typical juvenile justice regime over the past century has focused on youth under eighteen who have committed acts that would be a crime if committed by an adult, and has permitted transfer of youth over fourteen who have committed serious crimes and are considered unamenable to treatment in the juvenile system. But some states have experimented with other approaches, including establishing age cutoffs above and below eighteen, extending the juvenile courts' reach to youth who have merely misbehaved rather than committed a crime, and permitting or requiring transfer for children as young as seven for certain types of crimes.

However constructed, until relatively recently most juvenile court systems differed significantly from adult criminal court in virtually all respects, including their rationale, their dispositions, and their procedures. Punishment for adults is generally justified by the need to exact retribution, that is, to ensure that an offender receives his or her "just deserts" based on the perceived degree of culpability, and the goal of general deterrence, that is, the imposition of punishment sufficient to scare off would-be offenders. Although rehabilitation of the offender has from time to time been a strongly espoused goal in the adult system, dispositions in that system are often harsh, involving prison, and the procedures in adult court reflect that fact by imposing a heavy burden on the state to prove its case and providing criminal defendants with a plethora of rights. In contrast, in the traditional juvenile court system rehabilitation was the preeminent goal. Young offenders were often subjected to restraint, but usually for shorter, more indeterminate periods of time than adults, and much larger percentages of offenders were diverted out of the system to some type of treatment program. As a result, procedures in juvenile court were relatively informal, similar to an adult sentencing hearing rather than a criminal trial.

Between the late 1960s and the present, however, the juvenile system's philosophy and structure have increasingly come to mimic the adult system in full. Spurred, on one side, by courts and commentators worried about overuse and abuse of juvenile court jurisdiction, and on the other side, by a public concerned about increasing juvenile crime rates, legislatures have narrowed juvenile court jurisdiction, nudged what is left of that jurisdiction toward a punishment orientation that often downplays treatment, and imposed adult criminal trial procedures and determinate sentences. In at least some states, the two systems seem on the verge of becoming one, and many commentators advocate just such a merger, albeit usually with some special dispositional accommodations for children.[7]

Given this history, the usual story told about the juvenile justice system is that it must follow one of three paths. The "rehabilitation" path, which probably comes closest to the original motivation for establishing a separate court for juveniles, treats youths in trouble as innocent and salvageable beings who must be kept away from adult criminals to enhance their chances of becoming productive citizens. On this view, the triggering act need not be criminal, disposition is designed to make the child a better person, and confinement meant as punishment is to be avoided. The second path—what could be called the "adult retribution" model—heads in the opposite direction. In vogue among many state legislatures in recent years, it assumes that many young people who commit crime are fully accountable individuals who should usually be punished in the same fashion as adults. This path leads to broad transfer-to-adult-court jurisdiction, adult-like sentences in juvenile court, or both. The third option, which probably represents the consensus academic view as well as the practice in a number of jurisdictions, sits somewhere between the rehabilitative and adult retribution approaches. It treats juveniles as neither innocent nor fully culpable, but rather posits that their responsibility is diminished because of their youth. Under this "diminished retribution" model, dispositions are discounted proportionate to the juvenile's degree of immaturity, either on an individual basis or categorically.

These are, again, the usual alternatives put forward when juvenile justice is discussed. But there is a fourth option, an option this book will call "individual prevention." Under this model of juvenile justice, adolescents who commit crimes are not treated as though they are innocent or simply in need of redirection. But, once adjudicated guilty of an offense (a phrase we use in place of "convicted" for the same reasons most modern juvenile court systems avoid the latter term[8]), their dispositions are not designed to punish them, either. Rather the goal, pure and simple, is prevention of further crime. Framed in terms of the traditional purposes of the criminal justice system, the focus of the individual prevention model is specific deterrence through treatment and, if necessary, incapacitation. Because of its focus on treatment, the individual prevention path is closely related to the rehabilitation vision. Unlike the rehabilitative model, however, this path avoids claiming that juveniles are excused because of their youth, retains the retributive models' threshold requirement of a criminal act, and is narrowly focused on policies and procedures that promote recidivism-reduction rather than the broader goal of creating a well-socialized individual. The individual prevention model's primary divergence from the two retributive models is its rejection of relative culpability as the basis for the duration and type of disposition. Instead of that metric, the prevention model favors assessments of risk that vary the intervention depending on the most effective, least restrictive means of curbing future crime.

Under the individual prevention model, Charles Dutton and R. Dwayne Betts would not have been thrown in prison for years, and Luis Rodriguez would probably have been handled differently as well. While all three individuals would have been held accountable for their illegal behavior, long-term confinement would have been off the table, and even short-term confinement might not have been necessary. In cases like these, detention would be a last resort. Interventions, targeted at risk factors that are associated with crime, would usually take place in the community. Retrospective retributive punishment would take a backseat to forward-looking prevention.

This book takes the position that the individual prevention approach to juvenile justice is preferable to the other three models. After fleshing out the contours of the four models from a historical perspective, this chapter summarizes that argument. It ends with a chapter-by-chapter preview of the book.

The Early History of the Juvenile Court

The history of the juvenile court provides exemplars of all four models of juvenile justice, although legislatures and courts have not been as explicit about endorsing the individual prevention model as they have been in considering the other three models. The rehabilitative vision strongly informed the very first juvenile court, begun in the late nineteenth century in Chicago. Jane Addams, who helped establish the court, described its operation as follows:

> The child was brought before the judge with no one to prosecute him and with no one to defend him—the judge and all concerned were merely trying to find out what could be done on his behalf. The element of conflict was absolutely eliminated and with it, all notion of punishment.[9]

Ben Lindsey, an early juvenile court judge who wholeheartedly subscribed to this vision, similarly opined that "Our laws against crime were as inapplicable to children as they would be to idiots."[10] In the eyes of these progenitors, juvenile offenders were blameless. As summarized by one commentator, the original juvenile court movement "assumed that young people under an articulated statutory age (sometimes as high as 21 years of age) are incapable of rational decisionmaking and thus lack the capacity for moral accountability assumed by the punitive model."[11]

Under a rehabilitative model, then, the state is implementing its *parens patriae* (government as parent) power, not its police power.[12] The goal of the juvenile court is to help, not sanction. Although no court, not even the one championed by Addams, consistently endorsed the youth-as-innocents concept,[13] the rehabilitative model it spawned still heavily influences discussions of juvenile justice. The vision has both substantive and procedural implications, vestiges of which are visible today.

The principal substantive implication of the rehabilitative model is that the grounds for intervention are quite wide ranging. For instance, Judge Lindsey thought the court should ask, "Is the child . . . given to playing 'hookey' from school, or 'bumming' and running away, showing an entire lack of ambition or desire to work and settle down to regular habits?"[14] Julian Mack, another early juvenile court judge, asked, "Why is it not the duty of the state, instead of asking merely whether a boy or girl has committed a special offense, to find out what he is, physically, mentally, morally . . . ?"[15] From these types of sentiments rose an expansion of juvenile court jurisdiction beyond the law of (adult) crimes to include so-called status offenses, such as truancy, disobedience, and incorrigibility. For example, one statute defined as "delinquent" any youth who

> knowingly associates with thieves, vicious or immoral persons; or, who, without just cause and without the consent of its parents or custodian, absents itself from its home or place of abode, or who is growing up in idleness or crime; . . . or who patronizes or visits any public pool room or bucket shop; or wanders about the streets in the night time without being on any lawful business or occupation; or who habitually wanders about any railroad yards or tracks or jumps or attempts to jump into any moving train; . . . or who habitually uses vile, obscene, vulgar, profane or indecent language; or who is guilty of immoral conduct in any public place or about any school house.[16]

Reminiscent of vagrancy statutes eventually declared unconstitutional by the Supreme Court,[17] these types of laws gave juvenile court judges discretion to intervene in the lives of vast numbers of youth. And those interventions were sometimes quite intrusive. For instance, the "child-savers," as Anthony Platt dubbed them, believed that young offenders needed to be removed from their environment and detained in "reformatories."[18] These institutions were meant to be "guarded sanctuaries, combining love and guidance with firmness and restraint," and they were aimed at protecting their inmates "from idleness, indulgence, and luxuries through military drill, physical exercise, and constant supervision."[19] One still sees vestiges of the rehabilitative approach today in residential programs that focus on "milieu treatment" (involving residents in day-to-day interaction through psychotherapeutic discussion) and "behavioral token programs" (where youths are rewarded for conforming to rules), as well as in counseling programs that combine individual psychotherapy with close supervision.[20]

On the procedural side, the rehabilitative model counseled against procedures that would limit judges' ability to learn everything about their charges. Judge Mack described his view of the ideal juvenile court procedure as follows: "Seated at a desk, with the child at his side, where he can on occasion put his arm around his shoulder and draw the lad to him, the judge, while losing none of his judicial dignity, will gain immensely in the effectiveness of his work."[21] Since, as Addams put it in the language quoted above, "the element of conflict was absolutely eliminated" in the *parens patriae* juvenile court, no formal conflict resolution process was necessary.

Thus, the outline of the rehabilitative model is clear. Juveniles are to be excused and treated, not punished, for their antisocial behavior. That behavior need not amount to crime, because the primary goal is to improve the psychological well-being and socialization of the child, through isolation from the corrupting environment if necessary. Because the goal is treatment in the broadest and most paternalistic sense, procedures should not get in the way of finding out as much about the juvenile as possible. As one commentary described it, the progenitors of the juvenile court viewed it as "a legal bridge between the troubled child and the agencies of amelioration."[22]

Substantive Reforms

Most of the history of the juvenile court in the past half-century has consisted of backing away from the substantive and procedural implications of the rehabilitation vision. On the substantive side, much of the movement has been along the adult retribution path. Even in the early days of the juvenile court, judges found ways to transfer to adult court juveniles who committed serious crimes or appeared to be particularly dangerous.[23] The steadiest progression toward a harsher juvenile court, however, has been during the past thirty years. Since 1979, transfer jurisdiction has expanded dramatically in most states, in terms of both the age at which it attaches and the types of crimes that can trigger it. As a result, transfers of juveniles have increased at least 70 percent.[24] Further, the number of states that permit automatic transfer (rather than leaving that decision to the discretion of the juvenile court) has more than doubled to thirty-one, and thirteen states have lowered the age at which juvenile court jurisdiction ends to fifteen or sixteen. For those juveniles who remain in juvenile court, roughly half the states have adopted some version of "blended" sentencing that permits imposition of adult sentences on juveniles, albeit with the option of suspending a portion of the sentence under certain circumstances.[25]

There appear to be two dominant reasons that the adult retribution model has been so attractive during the last three decades. First, reformers believed that juvenile crime was increasing significantly (a perception that turns out to be inaccurate for most of that time period).[26] Second, advocates for a more punitive model assumed that juvenile offenders are, in the words of one prosecutor, "criminals who happen to be young, not children who happen to be criminal."[27] On this view, juveniles who commit adult crimes should pay the same price adult offenders pay, at least when the crimes are serious.

Not all who believed youth should be held accountable for their crimes endorsed this adult retribution stance, however. In the forefront of this group were the drafters of the American Bar Association's (ABA) Juvenile Justice Standards, which were promulgated in 1980. Consistent with a retributive, just desert stance, the standards recommended that juvenile court dispositions be based on the offense, not the offender; for the same reason, they also rejected status offenses. Specifically, the standards provided both that "sanctions should be proportionate to the seriousness of the offense [and] fixed or determinate as declared by the court after a hearing" and that "noncriminal misbehavior (status offenses or conduct that would not be a crime if committed by an adult) should be removed from juvenile court jurisdiction."[28] But the drafters of the standards also believed that juveniles' relative immaturity required lesser punishment than that meted out to adults who committed the same crimes. Thus, according to the standards, crimes requiring a twenty-year sentence in adult court might necessitate only a three-year sentence in juvenile court.[29]

More recent writers, supported by empirical findings that adolescents are more impulsive, less future oriented, and more subject to peer influence than adults, have made an even more nuanced case for maintaining a separate juvenile system grounded on this diminished responsibility assumption.[30] The standard conclusion of this view is that most youth who commit crime before age eighteen should be tried and sentenced in juvenile court, with transfer limited to only the most serious, mature offenders. Although in recent times the diminished retribution model has been less popular among legislatures than the adult retribution vision, its influence is apparent in the large number of states that mete out relatively short determinate sentences for juvenile offenders who are not transferred to adult court.[31]

Throughout these developments, the individual prevention model and the goal of recidivism reduction played a secondary, albeit influential, role. Judge Mack illustrated the subtle manner in which the *parens patriae* position approached the issue when he famously stated: "The problem for determination by the judge is not Has this boy or girl committed a specific wrong but What is he, How has he become what he is, and What had best be done in his interest *and in the interest of the state* to save him from a downward career."[32] The drafters of the Juvenile Justice Standards, although focused on just deserts, also obliquely recognized that protection of the public is a legitimate goal of juvenile justice; the standards do not specifically designate public safety as one of the purposes of juvenile justice sanctions,[33] but their dispositional provisions do indicate that probation conditions should take into account "whether the juvenile presents a substantial danger to others."[34] And the most punitive reforms of recent times were driven in part by the specter of the soulless juvenile "superpredator" who, unless confined, would routinely harm others.[35]

Thus, as one would expect, every approach to juvenile justice voices the desire to reduce juvenile crime. But the central focus of the other visions is elsewhere. The rehabilitative model hopes first and foremost to help the child, as Judge Mack's words indicate. The retributive models are, by definition, meant to punish for past acts, not prevent future ones, with the result that any achievement of the latter goal is an incidental effect of disposition. The individual prevention vision, in contrast, makes its primary objective the prevention of crime; helping the offender is an incidental goal, and interventions solely for the sake of exacting retribution are rejected.

In a regime where individual prevention is the guiding principle, the scope of the juvenile justice system would be significantly different than under the other models. Compared to the retributive models, it would be broader in some respects and narrower in others. Pre-teen children who might not be "blameworthy" enough to deserve significant punishment might nonetheless be thought to pose a risk and thus be in need of serious intervention in an individual prevention regime (although confinement in a detention facility would be the last resort under the individual prevention model, not the primary dispositional vehicle it is in a retributive regime). At the same time, many adolescents who commit serious offenses might be subject to minimal intervention if they pose minimal risk, despite the harm they have caused or their relatively significant culpability. Furthermore, transfer to adult court would never occur in a prevention regime because, regardless of how "culpable" a juvenile offender might be, the risk he or she represents can always be handled within the juvenile justice system, in confined space if need be.

Compared to the rehabilitative model, the scope of an individual prevention regime would be narrower in a different sense. Although in theory a preventive regime does not require any triggering conduct if risk can be proven in some other way, in fact the conduct underlying many status offenses and other "immoral" behavior is seldom strong evidence of risk (which will usually require some type of crime), and thus intervention will not be as likely in an individual prevention model. Nor is the scope of intervention likely to be as extensive as in a rehabilitative regime, since programs designed to "reform" and "educate" may go far beyond what is necessary to reduce crime, as the experience during the "child-saving" era illustrates.

Modern statutes tend to mix the four models together, with the result that none of them is found in its pure form. Most transfer statutes, for instance, either state or are interpreted to mean that waiver of juvenile court jurisdiction should be reserved for those juvenile offenders who are the most culpable *and* dangerous.[36] Blending of the models is even more evident in provisions describing the purpose behind dispositions of those offenders tried in juvenile court. For instance, in Idaho the juvenile code states that "the primary purpose of this act is to provide a continuum of programs which emphasize the juvenile offender's accountability for his actions while assisting him in the development of skills necessary to function effectively and positively in the community in a manner consistent with public safety."[37] Virginia's statute requires juvenile courts not only "to divert. . . , consistent with the protection of the public safety, those children who can be cared for or treated through alternative programs," but also requires the courts "to protect the community, . . . to reduce the incidence of delinquent behavior and to hold offenders accountable for their behavior."[38] Both statutes indicate that juveniles are to be held "accountable" but both also clearly emphasize rehabilitation, aimed primarily at protecting the public.[39]

Procedural Reforms

Reform of the procedural aspects of the juvenile system began in the 1950s, as scholars and courts began to criticize the informal nature of the rehabilitative model.[40] The reform movement came to its fruition in 1967, in the U.S. Supreme Court's decision in *In re Gault.*[41] Concerned that juvenile defendants were being subjected to long-term confinement via court proceedings that barely deserved the name, the Court held that juveniles charged with acts of delinquency are constitutionally entitled to counsel, notice of the charges, and the right to confront their accusers, as well as the right to remain silent.

Although this importation of adult criminal procedure into the juvenile court preceded by ten to fifteen years the most pervasive attempts to impose a retributive model on juvenile justice, it is nonetheless closely tied conceptually to both retributive visions. A system based on desert requires proof that a crime has been committed with the requisite degree of culpability and results in punishment commensurate with blameworthiness. Thus, in contrast to a rehabilitative model in which conflict is, at least in theory, minimized, the retributive models represent the "criminal prosecution" referenced in the Sixth Amendment, which mandates *Gault*-type rights in adult criminal court. In line with this view, the ABA's Juvenile Justice Standards not only required that juvenile offenders be accorded all the rights specifically guaranteed in *Gault* but also granted them a right to a public trial, in front of a jury, and mandated that the adult rules of evidence apply in juvenile court proceedings.[42]

The individual prevention vision of juvenile justice has somewhat different procedural implications. Because, like the rehabilitative model, it is not punishment oriented, the case for applying the full panoply of adult rights is not as clear-cut under such a model as it is under the retributive models. Of course, *Gault's* holding applies to juvenile court regardless of its substantive orientation. But it is important to note that despite its Sixth Amendment undertones, *Gault* was based on the due process clause, a much more flexible constitutional provision that does not necessarily require full-fledged adversarial procedures.[43] As a constitutional matter, therefore, adjustments to the adult procedural model flowing from the special aspects of juvenile court are possible, and an individual prevention regime would be likely to take advantage of that possibility if adult procedures such as juries, hearsay bans, and the right to remain silent made risk assessment difficult. At the same time, because determinations of risk must be as accurate as possible, those modifications are not likely to lead to the extremely informal processes that a paternalistic rehabilitative model would permit.

As in the substantive arena, the actual process followed in modern juvenile courts often represents a mix of paradigms. *Gault's* procedural reforms have dramatically changed the way most juvenile courts operate. The early juvenile courts "used informal procedures, excluded lawyers and juries, and adopted a euphemistic vocabulary to de-emphasize any resemblance to criminal proceedings."[44] The hearings tended to consist of dialogues between the judge and the youthful suspect, and the rules of evidence were ignored. Today, in contrast, states are required to provide juvenile defendants with lawyers in serious cases, the use of hearsay is limited, and defendants need not say anything in court if they assert their right to remain silent.[45] At the same time, *Gault's* prescriptions have not always been strictly implemented in practice, and indeed *Gault* itself cautioned that they should not be "ruthlessly administered."[46] As Barry Feld has noted, "despite formal changes of the 'laws on the books,' the 'law in action' lagged behind and most states failed to deliver legal services."[47] Whereas in theory the procedures associated with the retributive model are now the norm in juvenile court, in practice the juvenile court process in many states tends to resemble a watered-down version of the adult process.

The Thesis of the Book

The rehabilitative, adult retribution, diminished retribution, and individual prevention models of juvenile justice are just that—models; as the foregoing discussion made clear, most states have declined to adopt any of these models in their pure form, either substantively or procedurally. Nonetheless, with respect to the substantive focus of the juvenile court system, we believe the individual prevention model is superior to the other models. The procedural advantages of any particular model are less clear because of the paucity of relevant research, but here too there is reason to believe that neither the procedural formality of adult/retributive model nor the extreme informality of the rehabilitation-oriented court is optimal.

Below we summarize the case for preferring the individual prevention model as a substantive matter, a case that is developed in full in Chapters 2, 3, and 4 (our analysis of procedural issues and related prescriptions for reform are reserved for Chapter 5). There are three reasons for adopting the substantive focus of the individual prevention model. First, it fits best with our current knowledge about the causes and treatment of youthful offending. Second, it is the easiest to justify under current legal doctrine. Third, it provides the most persuasive explanation for maintaining a separate juvenile justice system. Such an explanation is essential if we want to take full advantage of advances in empirical knowledge about juvenile offending. It is also crucial if we want to resist the next—inevitable—swing of the pendulum toward a get-tough approach to juvenile crime.

The Implications of Recent Research

Consider first what we know about juveniles who commit crime. Recent research, described in more detail in Chapter 2, can be summarized in terms of three important findings, relating to the psychology, context, and treatment of juvenile offending. First, while juvenile offenders above the age of nine or ten normally can form criminal intent and understand the wrongfulness of their actions in a shallow sense, both pre-teen and teen offenders are less likely than adults—for a host of psychological and biological reasons—to consider the consequences of their actions or the prospect of punishment. Second, while juvenile offending, like adult offending, is in part the result of "internal" desires and beliefs, it is also particularly prone to the influence of context—peers, families, and neighborhoods. Third, following naturally from the second finding, the most successful way to reduce most juvenile offending is not incapacitation in a detention facility—a disposition that studies show is likely to increase recidivism—but rather intervention in the community specifically designed to ameliorate or eliminate the contextual risk factors, as well as psychological risk factors, associated with crime.

The first set of findings, on the psychology of juvenile offenders, indicates that adolescents are not "innocent" as a legal matter, thus undercutting the key premise of the rehabilitative model. But it also suggests that youthful offenders are less culpable than adult criminals, and thus are not ideal candidates for the adult retribution approach. These two conclusions might seem to support the diminished retribution model. But in fact they do not, because current criminal law doctrine requires very serious impairment before culpability mitigation can occur. For instance, adult criminal offenders with a mental disability rarely receive reduced sentences, yet their legally relevant capacities are substantially more diminished than those of the typical teenager. Moreover, the most significant traits of adolescent immaturity are not compromised cognitive abilities but rather impulsivity and a tendency to give in to peer pressure, traits that seldom support a case in mitigation for adults.

In contrast, the research on the psychology and context of juvenile crime strongly supports the premises of the individual-prevention model, which neither assumes that juvenile offenders are innocent, nor attributes significance to gradations in culpability between adults and adolescents. As we explain later, for prudential reasons an individual prevention regime would require an adjudication of guilt for a criminal act as a predicate for intervention and thus, unlike the rehabilitative model, would not treat the juvenile offender as blameless. At the same time, unlike the retributive models, the all-important dispositional decision in a prevention regime is focused on risk. Thus neither the outcome in individual cases nor the operation of the system as a whole relies on the proposition that juveniles are fully culpable (as contemplated by the adult retribution model) or the equally questionable proposition that they are substantially less culpable than adults (the premise of the diminished retribution model).

A similar analysis applies to the second set of empirical findings, to the effect that contextual factors heavily influence juvenile offenders. While perhaps useful as an explanatory matter and thus sympathy inducing, these types of research conclusions usually would not be given legally mitigating effect in the adult criminal justice setting. Thus, once again science is ignored by the adult-retribution model, which considers the debilitating effects of context irrelevant, and provides only tenuous support for the diminished-retribution model, which requires that those effects be seriously compromising. In contrast, the findings regarding the ecological etiology of juvenile offending are of much more relevance in rehabilitation and individual-prevention regimes, and particularly so in the latter type of system, where they can be extremely helpful in devising instruments for assessing risk and in designing post-adjudication programs that reduce the antisocial effects of immaturity and environment.

The third major research finding—that juvenile crime is most effectively reduced through community interventions specifically aimed at antisocial conduct—also fits more comfortably with an individual prevention approach than with the other three approaches. Because the goal under the individual prevention model is public safety, these community-based programs should be the disposition of choice. This conclusion is not as clearly warranted, however, in a purely rehabilitative regime, which might endorse any program, including segregation, that can help the juvenile "improve." And endorsement of a community-based dispositional regime is even more difficult under the adult and diminished retribution models. Adult punishment is usually associated with some type of imprisonment, not community-based programs. Even punishment that has been discounted due to juvenile immaturity is hard to square with such programs, especially if, as advocates of the diminished responsibility model contemplate, transfer to adult court is still on the table. Thus, an honestly applied retributive regime—adult or diminished—cannot take full advantage of advances in reducing juvenile recidivism and, indeed, is likely to lead to higher levels of recidivism given the finding that incarceration tends to exacerbate the reoffending rate.

Jurisprudential Considerations

The individual prevention model is also the easiest to justify as a jurisprudential matter. The foregoing discussion should make clear why the legal justifications for the other three options are weak. The rehabilitative model cannot be sustained by the myth that adolescent offenders are legally innocent of crime. The only alternative rationale for that model—that youth are more amenable to treatment and therefore can be coercively rehabilitated any time they need treatment—probably runs afoul of constitutional restrictions on the state's *parens patriae* power. The adult retribution model is also on shaky ground, because it fails to take into account the immaturity of most adolescents. Finally, the diminished responsibility model ascribes *too much* mitigating effect to juvenile immaturity. Fifteen-, sixteen-, and seventeen-year-olds, the age groups that commit most juvenile crime, are much closer to adults than preadolescents on the traditional measures of criminal desert.

Compared to these rationales, the justification for the individual prevention model—reduction of criminal recidivism—is more compelling. Because it is aimed at preventing crime, it more obviously benefits both youthful offenders and the public than does punishment meted out as a matter of desert. But it does so without endorsing the blunderbuss therapeutic approach associated with the rehabilitative model.

Moreover, the Supreme Court has endorsed the individual prevention rationale as a constitutional matter. In the 1997 decision of *Kansas v. Hendricks*[48] the Court upheld against a substantive due process challenge sexual predator statutes that permit post-sentence commitment, so long as they require proof that the offender has difficulty controlling his or her antisocial behavior. In other words, the Court held that individuals whose lack of volitional control makes them relatively undeterrable may be preventively detained if necessary to prevent recidivism. By analogy, one can argue that the same indicia of immaturity in juveniles that reduce culpability—impulsivity, attraction to risk, and peer-driven behavior—also decrease deterrability or responsiveness to social norms and thus would permit preventive intervention, ideally designed to increase deterrability.

Admittedly, a purely preventive system, or even one that, like the one proposed here, requires a predicate criminal act, is anathema to many because of its association with indeterminate detention and a dehumanizing therapeutic state. For instance, sexual predator statutes can and have authorized indeterminate, lifelong commitment for autonomous offenders who ordinarily would be subject to determinate punishment.[49] However, the potential abuses associated with an individual prevention regime are mitigated substantially when applied to juvenile offenders. Given the durational limitation on juvenile court jurisdiction, long-term indeterminate confinement would be rare. Nor would preventive intervention in the juvenile setting represent the insult to autonomy that a similar system in the adult context would, given the actual and perceived relative immaturity of juveniles.

In short, whatever its viability might be in the adult setting, the individual prevention model is a good jurisprudential fit with the juvenile justice system. The debate over whether a retributive approach to *adult* criminal justice is preferable to one that focuses on utilitarian goals of incapacitation, specific deterrence, and rehabilitation has a long pedigree and is in something of a stalemate today.[50] But in the special context of juvenile justice, the scale tips decidedly in favor of the latter agenda.

Political Arguments

The final advantage of the individual prevention model is that it is more likely to ensure the political future of a truly separate juvenile justice system, a goal that most observers of the system share. None of the other models explain as well why juvenile offenders should be handled differently from adult offenders. The adult retribution model obviously pushes in the opposite direction, given its equation of juveniles with adults. While the rehabilitative model does offer something quite different from the adult criminal justice system, it blatantly fails to satisfy the public's or legislatures' appetite for assuring accountability for crimes or their desire for protection against dangerous individuals.

The diminished retribution model appears to be a plausible compromise between the two. But, like the adult retribution model, it too ultimately fails to draw a significant enough distinction between adolescent and adult offenders. Even if, contrary to the assertion of this book, adolescents are less culpable than adults in a legally significant way, the most efficient method of recognizing that lesser culpability—and therefore a very tempting political option in an era of limited budgets and pressure to be tough on crime—is simply to try juveniles in adult court and reduce their sentence length proportionately. Under the diminished responsibility model there is no need for both a juvenile and an adult system because both use the same metric: culpability. The diminished responsibility model is understandably popular among juvenile advocates because it appears to avoid the harshness of the adult system, but it is flawed because it fails to distinguish juveniles sufficiently from adults.

A juvenile justice system focused on individual prevention, in contrast, is based on an entirely different construct than the criminal justice system. It is forward looking rather than backward looking. Its principal aim is reducing crime, not punishing it. The public and legislators can honestly be told that a separate juvenile justice system is necessary because its priorities are so dissimilar from those of the adult system. Moreover, the public is likely to perceive this message positively; at bottom, surveys show, the public is more interested in rehabilitating juveniles than punishing them, so long as the rehabilitation is focused on reducing crime.[51] As a leading criminological researcher stated, "I have found very few policy makers unwilling to at least listen to the empirical research when you frame it within the context of public protection."[52] The longevity of the juvenile justice system is more likely to be assured if its mission is framed in terms of prevention rather than treatment or punishment.

A Preview of the Book

The remainder of this book develops these arguments as follows. In Chapter 2, we summarize research on what is known about the causes of juvenile crime, how those causes might differ from those associated with adult crime, and the methods of reducing juvenile recidivism. Knowledge about these matters is much more extensive than it was just a few decades ago, allowing us to draw clearer distinctions between adults and juveniles and to fashion more effective treatment programs.

Chapter 3, the normative core of the book, expands upon the arguments outlined above. More specifically, it elaborates on the contention that the rehabilitative model is too paternalistic while the retributive model, whether in its adult or diminished responsibility form, does not provide a satisfactory rationale for a separate juvenile system. In contrast to the retributive models, the individual prevention model seeks an objective that is quite different from that of adult court and easily accommodates a treatment orientation. In contrast to the rehabilitative model, it limits such treatment to that necessary to reduce criminal recidivism.

Chapter 4 provides a detailed description of what a preventive system of juvenile justice would look like, including case studies that allow comparison between the rehabilitative, individual prevention, and retributive regimes. The individual prevention system would be administrative rather than criminal in nature and rely on modern risk-assessment and risk-management techniques. In further contrast to the current system, it would not permit transfer to adult court.

Chapter 5 changes focus from the substantive aspects of juvenile justice to its procedural framework. This chapter questions the post-*Gault* application of adult-like procedures to the juvenile court. It argues that procedures in juvenile court should comprise the optimal method of promoting fairness, accuracy, and efficiency, *whatever* that might be. The chapter then canvasses the relevant social science research, which suggests that these goals are not necessarily achieved by allegiance to the adult procedural model.

Chapter 6 summarizes the main points of the previous chapters and some of their implications. It also ponders ways in which policy makers and the public might be convinced to adopt these proposals. Initial resistance to a model that appears too lenient (to some) and too vulnerable to abuse (to others) can be overcome by emphasis on its crime prevention, therapeutic, and fiscal advantages.

2

Juvenile Crime and How to Reduce It

Antisocial conduct is so common among teenagers that some commentators consider it "normative" for that age group.[1] Yet only a fraction of these youthful offenders continue on this criminal path once they reach adulthood.[2] Why do so many juveniles engage in bad behavior? What distinguishes juveniles who engage in such behavior from those who do not? Why do most juveniles who engage in antisocial behavior desist once they become adults? Why do some of these juveniles continue their wayward path even after age eighteen? Are there interventions that, independent of the simple aging process, can reduce juvenile crime and the likelihood of crime in adulthood?

This chapter provides partial answers to these questions by describing current research about three topics: the biopsychosocial differences between juveniles and adults; the risk factors associated with juvenile offending; and the efficacy of interventions designed to reduce juvenile crime. The first two subjects are crucial to figuring out whether the assumptions underlying the retributive, individual prevention and rehabilitative models are accurate. The third topic is particularly important in assessing the individual prevention and rehabilitative models, as both rely on preventive interventions to succeed.

Our review of the research leads to the following conclusions. In terms of explaining criminal behavior, the primary distinguishing characteristic between adolescents and adults is that the former group, for a whole host of cognitive, neurobiological, and environmental reasons, is more prone to risk-taking and impulsive behavior. Youths who begin this antisocial behavior at an early age are the most likely to continue it into adulthood. Many youths who become law abiding in their twenties probably will do so regardless of how the legal system responds to them, but various interventions, in particular those that are community based, can reduce both the crime they commit while juveniles and the criminal propensities of those juveniles who are otherwise likely to continue to engage in antisocial conduct into adulthood.

This analysis of the existing research is guided by an ecological perspective, which posits that only if one understands the ongoing relationship between the individual and his or her social environment can one grasp the actor's motivation and behavior on any particular occasion.[3] A long line of experimental studies clearly demonstrates that human behavior is strongly influenced by social and contextual as well as individual factors.[4] This ecological model is reflected in the work of early twentieth-century social psychologists such as Kurt Lewin,[5] interpersonally oriented psychiatrists such as Harry Stack Sullivan,[6] behavioral scientists such as Rudolf Moos[7] and, perhaps most prominently, Urie Bronfenbrenner, who theorized that a child's development is heavily influenced by interconnected systems, including family members, peers, school and local community, as well as by more macro-level phenomena such as the legal system and the national economy.[8]

As Bronfenbrenner's work suggests, the ecological view of human behavior is particularly salient in connection with juvenile justice. The evidence indicates that compared to adults, children and adolescents may be more susceptible, receptive, and responsive to contextual factors, particularly dynamic or changeable risk factors.[9] That fact can have significant implications for juvenile justice, in terms of both understanding delinquent behavior and constructing interventions that can help reduce the likelihood of juvenile delinquency.

Biopsychosocial Influences on Juvenile Crime

The following brief review of the existing research on biopsychosocial influences on juvenile crime begins with a focus on individual risk and protective factors. It then extends the focus outward to include family, peer, neighborhood, school, and community and cultural influences on juvenile crime.[10] The research suggests that the biggest difference between adults and juveniles once they reach adolescence is their tendency toward reckless behavior. It also suggests that juvenile crime is as much the result of contextual influences as it is of personal characteristics of the juvenile.

Individual Factors

Behavioral science research on delinquent behavior traditionally has focused on individual psychological factors, especially cognitive functions that are thought to have some bearing on judgments of juvenile responsibility. More recently, researchers have expanded their focus to encompass more broadly conceived psychosocial factors that might affect judgment. More recently still, studies of the juvenile brain have enhanced our understanding of individual factors that can contribute to antisocial behavior. All three types of factors are explored here, with an emphasis on the differences between juveniles and adults.

Cognitive and Psychosocial Factors. The cognitive capacities of youth are clearly less developed than those of an adult. However, at a shallow level—involving the ability to perceive reality, understand information, and think in abstract terms—these capacities come on line at a surprisingly early age. Most of the research on juveniles' cognitive functioning suggests that by the end of the first decade of life people are able to understand society's rules. Thus, Laurence Steinberg and Elisabeth Cauffman, among the most prominent researchers in this area, have declared that "absent some sort of mental illness or retardation . . . anyone who is nine can form criminal intent and appreciate the wrongfulness of an action."[11] Additionally, by around age ten or eleven, children have acquired the basic capacity to make moral judgments based on intentions and motives, although this capacity continues to develop until the age of about seventeen.[12] By mid-adolescence (15 and 16), Steinberg and Cauffman state, the capacity of youth to understand information and engage in logical reasoning approximates that of adults.[13] As they put it, "there is substantial evidence that adolescents are well aware of the risks they take, and that increasing adolescents' awareness of various risks has little impact on their decision-making outside the laboratory. Moreover, there is little evidence that growth in the logical abilities relevant to decision-making occurs in any systematic way much past age 16."[14]

Other reviews of this area of research have reached similar conclusions. For instance, Deanna Kuhn's comprehensive review of empirical findings through 2008 concludes that "in the sense of being free agents—able to decide what they will attend to and what they will not, what they will invest themselves in and what they will not, what they will value and what they will not—adolescents are more like adults than they are like children."[15] Another recent review of the literature on social cognitive development concluded, "The results of these studies suggest that well before adolescence, children in different cultures develop concepts of rights in abstract situations . . . . Across ages, adolescents as well as adults balanced concerns with rights with other social and moral considerations."[16]

At the same time, adolescents are certainly not as adept at integrating and processing information as adults. Steinberg and Cauffman found that there are significant differences between young adolescents and adults in terms of what they call "psychosocial maturity"—the emotional and social influences on decision-making capacities. They evaluated the latter construct through three broad measures: responsibility (the capacity to make a decision in an independent, self-reliant fashion), perspective (the capacity to place a decision within a broader temporal and interpersonal context), and temperance (the capacity to exercise self-restraint and control one's impulses).[17] Their studies and follow-up studies conducted by others—ultimately involving thousands of subjects—indicate that, compared to adults, adolescents as a group score significantly lower on measures of self-reliance, consideration of future consequences, and self-restraint.[18]

Other research confirms these three tendencies in ways that are relevant to juveniles' propensity to commit crimes. Corroborating the finding that juveniles are less self-reliant than older individuals are multiple studies, discussed in more detail later in this chapter, concluding that adolescents are more likely than adults to give in to bad peer influence. The bottom line here is that as juveniles move toward the independence of adulthood they replace reliance on their parents with dependence upon their peers.[19]

The finding that adolescents focus on short-term consequences and rewards coincides with research indicating that youths are more sensation- and risk-seeking and do not assess punishment the way adults would.[20] As a group, adolescents value impulsivity and fun more than adults do, so they are more likely to see value where adults see only risk.[21] Moreover, they are much less adept than adults at planning and thinking about the future.[22] This relative obliviousness to long-term consequences may in part exist because reflectiveness is associated with a sense of identity, which does not begin to consolidate until the late teens or even the early twenties.[23] It may also stem in part from neurobiological immaturity and from having fewer stakes in life, both topics discussed further below.

The finding that juveniles find it relatively difficult to "manage" themselves is related to empirical work indicating that adolescents are more likely than adults to act on emotion and fleeting desires than deliberate thought,[24] and are also more susceptible to mood swings.[25] Thus, researchers speak of a "vulnerable 'time gap' during adolescence, during which risk seeking drives overpower regulatory and modulating mechanisms."[26] During this period, defying rules becomes part of adolescent experimentation with autonomy and identity development.[27]

Neurobiological Influences. The conclusion that there are significant differences between juvenile and adult decision making outside of the narrow cognitive context involving understanding and reasoning is supported and in part explained by research exploring neurobiological influences on child and adolescent development and behavior. For many years, scientists believed that most brain development occurred in the early childhood years.[28] But more recent studies utilizing advances in imaging technology indicate that adolescent brains are less well-developed than previously believed.

In particular, the frontal lobe undergoes significant change during adolescence and is the last part of the brain to develop. This process involves both "synaptic pruning," the elimination of unused brain cell connections in a way that improves brain functioning, and myelination, the development of myelin that insulates the neural circuits of the brain and makes electrical impulses more efficient.[29] Because the frontal cortices are responsible for higher order reasoning and "executive control"—fluid coordination of cognition and emotion, goal-directed planning and forethought, and impulse control—these findings suggest that adolescents may be somewhat less capable of controlling aggression and other impulses and less adept at engaging in goal-directed cognitive functioning such as long-term planning.[30]

Other neurobiological research has looked at age-related differences in the limbic system and subcortical regions of the brain. B. J. Casey and her colleagues hypothesize that in this domain there is a difference between adolescents and both pre-teens and adults, corresponding to heightened novelty-seeking and risk-taking behavior in the former group.[31] A number of other researchers claim to have found an "age-related pattern of regional brain activation [that] may explain the propensity for risk-taking and novelty-seeking behaviors in adolescents."[32]

Summing up this research, Steinberg suggests that changes in the limbic system may promote sensation-seeking conduct in early and mid-adolescence at precisely the same time the prefrontal cortex region of the brain—the part of the brain that controls executive functioning such as planning, regulation of emotions and impulses, and evaluations of risk—is maturing. This "temporal gap between the arousal of the socioemotional system, which is an early adolescent development, and the full maturation of the cognitive control system, which occurs later, creates a period of heightened vulnerability to risk taking during middle adolescence."[33] Adriana Galvan and her colleagues similarly suggest the adolescent's neural framework is similar to that which explains addiction, in that the still maturing prefrontal cortex is "'hijacked' by the subcortical system, which might render it unable to appropriately modulate decisions in the context of future consequences."[34]

Summary of the Impact of Individual Factors. In sum, the cognitive and neurobiological research on adolescent development does not suggest that adolescents lack capacity to formulate intent or are seriously compromised in their ability to recognize the wrongfulness of criminal behavior. But it does suggest that, as a group, they are less risk averse, less deliberate, and less likely to attend to the consequences of their actions, including criminal acts, than are adults as a group.[35] Of course, both of these conclusions are generalizations. Some adolescents reach maturity much earlier than others, while some adults still demonstrate adolescent-levels of risk-taking.[36] The fact remains, as one recent review of the literature indicated, that "impulsivity is a normative behavior during normal childhood development."[37] Echoing this view, June Arnett has stated that "reckless behavior becomes virtually a normative characteristic of adolescent development."[38]

Contextual Factors

Contextual influences can have profound effects on the development and continuance of delinquent behavior. These influences range from parents to peers, from schools to the broader community and the media. Although many of these factors are also associated with adult crime, their contribution to juvenile crime is both more proximate (as with family and school influences) and powerful (as with peer influences, and perhaps media and neighborhood effects as well). The significant impact of these factors suggests that individual decision making is only a partial precipitant of criminal behavior. More important, it reinforces the notion that juveniles who experience these factors may be compromised in their ability to obey the law and that attempts to improve that ability must take into account contextual factors.

Family Influences. Family dynamics are among the strongest predictors of risk for delinquent behavior.[39] The parent–child relationship is the major vehicle for the early socialization and moral development of the child. Insecure attachment between a parent (typically the mother or other primary caretaker) and an infant is a risk factor for later behavioral problems, particularly among boys.[40] Socialization also depends on the consequences the parent associates with positive and negative behaviors.[41] Thus, a wide range of parenting practices has been linked to risk for delinquent behavior, including poor or inconsistent parental monitoring and supervision.[42] For example, a study led by one of the authors found that adolescents who report that their parents do not treat them with personal respect are at increased risk for engaging in delinquent behavior.[43] Other studies have found that adolescents who state that their parents did not treat them fairly in the course of resolving conflicts were more likely to bully their peers[44] and more likely to associate with deviant peers.[45]

Child maltreatment, including abuse and neglect, also is associated with antisocial behavior, although perhaps not as strongly as one might expect.[46] In a comprehensive review of the literature, Cathy Widom reported that about 20 percent of children who were abused or neglected as children became delinquent as adolescents.[47] Abused children are at greatest risk of developing criminal careers, Anna Stewart and her colleagues found, when the abuse occurs in their adolescent years.[48] The pathway to violence after abuse is not always direct. For boys, the indirect path often leads from early aggressive behavior to alcohol abuse to violent delinquent and criminal behavior. For girls, alcohol abuse tends to mediate the relationship between maltreatment and violent criminal behavior.[49]

Another potential family risk factor is the witnessing of interparental or marital violence, especially if combined with maltreatment of the child.[50] Veronica Herrera and Laura Ann McCloskey found that, regardless of gender, children who witnessed marital violence were almost twice as likely to be referred to juvenile court for any offense, and were three times as likely to be referred for a violent offense.[51] Patrick Tolan and colleagues' study of 160 urban minority male youths and their mothers found that mothers who perpetrated violence on others (as opposed to mothers who suffered as victims of it) were also more likely to be harsh toward their children and monitor them less, which in turn was related to subsequent violence by the youths.[52] Parental substance abuse and psychopathology also are related to increased risk for delinquency,[53] as are higher rates of residential instability and paternal unemployment.[54] Finally, of course, parents influence their children's relationships by selecting the schools their children attend, the neighborhoods in which they live, and the extracurricular and other activities in which their children engage.[55]

Peer Influences. Peer influence probably plays an even more important role than family in contributing to adolescent crime,[56] and indeed may be the strongest risk factor for delinquent behavior.[57] Adolescence is usually a period in which reliance on parents regarding issues of identity and acceptance lessens as reliance on the peer group increases. As a result, adolescents are more likely than adults to be influenced by others, both in terms of how they evaluate their own behavior and in the sense of conforming to what peers are doing, with the peak of peer influence occurring around mid-adolescence.[58]

Peer interactions occur in almost all of the contexts in which adolescents find themselves—schools, neighborhoods, and social activities. In these contexts, social pressures continually shape ongoing behavior, including criminal activity. Most directly, peers facilitate the commission of crime. A majority of delinquent adolescent behavior occurs in groups.[59] Empirical evidence strongly confirms that young individuals take more chances when they are with peers than when they are alone.[60] In short, peer pressure to go along with the group can exert a powerful counterweight to the societal commands of the criminal law.[61]

Peers exert more indirect criminogenic influences as well, through their impact on the approval-seeking motives of the at-risk child.[62] As Jeffrey Fagan notes, "Witnesses are part of the landscape of social interactions and they influence adolescents' decisions on how to conduct social relations and which behaviors to value."[63] Unfortunately, Terrie Moffitt's research suggests, adolescents prefer to mimic their antisocial peers rather than their more law-abiding colleagues because those who engage in antisocial conduct appear to have attained adult status in many ways.[64]

School Influences. Schools provide an important context for adolescent behavior. Poor academic performance is related to the prevalence, onset, and seriousness of delinquency.[65] Additionally, minimal educational goals and poor motivation place children at risk for offending.[66] Other school characteristics that have been linked to antisocial behavior include poor student–teacher relations, the prevalence of norms that support antisocial behavior, poorly defined rules and expectations for conduct, and inadequate rule-enforcement behavior.[67]

Allison Payne found that students who attended schools with strong relationships among students, teachers, and administrators and a collaborative atmosphere were more bonded to their schools and engaged in less delinquency.[68] Similarly, several studies have found that school climates characterized by student perceptions of fairness and clarity of rules had less student delinquency and student victimization.[69] Indeed, high-quality school environments can substitute for poor parental attachment and involvement, especially among adolescents who are not strongly academically oriented.[70]

Socioeconomic Status and Poverty. Sociological theories have long emphasized the role of poverty and low socioeconomic status (SES) as key contributing influences on juvenile delinquency.[71] Yet systematic research has consistently failed to establish an empirical relationship between low socioeconomic status, by itself, and delinquency.[72] Recent investigators have suggested, instead, that various social and psychological factors may either moderate or mediate the link between SES and delinquency.

For instance, Robert Sampson and John Laub found that family practices such as harsh discipline, low supervision, and weak parent–child attachment explained about two-thirds of the effect of poverty and other negative social structural influences on juvenile delinquency.[73] Bradley Wright and colleagues likewise suggested that social/psychological factors mediate the relationship between SES and delinquency and that both low and high SES can cause delinquency, depending on the mediating factors addressed.[74] More recently, Carter Hay and colleagues sought to expand the scope of analysis by looking at the interaction of SES and environment, and found that adolescents who had a parent or parents who were unemployed were at greatest risk for delinquency when they came from *communities* that had high rates of poverty.[75]

Neighborhood Influences. As the last piece of research suggests, living in a high poverty or low-socioeconomic-status neighborhood has consistently been linked to delinquency.[76] Thus, one study found that impulsive boys in poor neighborhoods were at great risk for offending but that impulsivity posed little risk for delinquency for boys in better-off neighborhoods.[77] Yet it is also important to recognize, as Jeffrey Fagan has noted, that "social cohesion among individuals" can mitigate the effect of poverty.[78] Weak social controls and lack of community structure allow delinquent behavior to go on unchecked,[79] but strong social controls and parenting counter the risk for delinquent behavior even in the poorest urban neighborhoods.[80]

More specifically, the availability of neighborhood organizations serving youths and adults has been linked not only to lower levels of youth aggression but also to enhanced positive influences of peers, families, and mentors. For example, Beth Molnar and her colleagues found that the aggression-reducing benefits of the presence of positive peers were significantly stronger among youths living in neighborhoods with a high concentration of organizations and services. They went on to conclude that "certain family, peer, and mentoring resources may confer benefits *only* in the presence of neighborhood resources."[81]

Media Influences. Exposure to media violence also may contribute to delinquent conduct. Although theory regarding how this effect occurs and the differences between its short-term and long-term impact is still developing, scientists investigating this topic have found clear evidence that exposure to media violence increases aggressive and violent behavior in juveniles.[82] Further, highly aggressive individuals show greater effects of exposure to media violence than less aggressive individuals.[83] Research also has shown that children's perceptions of media violence as "lifelike" or "real" and their identification with aggressive characters is positively related to aggressive behavior.[84]

Age-Based Social Status. Finally, age-based minority social status, with the dependence and restrictions that this status brings, is correlated with antisocial behavior. This status differential might contribute to antisocial behavior in three ways. First, escape from risk-inducing environments is more difficult for dependent children than for adults. Second, adolescent autonomy is more restricted than that of adults because adolescents have less freedom to engage in "socially acceptable" outlets for risky behavior such as legal gambling, drinking, and risky financial investments. Lacking these legal outlets, adolescents may engage in unacceptable behavior. Third, minors are less integrated into the prosocial responsibilities, roles, and relationships of adulthood.[85] This reduced "stake in life" may lead them to feel they have less to lose than adults. Specifically, the "informal" costs of sanctions—stigma, the negative effects on employability and marriage, and isolation from mainstream institutions—may be weakened for adolescents.[86]

The Interaction of Individual and Contextual Factors—Early Starters

No one type of factor (individual or contextual) is going to explain juvenile crime, either generally or in particular. Consider, for instance, behavioral genetics research, which attempts to separate out the influence of nature and nurture by looking at the behavior of monozygotic twins (who share 100 percent of their genes), dizygotic twins (who share 50 percent of their genes), and adoptive children (who on average share about 50 percent of their biological parents' genes and none of their adopted parents' genes). Terrie Moffit's review of this literature concluded that about 50 percent of antisocial behavior is tied to genetic effects, 20 percent to shared family effects, and the remaining 30 percent to non-shared environmental experiences.[87] Thus, in the absence of intervention, the effect sizes for genetic and environmental influences on antisocial behavior may well be about 50:50.[88]

Behavioral genetics research also suggests that risk can be significantly increased by the combination and interaction of genetic factors and environmental influences. For example, whereas child maltreatment alone accounts for only a 2 percent increase in risk for conduct disorder, the combination of child maltreatment with genetic risk increases the overall risk for conduct disorder to 24 percent.[89] Overall, behavioral genetics studies of antisocial behavior suggest that gene–environment interactions are highly predictive of risk.[90]

A particularly important illustration of this phenomenon occurs in connection with what Moffitt has called "life-course persistent" offenders, as contrasted with "adolescent-limited" offenders.[91] The former type of offender tends to begin antisocial behavior at an earlier age.[92] In an effort to examine the differential impact of genetic risk on early and late-onset delinquency, Jeannette Taylor and colleagues used a longitudinal design with a twin sample of boys and found evidence that genetic factors had a greater influence on early starters, while environmental factors such as peer influences had a greater influence on late starters. Moreover, the early starters showed deficits in cognitive skills and executive functions in comparison to late starters and nondelinquents.[93]

The association of life-course persistent offending with certain genetic markers does not mean the early onset offenders are immune to rehabilitation that manipulates their environment, however. As is true of youth offending generally, environmental factors still play a significant role even in this context. For instance, Isabela Granic and Gerald Patterson have found that children with early onset behavioral problems tend to come from families with low SES and early coercive and rigid interactions with their parents, and tend to also experience peer rejection, academic failure, and depressive mood, all of which moves them toward a future of associating with deviant peers.[94] The influence of these associations then leads at ages twelve to fourteen to new, more covert forms of antisocial behavior such as truancy, stealing, lying, cheating, and alcohol and substance abuse.[95] This transition from overt to covert antisocial behavior is then associated with increased risk for adult criminal behavior.[96] Intervention at any of these points might help reduce the trajectory toward antisocial behavior (as the description of the Fast Track Program in the next section illustrates).

* * *

This discussion makes clear that we still have much to learn about why adolescents tend to be risk-takers compared to adults, why certain youths commit crime and others do not, and why some juvenile offenders persist in offending and others do not. But it is also important to note that even if we do not fully understand the causes of crime, interventions to prevent it can be effective. To take one classic example from a related field, consider how authorities ended a cholera epidemic in nineteenth-century London.[97] Long before medical breakthroughs in germ theory would revolutionize public health and explain how cholera infects individuals, John Snow, a physician in London, documented that people who were developing new cases of cholera shared a common experience—they drew their water from the Broad Street water pump. The raging epidemic was brought under control when authorities replaced the handle on the pump, which had been the source of contagion. This intervention was highly effective despite the lack of scientific knowledge about the true causal mechanism of the disease.

Likewise, in the field of juvenile justice we may be able to develop effective interventions to reduce juvenile crime in the absence of a complete understanding of underlying causal mechanisms. As the next section indicates, several successful intervention programs exist.

Reducing Delinquent Behavior

One of the traditional justifications for a separate juvenile justice system is the presumption that juveniles are more malleable than adults because they are "works in progress" who are more responsive to contextual influences, including rehabilitative interventions.[98] Although this premise has yet to be proven, it has encouraged more experimentation and evaluation of a wider range of intervention strategies for juveniles than for adult offenders. As a result, much is now known about how antisocial behavior by adolescents can be curbed.

An Overview

Four preliminary points about interventions designed to reduce juvenile offending are crucial. First, the overwhelming finding of researchers is that incarceration in prison or jail is less effective at reducing recidivism than most alternative programs. Mark Lipsey and Francis Cullen's recent comprehensive meta-analytic review of the empirical studies concluded that incarceration generally does little to curb criminal propensities, while nonresidential programs are fairly successful in this regard.[99] As a separate review by Lipsey put it, "interventions guided by therapeutic philosophies" are "more effective than those based on strategies of control or coercion—surveillance, deterrence, and discipline."[100] These findings make sense if offending is in some nontrivial respect due to contextual influences; if so, coercive interventions that take place in detention are not likely to address dynamic risk factors associated with crime or to generalize to the "real world" facing offenders once they are released.

Indeed, Lipsey and Cullen state that correctional sanctions "may *increase* the likelihood of recidivism."[101] Recent evidence confirms that secure detention and incarceration of youths contribute to mental health problems, impair future employment prospects, and foster crime.[102] Thus, one study found that prior commitment to a youth facility increased the odds of engaging in another crime 13.5 times, and was a stronger predictor for recidivism than membership in a gang, carrying a weapon, or a poor parental relationship.[103] Bringing troublesome youths in close contact with one another also has been shown to promote "peer deviancy training," which ultimately contributes to recidivism.[104]

Other ill effects of incarceration are legion. For instance, youths who are detained are more likely to end up in the deeper end of the juvenile justice system. One study found that juveniles who were detained were three times more likely than youths subjected to community-based alternatives to be subsequently committed to a juvenile facility, even after controlling for relevant factors such as the severity of the offense.[105] And even when youngsters have been able to benefit from therapy while in institutional settings, they tend to recidivate once they return to the same social environments that contributed to the development of their initial delinquent conduct.[106] Moreover, detention can impede the aging-out process that normally diminishes criminal behavior.[107] Finally, overcrowded conditions can lead to violence and unsafe living conditions (as well as leave the state open to costly litigation).[108] Overall, empirical evidence demonstrates that reliance on alternatives to detention has resulted in increased public safety and considerable cost savings.[109]

A second, equally important finding of meta-review research is that the treatments most likely to work in terms of reducing recidivism have three attributes: (1) they are applied primarily to high-risk (i.e., relatively dangerous) individuals; (2) they target treatment of dynamic risk factors (e.g., antisocial attitudes or peer relationships, criminal role models, lack of prosocial skill development) rather than vague personal or emotional problems (e.g., poor self-esteem); and (3) they focus on developing skills that offenders are capable of applying in the real world rather than adopting "nondirective" or "insight" approaches.[110] All three of these attributes suggest that treatment programs are least likely to be effective at reducing recidivism if they aim merely at improving the self-concept of the youth or in some other vague way are designed to "help" the youth become a "better person," as might be a primary focus of some interventions under a purely rehabilitative model.

Put another way, research evidence suggests that interventions that focus on trying to change the youngster's character or personality tend to be less successful than interventions directed at behavior per se or the situational and environmental factors that contributed to it. Indeed, one reason treatment interventions in the original juvenile court failed (with recidivism rates near 70%)[111] was that they tended to be rooted in psychodynamic theory. This sort of insight-oriented approach was developed primarily to understand and treat "internalizing" anxiety disorders among so-called YAVIS clients (for young, attractive, verbal, intelligent, successful) rather than "externalizing" conduct problems. Even if insight-oriented therapies are effective with YAVIS clients (which they may not be),[112] the typical delinquent child does not fit the YAVIS profile, particularly with regard to verbal competence and the tendency toward introspection.[113]

The third preliminary point about intervention strategies is that they vary widely not only in terms of content but also with respect to scope. Social scientists divide prevention programs into three types: primary prevention programs (which attempt to prevent a disorder from occurring); secondary prevention programs (which attempt to identify and treat a disorder as early as possible to reduce length and severity); and tertiary programs (which attempt to reduce the dysfunction created by a disorder that has already occurred).[114] Primary prevention interventions are universal in nature, and thus in the juvenile justice context seek to change individual and environmental risk factors through such vehicles as life skill training, promotion of good classroom behavior, and improvement of child–parent bonds in *all* children and families, through school- and community-wide programs.[115] Secondary prevention programs are more selective and are aimed at children who pose an enhanced risk of delinquency, typically those with high-risk characteristics and backgrounds who have not yet engaged in seriously delinquent behavior.[116] Finally, tertiary programs are targeted at individuals who have engaged in seriously delinquent behavior.[117]

A further distinction between the rehabilitation model and the individual prevention model, consistent with differences in their intervention goals, is that the former model is more likely to call for juvenile court involvement if any of these programs could be effective, whereas the individual prevention approach will usually be triggered only by strong risk factors of the type that are dealt with through tertiary intervention programs. Thus, the rehabilitation model is more likely than any of the other models to target nonoffenders, and in particular preadolescents. Note, however, that despite their focus on youths who have been involved in serious antisocial behavior, even tertiary programs could target a (small) number of very young children since, as the evidence described above suggests, some of society's more chronic offenders are "early starters."[118] These young offenders are most likely to become life-course persistent offenders, whereas those who start offending later in life often desist when they reach their twenties.

A final general point, already noted, is that while interventions should focus on the precipitants of offending to the extent they are known, they might still work even when causal factors are not known. Likewise, people or situations that did not play a contributing role in the development of criminal behavior may nonetheless be useful in its prevention. For instance, the parents of a child who is prone to criminal behavior may be part of a successful intervention even if they are indistinguishable in terms of parenting skills and general law-abidingness from parents of children who obey the law.

Specific Programs

We have come a long way from the pessimism of the "nothing works" era in juvenile justice.[119] Today there are many effective, evidence-based interventions aimed at treating and preventing juvenile delinquency. The Center for the Study and Prevention of Violence at the University of Colorado at Boulder has established a program called Blueprints for Violence Prevention, which is a national initiative aimed at identifying intervention programs that work to reduce criminal behavior, violence, and substance abuse.[120] To date, the Blueprints project has reviewed over 600 programs and identified eleven that it considers "model" because they meet rigorous scientific effectiveness criteria, as well as an additional eighteen programs that are thought to be promising. Programs are evaluated on three main criteria: demonstrated crime reduction using rigorous research methods; evidence of sustained effectiveness; and replication across multiple settings with diverse populations. Below are brief descriptions of the three Blueprints with the most direct relevance to the individual prevention model (a more elaborate description of each is found in the Appendix). We also review (with more detail in the Appendix) one of the "promising" Blueprints programs, the Fast Track Program, because of its focus on early starters who are among those who are at highest risk for delinquency and recidivism.

Functional Family Therapy (FFT). FFT was developed by James Alexander and Bruce Parson and is rooted in family systems theory and principles of behavioral change.[121] The program focuses on altering family-based risk and protective factors that are associated with delinquent behavior such as maltreatment and poor parental supervision, and tries to improve clarity of family communication and reciprocity in family relations. It also makes use of contingency contracts between parent and child aimed at modifying maladaptive and delinquent behavior.[122] FFT targets juveniles between the ages of eleven and eighteen and typically requires between eight and fifteen sessions, but sometimes necessitates up to twenty-six sessions for the most serious cases.[123] Overall, evaluation research indicates that FFT can reduce recidivism and out-of-home placement rates by 25 to 60 percent.[124] Further, a net benefit of over $10 is realized for every dollar spent on the program due to avoidance of costs typically associated with crime.[125]

Multisystemic Therapy (MST).[126] MST was developed by Scott Henggeler and his colleagues as an alternative to traditional interventions. Consistent with the principle that tertiary interventions should target the higher risk youth, MST has been particularly successful at decreasing rates of secure detention and out-of-home placement in chronic, violent juvenile offenders. The program involves a primarily family-based intervention that changes how juveniles function in the settings that can contribute to antisocial conduct, including home, school, peer, and neighborhood environments.[127] Therapists are assigned small caseloads (four to six families) so they can work intensively with offenders and their families over a relatively short period of time (approximately four months). The therapist delivers services in the juvenile's home and other natural settings such as the offender's school or neighborhood to increase the chances that behavioral change will endure and generalize across settings.[128]

A study with a four-year follow-up period demonstrated that recidivism rates among serious juvenile offenders who completed MST are substantially lower (22.1%) than the recidivism rates among a comparison group of serious offenders who completed individual therapy (71.4%).[129] A follow-up study almost fourteen years later revealed that these positive effects were durable—the MST group had 57 percent fewer arrests in comparison to the individual therapy group.[130] Subsequent effectiveness studies have indicated that the potency of MST may be significantly diluted when therapists do not adhere closely to the prescribed training model.[131] But the most recent summary of the overall effectiveness of MST reported in Blueprints indicates that MST reduces long-term recidivism rates by 25 to 75 percent, reduces costly out-of-home placements by 47 to 64 percent, and improves overall family functioning and the mental health of serious juvenile offenders, resulting in a benefit-to-cost ratio of $28.33 per dollar spent on MST.[132]

Multidimensional Treatment Foster Care (MTFC).[133] MST targets youngsters who are able to stay in their homes with their biological or legal parents. For those youths who do not have parents who are willing, able, or available to work with them in their own home, MTFC provides an alternative multisystems-oriented intervention. MTFC shares with MST many assumptions about the causes and consequences of human behavior, including the importance of family and peer influences.[134] However, in contrast to MST, which intervenes with delinquent youngsters and attempts to prevent the need for home removal, MTFC therapists work with foster parents and biological parents who have lost custody or control of their children in an effort to facilitate the youngsters' eventual transition back to their family of origin. Since most of these youths have multiple prior arrests, intervention is initially quite intensive, involving close supervision, consistent discipline, and reduced association with deviant peers. The average length of the intervention is seven months.

A comparison of youngsters assigned to MTFC with a group of offenders assigned to group homes found that those receiving MTFC were more likely to return to live with their relatives, were subject to fewer criminal referrals, and experienced fewer than half the contacts with police and the courts.[135] The cost of MTFC per youth is from one-half to one-third less than residential, group, or hospital placements, averaging approximately $3,900 per month. One of the main advantages of this approach is that it minimizes negative influences of deviant peers by avoiding congregate placements such as group homes and other residential settings that place together children with similar problems and criminal histories.[136]

Fast Track Program.[137] A program grounded in social-cognitive-behavioral theory that is more focused on internal psychological processes is the Fast Track Program, which is based on several decades of research on the relationship between social information processing and aggression in children, most of it conducted by Kenneth Dodge and his colleagues.[138] According to the Social Information Processing model (SIP), when children confront a potentially challenging social situation their reaction is heavily influenced by their memories of past experiences, such as parental maltreatment or other antisocial behavior, as well as their biological strengths and limitations.[139] As a result, some children develop what has been called "hostile attributional bias"—a pronounced tendency to attribute hostile intention to others in ambiguous and provocative situations—that is associated with aggressiveness.[140] Thus, for example, significant research confirms that, in comparison to nonaggressive youngsters, aggressive youngsters are less likely to pay attention to relevant social cues and rely instead on self-schemas and personal experiences such as familial abuse when attempting to interpret whether a peer who has engaged in provocative behavior did so intentionally.[141] Dodge and Frame found further that these attributional biases among aggressive boys were evident only when the aggressive child was the target of peer provocation; when these boys witnessed an ambiguous interaction between two other peers, they generally did not make biased attributions or faulty inferences.[142]

Further, according to SIP, even if cues are properly interpreted a youngster's goal specification can have an important influence on the likelihood of aggressive responding. Empirical evidence indicates that nonaggressive, socially adjusted youngsters are more likely to form relationship-enhancing goals than are aggressive youngsters, who are more likely to engage in relationship-damaging goals such as revenge or getting even.[143] For example, a child whose goal is to maintain status in a delinquent peer group may be more likely to respond to perceived provocation with aggression than would a youngster whose goal is to stay out of trouble. Furthermore, aggressive youngsters typically generate fewer potential responses to problem situations, and the responses that they do generate tend to be more aggressive than the responses generated by more socially competent peers.[144] They also tend to evaluate aggressive responses positively, to expect positive outcomes from aggressive behavior, and to select and enact aggressive responses to problem situations.[145] Many of these findings appear to be corroborated by neurobiological evidence.[146]

The Fast Track Program is based on SIP theory and is aimed at preventing serious conduct problems in school-age children and adolescents.[147] Much of it is aimed at primary or secondary intervention rather than youths who have committed serious crime, but it is included here because it targets children who are life-course persistent or "early starters" who might later commit such crime.[148] In grades 1 to 5, *all* children in the targeted school receive the universal components of the prevention program, aimed at improving "self-control, emotional awareness and understanding, peer-related social skills, and social problem solving to increase social and emotional competence."[149] Higher risk children, in particular those who have committed relatively serious antisocial conduct, participate in additional programs: child social skills groups, parent training groups, and parent–child sharing that promote positive parent–child relationships. Academic tutoring, peer pairing, home visiting, and adult mentoring are also provided to high-risk children on an as-needed basis. During the second, adolescence phase of the intervention, the intervention targets peer relations, academic performance, social skills and identity issues, and family/adolescent relations.

Evaluation of the intervention concluded that it was highly effective after the first year of intervention in improving child social and academic skills and improving parents' abilities to effectively discipline their children and establish more supportive and positive relationships with them. By the end of third grade, teachers reported significant reductions in aggressive behavior in the classroom; by the end of grades 4 and 5, significant intervention effects were noted even among high-risk children, with respect to both improvements in their social competence and reductions in their involvement with deviant peers and delinquent behavior. By grade 9, the evidence indicated that it was the highest risk children who were most responsive, in a positive sense, to the intervention, resulting in the prevention of 75 percent of potential conduct disorder cases. That result is promising, given that the cumulative social cost of a single life of crime has been estimated to total approximately $1.3 million.[150]

Summary. A conservative depiction of the research is that intervention strategies have improved to the point that multisystemic and other modern approaches aimed at risk management can reduce recidivism risk from around 40–80 percent to 20–50 percent.[151] These programs also represent an estimated net savings to taxpayers of between $7,000 and $18,000 per child in lieu of more traditional placements.[152] Overall, a fair appraisal of "state of the art" intervention strategies suggests that ecologically oriented, cognitive-behavioral interventions aimed at the multiple life contexts in which juveniles exist (family, peer, school, neighborhood) can be both clinically and cost effective. As a result, several states make use of these types of programs in their juvenile justice system, albeit often within a retributive rather than a rehabilitative or prevention framework.[153]

Conclusion

Adolescents as a group react differently to the world than do adults. Juveniles are less capable of mature judgment, impulse control, and foresight than adults. One reason for this difference appears to be differences in brain development. Adolescents are also more susceptible than adults to familial pathologies, peer pressure, and media violence, and they have fewer stakes in life, meaning they have less to lose if they make a bad choice.

Partly because we now better understand the etiology of adolescent misconduct, intervention strategies have improved to the point that modern multisystemic treatment aimed at community-based risk management can appreciably reduce recidivism. Given the availability of these promising intervention strategies, the next task is to ensure that state of the art interventions are adequately implemented and incorporated into the structure of juvenile justice administration. In Chapter 4, we demonstrate how multisystemic interventions lend themselves nicely to a risk management model, where the emphasis is on changing dynamic risk factors in various life domains that are associated with delinquent behavior. Before we get to that discussion, however, the legal and conceptual case for a juvenile justice system based on risk management needs to be made. The next chapter takes on that task.

3

The Implications of Science for Juvenile Justice

We argue in this chapter that the empirical facts about juvenile offending and intervention programs described in Chapter 2 most directly bolster the individual prevention vision of juvenile justice while providing only a modicum of support for the rehabilitation and retribution visions. Recall that the rehabilitation model of juvenile justice is based on the assumption that juveniles are innocents who should not be subject to punishment but rather should receive *treatment for significant emotional and behavioral problems.* The retribution models instead hold that youths are accountable for their actions and thus should be *punished for their crimes,* although under the diminished retribution model punishment could be mitigated because juveniles are assumed to be less culpable than adult offenders to a legally relevant extent. The individual prevention vision, in contrast, is focused on *prevention of crime.* It is premised on the assumption that juvenile offenders are relatively unaffected by the prospect of criminal sanctions and thus should not be subject to backward-looking punishment but rather are best handled through forward-looking interventions. At the same time, these interventions should be aimed at reducing (and are usually triggered by) criminal acts and thus are narrower in scope than those that occur under the rehabilitation model.

This chapter first shows why the rehabilitation model is flawed. It then does the same for the retribution models, focusing primarily on the diminished retribution variant, which has gained considerable support among policy makers. Finally, it presents the positive case for the individual prevention model, from both theoretical and pragmatic perspectives. The theoretical case for that model relies in part on *Kansas v. Hendricks,*[1] a much-maligned

Supreme Court decision upholding sexual predator statutes, but one that adopts a rationale for state intervention that is very useful in justifying a separate juvenile justice system and suggesting how it might function. The pragmatic case for the individual prevention model is based on a comparison of the retributive and preventive approaches to antisocial conduct. While both systems can be subject to abuse, the latter type of regime, with some important modifications, is much more likely to achieve optimal results without compromising core values.

The Overbreadth of the Rehabilitation Vision

The original juvenile court was grounded on the twin tenets that youths who commit crimes are not responsible for them and in any event can benefit immensely from therapeutic state intervention. The first assumption is incorrect for all but the youngest offenders. The second assumption cannot, by itself, justify a deprivation of liberty; a system that relies on treatability alone as the basis for coercive intervention would grant far too much power to the state and is not sufficiently related to the state's police power goals. Although most modern observers of the juvenile justice system probably agree with these points, it is worth fleshing them out to provide context for the rest of the discussion.

In adult court, conviction is warranted if an individual commits a criminal act with the requisite mental state (e.g., purpose, recklessness, or negligence) and is unable to proffer a justification, such as self-defense, or an excusing condition that causes a substantial lack of capacity to appreciate the wrongfulness of one's actions or conform behavior to the requirements of the law (such as insanity). It is important to recognize that, under current doctrine, these thresholds are met by the vast number of offenders. If one knows that one is causing a particular harm, understands that the harm is viewed by society to be illegal and wrongful, and has a minimal capacity to control one's behavior, one meets the minimum test for criminal liability.[2] For instance, even psychopaths, who clearly lack the emotional capacity to internalize the immorality of criminal conduct, are routinely considered criminally culpable,[3] as are pathological gamblers and others with personality disorders that are associated with very impulsive behavior.[4]

These bare criteria are doubtless met by all but the youngest adolescents. It turns out that the old common law rule—that children under eight cannot be held responsible for their crimes, that children over thirteen usually should be, and that those offenders aged eight through thirteen may or may not cross that threshold[5]—comes close to reflecting the empirically correct view of children's legally relevant mental capacities. At their youngest, children either do not intend to harm or, if they do, do not appreciate its wrongfulness. But, as Chapter 2 indicated, while children from eight through the end of adolescence are not as mature as adults, most of this group, and certainly its oldest half, can easily form the requisite mens rea (intent) for a crime and are fully aware that their criminal acts are illegal.

More will be said about the relative blameworthiness of children in the discussion of the diminished retribution model, which depends upon the allegation that juveniles are not as culpable as adults. For now the point need merely be made that youths older than ten are usually legally "responsible" for their actions; this group, which encompasses almost all juveniles who commit offenses, possesses the minimum capacities necessary for criminal liability. If the rehabilitation vision of juvenile justice is justifiable, it is not because juveniles are legally "innocent" of crime but rather because, despite their culpability, their greater treatability warrants a separate system for them. Indeed, despite their youths-as-innocent polemic, those who developed the juvenile court were probably motivated primarily by their perception that youths are unusually malleable and vulnerable, and thus are both more treatable and in need of isolation from adults.[6]

Whether children *are* more "treatable" than adults is not clear.[7] But even if that assertion is true, alone it cannot legitimize a system that can result in imprisonment. The rationale of *O'Connor v. Donaldson*,[8] a 1975 Supreme Court decision, establishes an important, if somewhat vague, constitutional threshold for state intervention of this sort. In *Donaldson* the Court held that the government may not commit people to a mental hospital merely because they are mentally ill or because such deprivation might "raise [their] living standards."[9] Elsewhere the Court stated: "There is… no constitutional basis for confining [people with mental illness] involuntarily if they are dangerous to no one and can live safely in freedom."[10] Applied to juveniles, this language would not permit a deprivation of liberty—even one involving a "treatment facility" rather than a jail or prison—merely because it can benefit troubled youths. Instead, this most coercive of state actions may occur only if juveniles pose a danger to others (in which case the state's police power is triggered) or are in an unsafe situation (in which case the state's parens patriae authority is implicated).

Of course, many juveniles who do not pose a risk to others might be unable to "live safely in freedom," an endlessly manipulable phrase. And there is no doubt that government owes a special duty to children because of their vulnerable status. The Supreme Court clearly endorsed this proposition in *Pierce v. Society of Sisters*[11] when it stated that "the child is not the mere creature of the state; those who nurture him and direct his destiny have the right, coupled with the high duty, to recognize and prepare him for additional obligations."[12]

However, as established by numerous cases in the civil commitment context (involving both adults and juveniles), short of seriously self-harming actions akin to suicide or a failure to take care of basic needs, the parens patriae power does not justify a deprivation of liberty, if only because such a deprivation is more likely to hurt than help.[13] Exercise of this power is best carried out through other less intrusive mechanisms, including the primary and secondary prevention programs described earlier, dependency courts, compulsory education laws (the subject of *Pierce*), welfare rules, and the like. While the absence of these alternatives at the turn of the twentieth century may explain why the original juvenile court eagerly sought the parens patriae authority, their existence today means the juvenile court can focus on manifesting the state's police power.

In short, the conceptual flaw in the rehabilitation vision is that it seeks to obtain treatment for both troublesome youths and those who are merely troubled. That mixture of purpose explains much of the history of the juvenile court, which has bounced back and forth from wide-open jurisdiction to a focus on adult-type crimes. It is also reflected in the strange insistence among many commentators that juvenile justice remains a manifestation of the state's parens patriae authority, when in practice it is often anything but. We need to stop thinking of the juvenile court as an appendage of the welfare state and aim it toward the goal of dealing with juvenile crime.

The Misplaced Focus of the Retributive Models

The retributive models, in their pure form, avoid this conceptual conflation. Leaving parens patriae matters to other legal systems, these models are meant to implement the state's police power through punishing juveniles who harm others. Treatment of juvenile offenders is not necessarily ignored, but it is not necessary for, and in a sense is a distraction from, assigning culpability and assuring accountability for one's offenses. This latter fact ends up being the primary problem with the retributive approach. Its focus on backward-looking attributions of blame blinds it to the benefits of a forward-looking prevention approach, while making dangerously tempting the abolition of the juvenile court.

The latter tendency is most obvious if one subscribes to the *adult* retributive vision of juvenile justice. Under that model, juveniles who commit crime are considered no less guilty than adults who commit the same offense. Thus, they should receive the same punishment. If they do not, then the system is not really an adult retribution system but some sort of hybrid (about which more will be said later in this chapter). Under a pure adult retribution model, a separate juvenile justice system is pointless except as a way of keeping young offenders away from older ones.

The diminished retribution vision is meant to redress this problem by adapting desert analysis to the juvenile justice context. Pointing to the research on differential maturity and judgment canvassed in Chapter 2, the proponents of this vision argue that a separate juvenile justice system is necessary as a means of recognizing the diminished blameworthiness of juveniles. Championed by the drafters of the Juvenile Justice Standards,[14] Franklin Zimring[15] and most recently Elizabeth Scott and Laurence Steinberg,[16] this view has even influenced the Supreme Court. In its decision in *Roper v. Simmons* exempting individuals under eighteen from the death penalty, the Court pointed to the psychological and neurobiological research suggesting that juveniles are immature and concluded that, compared to adult offenders, juveniles who offend demonstrate "lesser culpability."[17]

The diminished retribution model does concededly support the holding in *Roper*, because execution should be reserved for the worst of the worst, and no youths under eighteen, regardless of how egregious the killing, fits into that class of individuals.[18] But as long as traditional culpability notions are in place, the diminished responsibility rationale cannot justify an entirely separate juvenile justice *system*, for all crimes and all sentences. Even juveniles as young as ten can be culpable under today's criminal law standards, and most juvenile offenders over thirteen probably do not deserve any mitigation under those standards. While mid-adolescents are not as mature as adults, their lack of maturity does not mitigate their culpability as that concept is typically defined in noncapital cases.

Advocates of the diminished retribution model often analogize the immaturity of juveniles to the impairment caused by mental illness.[19] But adolescents who are not themselves suffering from mental disability are rarely as impaired as people with schizophrenia and like disorders, which involve delusions, hallucinations, and other significant cognitive and volitional disturbances.[20] Moreover, even people with fairly serious mental disability at the time of the crime are convicted, and those who are convicted usually do not obtain a reduction in sentence.

Consider, for instance, practice under the Federal Sentencing Guidelines, which apply in all federal cases and are the model for many state sentencing systems. Although the Guidelines do permit a downward departure from the typical sentence upon proof of "significantly reduced mental capacity not resulting from voluntary use of drugs or other intoxicants,"[21] the Sentencing Commission's policy statement also declares that mental and emotional conditions are not "ordinarily relevant" in determining whether a sentence should be outside the Guidelines' ranges.[22] In practice, Michael Perlin and Keri Gould found in their study of federal cases, "departures from the Guidelines based on mental disability have been few, and more often than not, have come in cases in which a defendant's mental state more closely approximates that of a potentially successful insanity plea."[23] As a leading case put it, the mental disability must be "extraordinary" or "atypical" to warrant a downward departure.[24] Even when a downward departure for mental disability is granted, it often amounts to only a few years and seldom approximates the huge discounts contemplated by diminished retribution advocates. Recall, for instance, the Juvenile Justice Standards' recommendation that a juvenile who committed a crime that would require a twenty-year sentence for an adult be sentenced to only three years.[25]

In the states as well, mental illness rarely results in a significant reduction of sentence.[26] One review of state practices notes, for instance, that mental disability short of insanity rarely results in mitigation.[27] Although such a stance may seem unduly harsh, note that a more lenient position would mean that significant numbers of "ordinary" offenders would be entitled to a sentence reduction, including offenders suffering from depression, impulse disorders, mild mental retardation, and perhaps even psychopathy and other types of personality disorders.[28]

Consistent with this reasoning, courts rarely consider immaturity a mitigating circumstance. While the Supreme Court's recent decision in *Graham v. Florida* extended *Roper* by prohibiting a sentence of life without parole for most juveniles, it continued to permit such sentences for juveniles convicted of murder.[29] Lower courts are very unlikely to strike down juvenile life sentences for any serious crime if parole is available.[30] Additionally, a number of courts have rejected the argument that mandatory and prosecutorial transfer schemes that remove the transfer decision from the trial judge are unconstitutional because they deprive youths of the opportunity to prove their immaturity.[31]

Perhaps the biggest disappointment for advocates of the diminished responsibility model has been the courts' almost uniform rejection of arguments based on the research indicating that adolescent brains are less developed than adult brains. The most recent survey of the case law, conducted by Terry Maroney, concluded that "contrary to many predictions, adolescent brain science has had no deep impact in the courts," even at the sentencing stage.[32] This judicial nonchalance toward the new neurobiological findings, however unexpected among juvenile advocates, is perfectly consistent with the observation made earlier that intentional conduct that is not the result of significant mental impairment is generally seen as fully culpable; as Maroney notes, as far as the courts are concerned, brain-based arguments are "doctrinally irrelevant," "have been foreclosed by legislatures," or clash with observation and common sense.[33] The courts' bottom line sentiment with respect to the argument that immaturity of judgment should be factored into culpability assessments was captured by the Connecticut Supreme Court when it stated that, taken to "its logical conclusion," the argument would "require this Court to rewrite the entire Penal Code, crimes and defenses, to necessitate consideration of the age of young offenders for the ultimate purpose of defining their culpability."[34]

One can plausibly argue, of course, that despite its likely massive impact, a more generous mitigation scheme is precisely the dispositional calculus justice systems should have. Perhaps lesser forms of adult disability as well as adolescent immaturity should routinely result in sentence reductions. Further, just as offenders with mental disability can be diverted post-conviction into a separate system (consisting of mental hospitals or psychiatric units on prison wards), an advocate of the diminished responsibility vision can argue that juveniles should be handled in a system or in units that keep them separated from adults, at least at the dispositional stage. In essence, Scott and Steinberg, who have developed the best defense of the diminished responsibility position, endorse this view. They assert that young people who offend are entitled to mitigation not only because of diminished judgment but also because they are more vulnerable to coercive circumstances and peer influences and because their character is undeveloped, in a state of flux, and very likely to change as they reach adulthood. Further, they contend that this mitigation should take place in a system separate from the adult criminal justice system.[35]

There is no dispute that adolescents not only are less capable of deliberate decision making but also are more peer driven and unformed in character than adults. But to accord these latter two differences any more mitigating weight than the first (decision making) difference would, again, be a radical departure from traditional understandings of culpability. Typically, coercion short of duress is not a defense and seldom leads to a reduction in sentence unless it involves a serious threat of violence to the offender;[36] even then the sentence reduction is not particularly significant.[37] Allegations that a person has a "good" character is not a defense at trial unless the defendant is claiming that he or she is not the type of person who would commit a crime;[38] in the typical juvenile case, that element is usually conceded. More generalized claims of good character provide mitigation only at sentencing and, for reasons suggested above, they rarely mitigate culpability even there, at least at the federal level.[39] The examples of character mitigation proffered by Scott and Steinberg (for instance, mitigation based on reputation, restitution, and remorse[40]) are different in kind from the type of mitigation that an immaturity argument posits.

In any event, acceptance of the proposition that Scott and Steinberg imagine—that evidence of immaturity should have a vastly expanded impact on legal accountability rules—would not provide a reason to *try* juveniles separately.[41] Rather, it would merely support a system in which juvenile offenders are adjudicated in adult court and then shunted into a different dispositional system. Indeed, that is the approach that Barry Feld, a prominent advocate for the diminished responsibility approach, has candidly admitted probably makes as much sense from that perspective. As he concedes, "while younger offenders may be less criminally responsible than more mature violators, they do not differ as inherently or fundamentally as the legal dichotomy between juvenile and criminal courts suggests."[42]

Finally, it is not clear that those who endorse the diminished responsibility vision are really willing to adhere to it even at the dispositional stage. This last conundrum for the diminished retribution model arises because under an honest application of that approach, juveniles must serve whatever sentence their blameworthiness indicates they should receive regardless of whether treatment or any other phenomenon (including growing older and more mature) changes the likelihood they will reoffend. On the one hand, those who insist on this just deserts regime are willing to permit results that would be unpalatable to many: premature release of juveniles who may pose a grave risk and, more commonly, overlong confinement of those who could be safely released or put on probationary status. On the other hand, those who are comfortable with taking into account juvenile offenders' risk potential in fashioning disposition—probably most of those who claim to adopt a diminished retribution view—are in effect abandoning the premise of that model and are instead moving toward the individual prevention vision of juvenile justice.

For instance, Scott and Steinberg assert that "punishment calibration should be based on the seriousness of the offense" and "the culpability of the offender,"[43] but they also state that "the case for a separate mitigation-based justice system for the adjudication and disposition of juveniles rests not only on proportionality but also on evidence that such a system is the best means to minimize the social cost of youth crime."[44] They devote an entire chapter to describing research suggesting the worth of community-based programs and the criminogenic effects of detention,[45] thus appearing to favor these types of dispositions despite their potential conflict with culpability principles. Furthermore, because they endorse transfer of "severely antisocial youths" based on amenability to treatment and response to past treatment efforts rather than simply crime seriousness,[46] Scott and Steinberg are willing to dispense with proportionality analysis altogether when making transfer decisions about a group that, while representing only a small portion of juvenile offenders,[47] commits a disproportionate amount of juvenile crime.[48] In short, their proposals, examined closely, seem to be remarkably consistent with a preventive regime. It is now time to take a closer look at that model.

The Theoretical Basis for Individual Prevention—Relative Undeterrability

One reason to be reticent about explicitly adopting an individual prevention approach is its questionable pedigree. Although its focus on the police power goal of preventing harm to others avoids the open-endedness of a rehabilitative, parens patriae regime, it is still associated with images of the "therapeutic state," endless confinement, and totalitarian abuses. Nonetheless, a well-conceptualized individual prevention model is, in the juvenile context, theoretically more justifiable and practically more attractive than any of the other models.

The theoretical piece relies in large part on *Kansas v. Hendricks*.[49] In *Hendricks*, the U.S. Supreme Court upheld a statute that permitted preventive detention of sex offenders who are shown to have a "mental abnormality" that predisposes them to commit acts of sexual violence. The Court also held that because the state's objective in establishing such preventive schemes is not retribution or general deterrence but rehabilitation and incapacitation—individual prevention goals—it is not engaging in punishment despite the significant deprivation of liberty involved.[50] While on the surface seemingly far afield from juvenile justice, this decision, once dissected, provides a provocative prism through which to view it.

Hendricks marked an important shift in the jurisprudence of preventive detention. For some time, most theorists subscribed to the notion that the only individuals who may be subjected to long-term intervention for the purpose of prevention, as opposed to punishment, are those who are seriously mentally ill (i.e., those suffering from psychotic symptoms). Two grounds were advanced for this view. First, given their distorted perceptions of the world, people with serious mental illness are oblivious to the dictates of the criminal law. When people are literally undeterrable by criminal sanctions, society may protect itself through preventive action.[51] Second, we express our respect for the principle of individual autonomy by generally refusing to confine a person, even one who is dangerous, until he or she has chosen to commit an antisocial act. But preventive confinement of dangerous people who are insane does not denigrate their autonomy because they are presumed to have none when seriously symptomatic.[52]

In *Hendricks*, the Supreme Court implicitly rejected these limitations on preventive detention. Instead, it put its imprimatur on a system that applies to a category of people (sex offenders) who are *not* seriously mentally ill (they are usually said to have "personality disorders"[53]), are more deterrable than the latter group (they usually plan their crimes and try to avoid apprehension[54]), and are viewed as autonomous (as indicated by the fact that they are virtually never found insane[55]). So long as the individuals detained under these so-called sexual predator statutes are "dangerous beyond their control," their detention on dangerousness grounds is permissible.[56] Further, in the later case of *Kansas v. Crane* the Court made clear that the "dangerous beyond control" language does not require *un*deterrability or equate to what insanity doctrine sometimes calls an "irresistible impulse." As the Court explained in *Crane*:

> [In *Hendricks*,] we did not give to the phrase "lack of control" a particularly narrow or technical meaning. And we recognize that in cases where lack of control is at issue, "inability to control behavior" will not be demonstrable with mathematical precision. It is enough to say that there must be proof of serious difficulty in controlling behavior. And this . . . must be sufficient to distinguish the dangerous sexual offender whose serious mental illness, abnormality, or disorder subjects him to civil commitment from the dangerous but typical recidivist convicted in an ordinary criminal case.[57]

Courts that have interpreted this language routinely permit commitment not only of sex offenders with "serious mental illness" such as psychosis but also of those diagnosed with some sort of personality disorder.[58] Thus, while *Hendricks* and *Crane* do limit the state's authority to detain preventively by requiring that those detained be less deterrable than the "typical recidivist" in the "ordinary case," they also established that the state may confine people for what they might do rather than what they have done even when they are not disordered in the sense required for exculpation.

Hendricks did suggest a few other limitations on this preventive power. First, the state must attempt rehabilitation of those who are preventively confined.[59] Second, implicit in this first requirement is the idea that the state must make good faith efforts to limit the confinement in any way it can (including treatment). Third, the state must periodically review the status of individuals so confined and release them if they are no longer dangerous.[60]

With these caveats, *Hendricks* makes clear that, as a constitutional matter, a system based on individual prevention goals can exist separately from the criminal justice system *and* separately from a prevention system for people with serious mental illness. The decision makes inadequate control of behavior—what this book calls "relative undeterrability"—the principal determinant of whether a preventive system is justified in a particular case. The question addressed here is whether juvenile offenders are suited for such a system.

The answer, in short, is yes. The assumption of relative undeterrability that is required for the individual prevention model is a much better fit with what we know about juvenile offenders than the assumptions associated with the other models. Under the rehabilitation model juveniles are innocent, under the adult retribution model juveniles are as culpable as adults, and under the diminished retribution model adolescents have difficulty appreciating the wrongfulness of their criminal conduct or are coerced into criminal activity to a legally relevant extent. None of these images of juveniles reflect reality. Much closer to the truth is the assumption underlying the individual prevention model: juveniles are less likely than older offenders to be affected by the prospect of punishment. As Chapter 2 indicated, compared to older individuals, adolescents are less risk averse, more prone to give in to peer pressure, less likely to have a stake in life, more oriented to the present, less likely to have perspective, and more likely to rush to judgment. All of these traits tend to produce offenders for whom the deterrent force of the criminal law is likely to be, literally, an afterthought.

Of course, *Hendricks* requires individualized determinations of inadequate control before government intervention may take place, whereas the prevention regime proposed here governs an *entire group* of offenders, many of whom have little difficulty controlling their behavior (or experience such difficulty due to a completely different etiology than is associated with committable sex offenders). But juveniles as a whole are much more likely than adults to feature the relevant attributes; research makes clear that the traits of impulsivity and recklessness are normative aspects of childhood development. Scott and Steinberg provide additional persuasive justifications for a categorical approach: the difficulty of differentiating between those who are compromised and those who are not, and the fact that the law routinely treats juveniles as a category in other contexts.[61] But whereas their category is based on the faulty assumption that adolescents' responsibility is diminished to a legally significant extent, this book relies on a more accurate generalization about juveniles' relative undeterrability.

Ironically, given the common perception that it represents a triumph for the diminished responsibility position, *Roper v. Simmons* provides less support for that view than it does for the view that juveniles are less deterrable than the "ordinary recidivist." In exempting juveniles from the death penalty, *Roper* not only relied on its finding that juveniles are less culpable but also on its conclusion that "the same characteristics that render juveniles less culpable than adults suggest as well that juveniles will be less susceptible to deterrence."[62]

And while the lesser culpability of juveniles is, under current law, at most sufficiently mitigating to avoid a sentence of life without parole, the lesser deterrability of juveniles is not sentence specific: indeed, if the Court is right in its suggestion that even the death penalty does not have "a significant or even measurable deterrent effect on juveniles,"[63] juveniles are presumably relatively less likely to be deterred by *any* specific criminal punishment.

As the *Roper* Court noted, deterrability is very closely related to culpability. If adolescents tend to act impulsively or with little thought, they can be seen as both less deterrable *and* less culpable. But to the extent that culpability and deterrability do intermingle, again it is the latter concept that best describes the import of what is known about juveniles. Consider the following example offered by Scott, one that she believes illustrates a situation involving diminished culpability:

> A youth hangs out with his buddies on the street. Someone suggests holding up a nearby convenience store. The boy has mixed feelings about the proposal, but cannot think of ways to extricate himself—-although perhaps a more mature person might develop a strategy. The possibility that one of his friends has a gun, and the consequences of that fact, may not occur to him. He goes along with the plan partly because he fears rejection by his friends—a consequence that he attaches to a decision not to participate—and that carries substantial weight in his calculus. Also, the excitement of the holdup and the possibility of getting some of the money are attractive. These considerations weigh more heavily in his decision than the cost of possible apprehension by the police or the long-term costs to his future life of conviction of a serious crime.[64]

The boy in this scenario clearly can be said to demonstrate, as Scott puts it, "immaturity of judgment."[65] But the symptoms of this immaturity—the "mixed feelings," the inability to come up with options, the vulnerability to peer pressure, and the urge for excitement—most obviously compromise the boy's capacity or willingness to obey the law, not his capacity to formulate intent or appreciate the wrongfulness of his actions. In this typical juvenile crime scenario, the case for diminished deterrability is much stronger than the case for diminished culpability.

Compared to diminished retribution theory, the relative undeterrability rationale offers two conceptual advantages in making the case for a juvenile justice system. First, the relative undeterrability rationale is now officially recognized doctrine. Before *Hendricks*, one could have well concluded that, similar to the criminal law's rejection of the principle underlying the diminished responsibility model, any difference between adults and juveniles in terms of deterrability should have no legal implications. After all, just as the empirical findings indicate that most teens meet the minimum culpability threshold, none of the research on deterrability suggests that any but the youngest children are so volitionally impaired that they are analogous to those found insane as a result of an irresistible impulse. In other words, juveniles are less deterrable, not *un*deterrable. But, in contrast to the judicial and legislative refusal to broaden significantly the scope of diminished responsibility, *Hendricks*, *Crane*, and the lower court decisions construing these cases legitimize a more expansive type of preventive regime, one that can easily apply to juveniles.

The second way in which allegiance to an individual prevention model can make the case for a separate system of juvenile justice more convincing is political rather than theoretical. To say that we need such a system because juveniles do not deserve as much punishment as adults is only weakly persuasive; although it coincides with popular views about youth, it admits that adjudications of juvenile offenders are to use the same metric courts apply to adults. The diminished responsibility model is thus easily characterized as merely a softer version of adult court, a view that smoothes the path for mechanisms, like transfer and blended sentences, that treat like adults the large number of juveniles who commit adult-like crimes. In contrast, to say that we need a separate juvenile system because the greater impulsivity and heedlessness of youth requires that we focus on prevention not only resonates with common intuition but also is clearly built on something other than the (adult) punishment model, and thus more strongly suggests that juveniles need a different type of intervention altogether. The latter view also coincides more closely with what the public wants and expects from the juvenile justice system. As Scott and Steinberg's own study indicated, "adult punishment and long incarceration are approved, for the most part, only as a means to protect the public from violent young criminals; however, if other more lenient sanctions are effective, they are favored over incarceration."[66]

That the Supreme Court has endorsed a version of the individual prevention model or that this model may be better than competing models at justifying a separate juvenile justice system does not necessarily mean, of course, that the individual prevention model is the best approach to the problem of juvenile offending. In fact, as detailed below, the preventive approach as it currently operates in the adult setting is seriously flawed. But an individual prevention model in the juvenile setting is much preferable to its primary competitor, the diminished retribution model. Once a few adjustments are made, the individual prevention regime better promotes and reconciles the most important state and individual interests that come into play when a juvenile has caused or is likely to cause harm to others.

Objections to and Benefits of the Prevention Model

The pure prevention model approved in *Hendricks* is simple to outline. The state is authorized to act when an offender poses a significant enough risk to others to warrant intervention. The intervention (not "punishment," since the goal is to prevent acts in the future, not rectify past wrongs) is individualized and should be no more restrictive of liberty than necessary to achieve the prevention aim.

Individual prevention regimes of this sort have given rise to several objections, which can be boiled down to six essential complaints. Such a regime, it is said, (1) relies on suspect risk assessments and risk-management techniques; (2) is highly prone to abuse by government officials; (3) tends to dehumanize its subjects; (4) ignores the universal urge to punish, which undermines norms and creates disrespect for the law; (5) fails to produce sufficient deterrent effect; and (6) is costly. Each of these objections is weighty. Many of them diminish in strength, however, when one looks at analogous problems with retributive approaches. More important, however persuasive these objections are in the adult context, in the juvenile setting they lack the same force. Nonetheless, addressing these objections helps flesh out some crucial legal limitations that must be in place for the preventive approach to be consistent with society's moral values and legal principles. Additionally, evaluating these criticisms helps to clarify the practical benefits of the individual prevention model.

Evaluating Risk

The objection most frequently lodged against any regime based on prevention is that we are not sufficiently adept at evaluating risk or at managing it to justify deprivations of liberty. The common wisdom since the early 1970s, accepted even by courts that enthusiastically endorse risk assessment, is that predictions are wrong at least as often as they are right.[67] And when it comes to treatment programs, many still adhere to Robert Martinson's famous conclusion in 1974 that "nothing works."[68]

There are several responses to these concerns. At the outset, it is important to acknowledge that both prediction science (in particular, actuarial-based risk-assessment instruments) and intervention modalities (in particular, community-based treatments) have improved immensely over the past couple of decades. The efficacy of community-based treatments has already been described; we discuss developments in risk assessment in the next chapter.

More important, while predictive judgments will admittedly always be suspect even if these advances continue, opponents of prevention regimes seldom recognize the possibility that those judgments are no less accurate than the retrospective assessments necessary to implement the primary alternative to prevention—punishment based on relative culpability. Mens rea concepts—the primary means of grading responsibility for crime—are notoriously difficult to define and apply. Legislatures and courts have yet to develop a neutral or coherent doctrine of blameworthiness that approaches the transparency of actuarial-based instruments used in risk assessment, nor have they devised a nonarbitrary hierarchy of punishments. The best effort in this regard to date comes from Paul Robinson, who describes research indicating a high level of agreement among various groups regarding the rank ordering of crimes.[69] But Robinson also notes that there remains noticeable disagreement about the relative rank even of core crimes and that the absolute punishment will still vary substantially depending on the maximum penalty (e.g., the death penalty v. 15 years) that one is willing to countenance as a retributive matter.[70] These findings mean that the actual time spent in prison can vary enormously depending on the particular legislative and judicial agents making the decisions.

Even if agreement can be reached as to the proper "desert" for a given crime in the abstract, the inscrutability of past mental states means that judges and juries at best can only guess how blameworthy a person is or whether a particular punishment is deserved. Culpability determinations depend upon the ability of the fact finder to divine whether a crime was "premeditated" or simply intentional, reckless or merely negligent. These terms are not self-defining, and even defendants may not be able to describe the precise thoughts and beliefs that preceded the crime.[71] The assumption that one's degree of culpability can be proven beyond a reasonable doubt is a legal fiction, necessary to obscure the fact that sentence differentials measuring in the decades depend on mere guesses. This jurisprudential sloppiness is exacerbated if one is led to conclude, based on the research reported in Chapter 2 about the extent to which criminal conduct is attributable to ecological factors, that the law's method of measuring culpability is skewed by its focus on endogenous causes.

A third reason that the imprecision associated with risk assessment should not doom an individual prevention regime has to do with how we respond to the inevitable errors that occur. Again comparing the prevention and retributive approaches, mistakes about risk are, at least in theory, much easier to correct than mistakes about culpability. As *Hendricks* held, preventive interventions must be justified through periodic review, at which the state shows that the individual continues to pose the requisite risk. In contrast, periodic review is inconsistent with the notion of punishing a person for past conduct.

Finally, the cost of any error that does occur may not be as great in a preventive regime as it is in a regime focused on retribution. The latter system demands punishment, which usually involves some type of confinement (and, when it does not, begins to look much more like a preventive regime). A preventive system, in contrast, does not require confinement but can often, as the description of community-based intervention programs in Chapter 2 suggested, achieve its aims through some less restrictive means.

Indeed, to be constitutionally legitimate, preventive regimes *must* achieve their preventive aim using the least drastic means available. This conclusion follows from the Supreme Court's decision in *Jackson v. Indiana*, which required that "the nature and duration of commitment bear some reasonable relation to the purpose for which the individual is committed."[72] This language places two limitations on preventive interventions by the state. First, the nature of the government's intervention must bear a reasonable relation to the harm contemplated. For instance, as already noted, most individuals who pose a risk do not require long-term institutionalization, especially when the harm posed is toward the less serious end of the spectrum or the risk is low. Second, the duration of the intervention must be reasonably related to the harm predicted. Discharge is required when the individual no longer poses a danger, and treatment is required if it will shorten the duration of confinement. While *Hendricks* did not have occasion to address the first limitation, recall that the Court explicitly affirmed the second set of restrictions in that case.[73]

Admittedly, dispositions under the type of sexual predator statutes approved in *Hendricks*, which tend to amount to long-term incarceration in prison-like settings, do not always follow these dictates. But long-term detentions are much less likely to occur in the juvenile setting, not only because interventions in the community can often be successful with this group but because the duration of any detention that does occur will be inherently curtailed by the limitations of juvenile court dispositional jurisdiction, which in no state extends beyond age twenty-five.[74] Note also that given the criminogenic effects of confinement with adults and the rejection of culpability as a determinant of disposition, in a prevention regime even the most serious juvenile offenders would never be transferred to adult court. Thus, de facto life sentences of the type that may occur under a *Hendricks* statute are not possible under a system that is devoted to dealing solely with young people. Just as important, confinement that *does* occur in such a regime will bear a direct relationship to its usefulness as a public safety measure, as compared to confinement in a retributive regime, which is at best fortuitously related to public safety and thus can lead to either premature release or unnecessary restraint.

The conclusion that difficulties in measuring and treating risk do not preclude preventive interventions does not mean, of course, that such interventions are permissible upon any showing of risk. There should be both qualitative and quantitative restrictions on the government's efforts to prove the requisite level of dangerousness and, if intervention occurs, on how long that intervention may last. For instance, risk assessments leading to confinement should rely on structured clinical-assessment instruments or actuarial devices, and interventions should be proportionate to risk. The nature of these limitations is discussed at length in Chapter 4.

Abuses of Discretion

Even if fears about the uncertainty connected with risk assessment and management can be allayed, or at least put in perspective through comparison with the vagaries of culpability assessment and punishment, an individual prevention approach remains vulnerable to the criticism that it expands the opportunities for government officials to misuse their power. In particular, clarification is necessary with respect to (1) the type of predicted harm that authorizes preventive intervention (only crimes, or any behavior that might be called antisocial?); (2) the type of act, if any, that triggers it (only serious crime, any antisocial act, or the presence of biological or environmental "static" risk factors as well?); and (3) the criteria for determining when the state must release an individual from its control (since any offender probably poses some degree of risk, regardless of the duration or type of intervention that has occurred).

The first question can be answered relatively easily. Interventions designed to reduce harm to others should be aimed only at preventing harms that are defined as such by the substantive criminal law. Allowing intervention simply to prevent vaguely described or minor antisocial acts would give government officials carte blanche to round up undesirables who are only trivially risky. By approving preventive detention only for the "particularly dangerous" *Hendricks* may have endorsed this limitation when confinement is sought.[75] We would expand this limitation to all forms of coercive intervention.

The second question, which *Hendricks* did not address, requires a more elaborate answer. Although earlier discussion indicated that a tertiary prevention approach of the type we propose will generally be triggered by a serious antisocial act, as a theoretical matter a preventive regime does not *require* proof of such an act. The logic of prevention discussed earlier would permit the state to protect itself from undeterrable people without having to wait for any particular conduct.

However, the principle of legality—one of the most venerable principles of law—imposes a side constraint that requires modification of this aspect of the preventive approach. The legality principle, which the Supreme Court has endorsed as a matter of due process, dictates that any law, civil or criminal, that deprives individuals of liberty or property must be sufficiently clear that it gives potential violators and government officials adequate notice of the circumstances under which it operates.[76] A vague law chills innocent behavior by citizens, but even more insidiously, it increases the potential for abuse by officials.[77] Thus, for instance, the Court has struck down a loitering statute because it "contains no standard for determining what a suspect has to do in order to satisfy [its] requirements" and therefore "vests virtually complete discretion in the hands of the police to determine whether the suspect has satisfied the statute."[78]

In retributive systems, inchoate offense doctrines like attempt try to cabin government power by demanding evidence that even the most evil-intentioned actor committed some sort of corroborative conduct before conviction may occur. Similarly, an individual prevention regime should require triggering conduct as a curb on government power. If the government could intervene based solely on the nature of one's thoughts, condition, or environment, individuals with the relevant characteristics would have no way of avoiding the intervention, at least when those characteristics are either unchangeable or cannot realistically be changed. Further, the government could prosecute such individuals whenever it wanted to do so.

There are at least three other reasons, besides limiting official power, for an act requirement as a predicate for preventive intervention. First, proof of an antisocial act reduces the potential for mistake by providing evidence useful to the risk determination.[79] Second, absent proof of an act, intervention is likely to appear unfair, both to the offender, thus possibly undermining cooperation with and efficacy of treatment, and to society, thereby undermining the legitimacy and potency of the system as a whole. Finally, this requirement would make clear to would-be offenders the precise point at which the state can intervene, which provides the notice that the legality principle demands.

Application of the legality principle and these other considerations to a prevention-oriented juvenile justice system necessitates some sort of threshold act before intervention may take place. Under the rehabilitative model, the triggering event could be a so-called status offense, such as incorrigibility, or conduct that would not be a crime if committed by an adult, such as running away, truancy, or violating a curfew.[80] Under a pure prevention theory these types of acts would authorize intervention only if they were significant risk factors indicative of serious criminality, which is unlikely to be the case.[81] But even if the necessary relation between these acts and risk existed, legality-related concerns about excessive government power might still impose limitations on a pure expression of the prevention model (as they limit retributivism, which in its pure form would penalize evil thoughts). Low intervention thresholds might be permissible if juveniles were really treated like innocents and the interventions were trivial, as is the case in many primary or secondary prevention programs. But when serious restrictions on freedom are possible, even if part of a community-based program, interventions should be prohibited unless the state can show that the individual has committed an act that would be criminal if committed by an adult. Similarly, some acts that are clearly risk factors, such as associating with a gang, should not, by themselves, authorize tertiary interventions because the adult system would forbid criminalizing them on constitutional grounds.[82] This position, which is also consistent with the individual prevention model's rejection of parens patriae as the basis for intervention by the juvenile justice system, imposes a significant brake on state power at the front end of the preventive intervention process.

Corrupt or discriminatory decisions can also occur at the dispositional stage, especially during periodic review. Here too there must be restrictions on the government's efforts to continue intervention. First, the legality limitation must apply here as well. This means that, at least when they lead to continued confinement, risk assessments should be based on structured clinical assessment instruments or actuarial devices because they rely on criteria that are relatively clear and transparent. Additionally, as discussed in detail in the next chapter, interventions should be proportionate to the offender's degree of risk, meaning that the government must demonstrate increasingly stronger proof of risk as the intervention continues.

Even with these limitations, mistakes and abuse are likely to occur, which may make a retributive regime, with its determinate sentences and similar sentences for similar crimes, more attractive to some. But these desert-based limitations at the back end are effectively nullified by discretionary actions at the beginning of the process, where prosecutors are granted extremely broad discretion that is not subject to judicial or any other type of monitoring. The Supreme Court has stated that "so long as the prosecutor has probable cause to believe that the accused committed an offense defined by statute, the decision whether or not to prosecute, and what charge to file or bring before a grand jury, generally rests entirely in his discretion."[83] This uncabined authority of the prosecutor can produce wildly disparate dispositional results.[84] Thus, the potential for abuse is unfortunately nontrivial in both types of systems.

One case that critics of the current approach to juvenile offenders are fond of describing is that of Lionel Tate, who killed a six-year-old girl when he was twelve years old, apparently while simulating wrestling that he had seen on TV. After transfer to adult court, he received a life sentence (later affirmed on appeal, although the verdict was overturned on other grounds).[85] The typical reaction to this case is that the sentence was "disproportionate" to Lionel's culpability, given his immaturity; [86] indeed, given the fact that he was later determined to be incompetent to stand trial and to have a mental age of nine,[87] he may have lacked even the appreciation of his offense's wrongfulness that is required by current criminal law doctrine for a bona fide excuse. What is less seldom remarked is the equally incredible fact that the prosecutor first offered Lionel and his mother a three-year sentence to be served in the juvenile system (which the mother turned down).[88] Whatever disposition was appropriate for Lionel, allowing the prosecutor discretion to choose between seeking a three-year juvenile sentence and a life sentence in the adult system is an open invitation for unconscionable results.

Furthermore, the retributive goal of equal, determinate sentences for identical offenses, even if it could be achieved, makes little sense. In fact, the desert visited by a particular term of imprisonment for, say, robbery may vary from robber to robber, depending on the conditions of imprisonment and the nature of the robber.[89] A system that stresses consistency based on risk is probably *more* equitable than one based on culpability, given the malleable nature of the latter concept.

Dehumanization

A third objection to prevention regimes—one the Court implicitly rejected in *Hendricks* but which nonetheless should be given serious consideration—is that they undermine the autonomy premise upon which the criminal justice system and our entire society are built. Whether or not our actions are determined, the argument goes, it is morally and practically important to treat people as if they are responsible moral agents.[90] Preventive regimes limited to the incapacitation of those with extreme cognitive or volitional impairment do not threaten this imperative because they preventively confine only those who have been adjudged legally nonresponsible. But preventive schemes like those endorsed in *Hendricks* send a different message. The more categories of people that are confined based on future rather than past acts, the greater the insult to the moral claim that individuals control their fate and conduct.

This dehumanization concern is difficult to evaluate because it is so abstract. It seems most potent when the government creates two systems of liberty deprivation for those who commit antisocial acts—one designed to punish and the second designed to preventively detain—and then chooses the latter option. In this "two-track" situation, exemplified by sexual predator systems that co-exist with the criminal process, preventive detention palpably signals that the person is different, a harmful "predator" rather than a rational actor who has chosen to commit culpable harm. Research suggests that this type of stigmatization may even have criminogenic consequences.[91]

The dehumanization objection is less powerful, however, when there is only one track, entirely devoted to the prevention goal, as under the juvenile system proposed here. In such a setting, all offenders are evaluated along a continuum of risk, thereby avoiding the explicit and offensive "dangerous being" label that characterizes the separate sexual predator regime. Moreover, in contrast to the latter regime, intervention based on dangerousness in a single-track system would, if earlier prescriptions are followed, occur immediately after proof that the individual caused harm. In this way, the individual-prevention system resembles punishment based on desert, even if in fact it is forward-looking in focus.

In any event, the argument that a *Hendricks* regime would undermine society's presumption of individual autonomy loses much of its force in the juvenile setting. As discussed earlier, while most children can justly be held legally responsible for their criminal actions, the research suggests that on the autonomy scale they fall somewhere between adults with severe mental illness and non-mentally ill adults. More important, the perception that juveniles are less autonomous than adults is widespread. Several surveys indicate that the public is comfortable with a juvenile system that focuses on reduction of juvenile crime, even if that means more lenient sentences and an emphasis on rehabilitation.[92] Thus, treatment of children as relatively nonautonomous does not significantly undercut society's belief in the concept of "free will" or dilute its ability to condemn adult offenders.

Societal Need for Desert

Related to the dehumanization objection is the concern that a system aimed at prevention pays insufficient homage to society's need to express its repugnance toward offenders, which is said to have a variety of bad consequences. These critics correctly note that a preventive system would not always impose the "punishment" demanded by desert principles. In some cases, it could impose a sanction that, when viewed from the desert perspective, is too lenient, thus allegedly failing to vindicate the interest of either the victim or society in expressing outrage at the harm done. In other cases, the intervention may appear disproportionately long from a retributive perspective. If these instances multiply, the argument goes, there could be an increase in vigilante justice, a weakening of norms regarding antisocial behavior, and even a burgeoning belief that individuals are not responsible for their actions, all developments that might make citizens less compliant with societal prohibitions.[93]

These latter claims are speculative even when applied in the adult context.[94] If the preventive approach is limited to the juvenile setting where, as just noted, the public is not as concerned about desert, they seem even less salient, particularly when, as would occur in the type of regime proposed here, a statement of accountability is made in connection with adjudication, *some* intervention usually takes place after adjudication, multiple offenses are subject to greater intervention, and the overall goal of prevention is made clear to the public. With these characteristics in place, a preventive juvenile system should provide enough of a bow to desert to avoid the hypothesized harms of ignoring it. Support for that conclusion comes from the apparent absence of these harms (e.g., vigilante justice) in the many jurisdictions that administer or used to administer preventive-style juvenile justice systems.[95]

It must be admitted, however, that, in rare instances, a particularly serious case will cause significant tension in a system based on risk rather than desert. For example, the case of Willie Bosket, a fifteen-year-old who killed two subway passengers in the course of a robbery, occasioned an uproar in New York state when it was handled through the juvenile court system, which at that time had exclusive jurisdiction over such crimes.[96] But the response to Bosket's disposition also makes clear why a desert-based system can badly malfunction. Within two weeks of Bosket's sentence, the legislature rewrote state law to permit transfer of juveniles as young as thirteen if they committed a serious crime.[97] From a crime prevention perspective, the better approach would be to keep someone like Bosket in the juvenile system but recognize that such an individual should be subject to intervention as long as he or she poses a high risk of committing serious crime. That intervention might well involve confinement (if community-based intervention were deemed unfeasible), could last a number of years (depending on the differential between act and dispositional jurisdiction of the juvenile court), and in extreme cases could even extend beyond the end of typical juvenile court jurisdiction if the individual poses a particularly high risk. If the public understands that indeterminate confinement is a potential disposition in the most serious cases, it will be less inclined to demand wholesale counterproductive changes of the type associated with Bosket's case.

Eventually, a possible reconciliation of desert and risk principles may come from work attempting to discern the extent to which the public is willing to equate nonincarcerative interventions with prison time in terms of desert.[98] Conceivably, for instance, six months of Multisystemic Therapy could have as much "punitive bite" as a similar term of imprisonment in the public's mind. Research exploring this possibility is still in its nascent stages, however. And it is likely that even if desert can be equated with alternative sanctions, in many cases it will require far more intervention than is necessary to complete an effective preventive program. If so, it makes little sense, at least from a utilitarian perspective, to extend the intervention simply because some segment of the public will be bothered by a shorter, less punitive disposition, unless and until more solid evidence exists that not doing so will lead to vigilantism and other types of noncompliance.[99]

Even if such evidence surfaces, it should not necessarily dictate rejection of a preventive approach in these tough cases. Rather, as occurs with indeterminate sentencing in the adult system, the best response from a prevention perspective would be to impose a *potential* maximum sentence. The public could be told the juvenile offender will spend up to a particular number of years in confinement. But ultimate release would depend on assessments of risk. Although the Supreme Court probably did not mean its language in *Graham*—the life without parole case—to be read this broadly, it still states the relevant proposition: "What the State must do . . . is give defendants like Graham some meaningful opportunity to obtain release based on demonstrated maturity and rehabilitation."[100]

Deterrence

The first version of the deterrence argument against the individual prevention model is simple: because intervention for prevention purposes is, by definition, not punishment and, as suggested above, tends to rely on dispositional vehicles other than confinement, it will fail to deter juveniles from antisocial behavior. This objection has some merit. Certainly if there were no consequences to a criminal act, general deterrence would be lacking. Furthermore, it is probably the case, as authorities have reported anecdotally, that the relatively "softer" penalties in the juvenile justice system reduce young offenders' concern about getting caught.[101] But assuming the potential for some type of coercive intervention after a crime occurs and that this intervention becomes more onerous for repeat offenders—both characteristics of an individual prevention system—a general deterrent effect similar to that which can be expected from a robust punishment regime is likely.

This perhaps counterintuitive conclusion derives from the extensive literature showing that even adult criminals are not affected by legislative increases or decreases in sentences.[102] Whether because they are not aware of sentencing differentials, are governed by (im)moral rather than legal considerations, do not believe they will be caught, or simply ignore their best interests due to social, situational, and chemical influences, most criminals "are undeterred by harsher punishments."[103] If that is true for most adults, than it is certainly true for juveniles, who are less likely to be deterred by *any* type of punishment. In other words, as long as the possibility exists of some form of liberty-restricting intervention after an antisocial act, a prevention-oriented juvenile justice system will probably generate as much general deterrence as it is possible to get in most cases.

Corroborating this assertion is research on inner-city youth suggesting that peer behavior and mores have a much more powerful influence on potential juvenile offenders than does the threat of legal sanctions,[104] as well as research carried out in a number of different locales finding that, contrary to their statements, youth in adult prison are not deterred by it.[105] Indeed, juveniles who have the most experience with the criminal justice system apparently are the least concerned about punishment, suggesting that prisons do not carry the threat that deterrence theorists would like them to have.[106] The most substantial study concluding that harsher sanctions do have a significant effect on juvenile offending is based on finding a 23 percent increase in crime by eighteen-year-olds in states with a relatively harsh juvenile system and a relatively lenient adult system.[107] Putting aside the low likelihood that a juvenile justice system could be appreciably harsher than an adult system (the author doesn't indicate the criteria used to assign these categories) the observed increase in crime rate could easily be due to the criminogenic effects of detention in harsher juvenile regimes rather than the result of an informed calculation by eighteen-year-olds that their penalty will be relatively more lenient now that they are subject to adult jurisdiction.[108]

But the deterrence argument can be recharacterized, in terms that overlap to some extent with the dehumanization objection. As Henry Hart put it, a preventive regime might defeat deterrence in the sense that it "would undermine the foundation of a free society's effort to build up each individual's sense of responsibility as a guide and a stimulus to the constructive development of his capacity for effectual and fruitful decision."[109] Others have echoed this view.[110]

This assertion about the character-building function of punishment is no more convincing, however. Consistent with our discussion of the contextual nature of crime in Chapter 2, research shows that the combined effect of families, peers, churches, schools, and other institutions is more effective than the criminal law at teaching citizens the difference between right and wrong. As Tom Tyler states in his summary of this literature, "people are reluctant to commit criminal acts for which their family and friends would sanction them[;] individuals look to their social groups for information about appropriate conduct."[111]

Moreover, as one of us has noted in other work, if the goal is to inculcate sound practical judgment in the individual offender, punishment through a judicial or jury verdict of "guilty" is a "blunt instrument for doing so."[112] An individualized prevention regime has a much better chance of developing good judgment:

> Risk management, properly conducted, explores the causes of antisocial behavior and continually stresses the offender's ability to change that behavior through cognitive restructuring, avoidance of risky behavior (such as drinking or fraternizing with gang members), and adjusting relationships. A regime based on prediction does not have to insult the notion that past choices have consequences and that the offender is responsible and held accountable for them. There is a difference in message, however. The punishment model says to the offender: "You have done something bad, for which you must pay." The prevention model says: "You have done something harmful, which you must not let happen again."[113]

Arguably the latter message is much preferable to the former, especially when dealing with juveniles. In any event, it is not clear that the message sent by a diminished retribution regime is any stronger; arguably that regime counterproductively dilutes accountability by telling juveniles they are considerably less culpable than adults. Youthful offenders need to be held accountable for their actions. But accountability need not be equated with punishment or prison time.

Perhaps, though, the process of punishment itself builds character. This claim is that doing one's time instills dignity and allows the released offender to reenter society with a guilt-free conscience. That process compares favorably, it is argued, to an indeterminate disposition, which can be demoralizing and breed cynicism.[114]

There is anecdotal evidence supporting the latter view. Yet there is also anecdotal evidence supporting the view that risk-management programs can instill a greater sense of worth. Because these programs are premised on the idea that time of release depends upon the offender's willingness to achieve specific treatment goals, they may enhance individual responsibility and energize those with the potential to be law abiding. As observers of the adult parole system have noted, discretionary parole release is a much better mechanism than mandatory parole for achieving rehabilitation because "mandatory releasees are given an automatic release date and therefore have no system incentives to seek programs and treatment to facilitate change."[115] Researchers have also concluded that good time credits in adult prisons can dramatically increase participation in rehabilitation programs, provide incentives to cooperate with prison authorities, and give prisoners reason to believe they control their fate at least to some extent, thus enhancing their "ability to operate as independent actors."[116] At the least, it can be said that we have no clear evidence that retributive punishment is better at "building character" than a risk-management regime.

Cost

Even if one accepts prevention as the primary goal of juvenile justice, a final reason to be reticent about an individual prevention regime is that all but the least ambitious versions of it could be enormously expensive. For instance, the state of Illinois estimated that implementing a sexual predator statute in that state would cost more than $1 billion over a ten-year period.[117] The key policy question about such expenditures is not whether they improve public safety; surely they buy some added protection. But compared to what? The concern is that the amount of money spent on such programs diverts support from other, more effective preventive mechanisms (to wit, punishment under a just deserts model).

That seems unlikely in the juvenile setting. As recounted in Chapter 2, compared to prison, community intervention programs for juveniles are not only better at reducing recidivism but less costly. The Surgeon General's Report on Youth Violence echoed these claims, concluding after a review of the relevant research through 2000 that preventive programs "cost less over the long run than mandatory sentences and other get-tough approaches."[118]

Even if expenditures are the same on a per capita basis, rehabilitation of juveniles is likely to be more cost effective than rehabilitation of adults, for at least two reasons. First, if juvenile rehabilitation works, the overall crime rate will be reduced more significantly because individuals will end their antisocial conduct earlier. Second, individuals will be crime free for a longer period of time, allowing more productive lives on other fronts.

A third intuitively appealing reason—that children are less set in their ways than adults and thus easier to rehabilitate—is based on an unproven empirical assumption. But there is little doubt that adolescents are more treatable than the average offender committed under the sexual predator laws authorized by *Hendricks*,[119] providing still another distinction between those laws and the prevention-oriented juvenile justice system proposed here. If states are willing to spend money on treatment and preventive intervention, they should make sure to spend a disproportionate amount of it in the juvenile justice system.

Conclusion

The new police power paradigm contemplated by *Hendricks*, although suspect in its application to adults, provides a coherent and defensible justification for a preventive juvenile justice system. Because children are less deterrable than adults, they can be subject to preventive intervention. Because the juvenile court has limited jurisdiction, because children are perceived as less autonomous than adults, and because the treatment of youth is relatively cost effective, a preventive system applied to juveniles does not have the serious shortcomings associated with its application in the adult context.

This individual prevention model of juvenile justice is preferable to the rehabilitative and retributive models that have dominated discussion of the juvenile justice system throughout the past century. The rehabilitative model is based on untenable assumptions about juvenile offenders' innocence and the scope of government power to socialize youth, and the adult retribution model is a recipe for exacerbating juvenile recidivism. The diminished retribution model, while superior to these two models, rests on assumptions about juvenile capacities that are inconsistent with current criminal law doctrine, and in any event does not provide a persuasive theoretical basis for a segregated juvenile justice system that takes full advantage of the new recidivism-reducing community interventions.

In the spirit of compromise one could nonetheless construct a system that reconciles all four of these options, combining the preventive model with various elements of the rehabilitative and retributive models. Some sort of hybrid approach exists in a number of American jurisdictions today, even the toughest of which have not completely rejected the rehabilitative ideal.[120] But the arguments presented in this chapter push against such a hybrid. In contrast to the rehabilitative model, youths should not be the subject of juvenile court jurisdiction unless they have committed serious antisocial conduct and represent a high risk. In contrast to the retributive models, an emphasis on prevention should lead to the elimination, not just the reduction, of transfer jurisdiction and "blended" sentencing for older youth.[121] Finally, in contrast to all three of the other models, once found deserving of a guilt adjudication for a criminal offense, juveniles of all ages should be subject to juvenile court intervention only according to assessments of risk and risk management principles. In particular, juveniles should not receive a sentence based on retributive principles, because if such sentences achieve public safety and recidivism-reduction goals, they do so only serendipitously, while offering too much of a temptation to fold juvenile justice into the adult criminal justice system. Prevention of recidivism, not vaguely defined "rehabilitation" and not culpability-based punishment, should be the rallying cry for advocates of a separate regime for youthful offenders.

The discussion in this chapter has provided only an outline of a prevention-oriented juvenile justice system. As a result, it has only hinted at the benefits of such a regime. It is now time to provide more detail.

4

A Preventive Risk-Management Model of Juvenile Justice

The next two chapters lay out our vision of how an individual prevention regime of juvenile justice would work. This chapter describes its substantive scope, while the next chapter discusses its procedural components. Before delving into the specifics, we outline below some of the broad legal and behavioral science principles underlying the preventive risk management model of juvenile justice.

The first guiding principle, one that we have already stressed, is that a preventive risk-management model of juvenile justice is forward looking. The primary goal is to prevent recidivism and future crime. Conduct and experiences in the past are relevant primarily as data that can be used to make good legal, clinical, and policy decisions affecting future outcomes.

The second guiding principle is that administrative models of justice are better than adjudicative models at implementing policy and program objectives (such as those relevant to prevention). Backward-looking, adjudicative models of justice serve well the aim of making people pay for past offenses. But administrative models are better suited to effectuating a system organized around risk management.[1]

The third guiding principle is that the juvenile justice system should provide a natural laboratory for basic and applied research on issues relevant to adolescent development, delinquency prevention, and procedural justice.[2] The administrative entity that runs the juvenile justice system must seek and take advantage of empirical analysis of different prevention mechanisms. It should incorporate intervention models that are grounded in and guided by evidence-based practices while allowing for the systematic development and empirical evaluation of promising and innovative intervention programs. In other words, the juvenile justice system should be performance-based both substantively and procedurally.

The fourth guiding principle is that decision making in an individual prevention-oriented system is best made by individuals and teams of individuals with expertise across a number of domains. Expertise in juvenile law may be necessary but is certainly not a sufficient knowledge base for primary decision makers in a performance-based risk management system of juvenile justice. Basic organizational management skills, the ability to function as a critical consumer of behavioral science research, and the ability to oversee the ongoing monitoring and evaluation of outcomes at the individual, program, and system-wide levels are all skill sets needed to supplement the traditional legal expertise of the traditional juvenile court judge.

The fifth guiding principle is the recognition that the juvenile justice system does not function in a vacuum. Primary decision makers in the juvenile justice system must have ongoing and mutually informative relationships with other youth-socializing institutions such as families, schools, communities, and the child welfare, health care, and adult criminal justice systems.[3]

With these guiding principles in mind, we can turn to the issues surrounding the substantive scope of a preventive risk-management model of juvenile justice. The first part of this chapter addresses the eligibility criteria for an individual prevention regime: when would such a juvenile court have jurisdiction? The second part of the chapter looks at the dispositional consequences of a decision to intervene in the life of a youth: how would a performance-based risk-management system work?

Juvenile Court Jurisdiction

Traditionally, the juvenile court exerted "act jurisdiction" over those who allegedly committed crimes or status offenses prior to age eighteen and "dispositional jurisdiction" over convicted individuals until age twenty-one or so. But it also had "transfer jurisdiction" over youths above fourteen or fifteen, which permitted the court to transfer juveniles out of juvenile court to adult court if they were considered unamenable to treatment. More recently, while a number of states have eliminated status offenses, most have also lowered the maximum ages for act and dispositional jurisdiction or the minimum age for transfer eligibility, or both, and the transfer decision now is focused more on culpability than treatability.[4]

In an individual prevention regime, the maximum age for act jurisdiction might increase *beyond* eighteen, the maximum age for dispositional jurisdiction would definitely increase, and transfer jurisdiction would disappear. At the adjudication stage, in addition to criminal acts typically prosecuted in adult courts, low-level crimes that are normally not prosecuted but that are associated with high risk for future crime would become an explicit basis for jurisdiction and a high priority for intervention and risk management. At the dispositional stage, assessments of risk and treatability would dominate; culpability determinations would not be relevant. Furthermore, if a juvenile's recidivism can be reduced through available treatment and the treatment is not provided, release or an injunction forcing the treatment would be the proper relief.

The Age Requirement

If undeterrability provides the rationale for intervention, as it would under the individual prevention approach we propose, the age of eligibility for that regime should end when relative undeterrability ends. Of course, the various personal characteristics and circumstances associated with a significant degree of undeterrability do not disappear suddenly at a particular age and will vary in strength at different ages for different people. The research is ambiguous as to when these characteristics change for most people.

At this point, all that can be said is that the traditional cutoff age of eighteen would not be inconsistent with research regarding risk perception, temporal perspective, the effects of peer pressure, or one's stake in life. However, the maximum age for act jurisdiction could ultimately be extended beyond eighteen for policy reasons grounded in research. For example, social scientists have noted that our culture has nudged the dividing line between adolescence and adulthood forward to the mid-twenties as young people take longer to acquire the education and skills necessary to compete in our modern economy.[5] Neuroscience research indicating that frontal lobe development continues well into the third decade of life also tends to support arguments for expanding act jurisdiction beyond eighteen to sometime in the early twenties.

Additionally, dispositional age should extend well beyond eighteen. Some states allow juvenile courts to exercise dispositional jurisdiction up to age twenty-five. A significant differential of seven years or so between age and dispositional jurisdiction makes sense for several reasons. First, for juveniles who commit a crime in their later adolescence, an intervention program lasting into the early twenties may be necessary. Under the juvenile system as it operates now, juvenile offenders are often transferred to adult court simply because a treatment program cannot be completed by the time a juvenile offender "ages out."[6] The pressure to engage in this counterproductive practice would be eliminated by a differential between act and dispositional age jurisdiction (of course, this pressure would also be removed by the elimination of transfer jurisdiction, a move that we discuss later).

A second reason for such a differential is the converse of the situation just described. Sometimes a person who commits a crime after age eighteen could nonetheless benefit from juvenile programs. The act/dispositional age differential would permit adult courts to engage in "reverse transfer" at the dispositional stage in those cases where the court believes a juvenile facility would be more appropriate and less criminogenic than an adult prison.

Third, a differential between age and dispositional jurisdiction would allow longer detention of those juvenile offenders who are at very high risk for violent offending and have failed to respond to community-based, multisystemic interventions. Indeed, for extremely dangerous juveniles, extended detention, beyond even age twenty-five, might be prudent. However, as we discuss below, proportionality reasoning would impose an outer limit to such detentions.

A final and related reason for establishing a significant gap between age and dispositional jurisdiction is that it would provide a safety valve in those high profile cases, such as that of Willie Bosket described in the previous chapter, when a juvenile offender commits a horrific crime and the public demands "justice." In such cases, the differential of up to seven years might help assuage the public's desire for prolonged detention. It is of course possible that authorities might feel pressure to prolong detention of these types of individuals even if they do not pose a high risk. That outcome would be inconsistent with individual prevention principles and ideally could be avoided. But, as unjustifiable as it is, such detentions would be preferable to the alternative—the open-ended transfer regime that we have today, where young offenders like Bosket would spend most, if not all, of their lives in adult prison at public expense, with little or no effort to return them to society as responsible citizens.

The Act and Mental State Requirements

The previous chapter provided several reasons as to why a prevention regime should require a triggering act. But the precise nature of this conduct was left vague. Certainly commission of an act that would be prosecuted as a crime in adult court would satisfy this requirement. Additionally, however, some antisocial behaviors associated with relatively trivial crimes that are typically not prosecuted or not taken seriously could form the basis for juvenile court jurisdiction under a system focused on individual prevention if they have been linked in the empirical literature with high risk for future crime. Some examples of such acts might include behaviors associated with "early starter," life-course persistent offending, such as bullying[7] (assault) and cruelty to animals,[8] as well as complicity in theft crimes that occur in association with delinquent peers. These types of offenses, often ignored or minimized in adult court, might well be common triggering acts in an individual prevention regime.

At the same time, to meet the demands of the legality principle, all acts that serve as the basis for juvenile court jurisdiction would need to be codified by statute. Furthermore, vague "status offenses" like incorrigibility or constitutionally protected activity such as gang membership should not be grounds for intervention, even if they are associated with risk. As the Supreme Court has recognized, limitations on the threshold for deprivations of liberty are necessary to curb abuses of discretion and provide concrete notice.[9] A more instrumental reason for equating juvenile court act jurisdiction with adult crimes is the goal of protecting the integrity of juvenile justice and government as a whole. The previous chapter discounted the possibility that ignoring desert at the dispositional stage, *after* a guilt determination, would so undermine public confidence that general compliance with the law would be undermined. But any system that permitted *intervention* for behavior that is considered innocent is much more likely to occasion community outrage.

Even at the adjudication/intervention stage of the process, however, an individual prevention regime would institutionalize one significant difference between juvenile crimes and the typical adult crime, specifically in connection with the mens rea, or mental state, requirement. The mens rea requirement prevents conviction for harms that are purely accidental. Moreover, in some jurisdictions even harms that are negligently caused cannot lead to criminal liability in adult court.[10] In these jurisdictions, only harms that the perpetrator intended to occur or was aware might occur as a result of his or her actions can be the basis for an adjudication of guilt; harms that a reasonable person in the perpetrator's shoes would have anticipated—say, an injury due to speeding or resulting from a shot fired near a group of people—but that the actor did not actually anticipate or foresee cannot lead to criminal liability.[11]

The type of individual prevention regime we envision would continue to prohibit guilt adjudications for merely accidental harm, both because it is not likely to be a risk factor and because liability in this situation would be anathema under legality reasoning. But we would permit adjudications of guilt for negligent crime. Many theorists believe that this type of crime deserves punishment.[12] More important for our purposes, it can be a significant risk factor. As Chapter 2 indicated, juvenile offenders may often engage in behavior oblivious to risks that adults could easily foresee. When an adolescent commits an act that harms or endangers someone, an unawareness that the harm would occur or that the risk was present should not prevent assertion of juvenile court jurisdiction for the purpose of reducing the likelihood of repeat occurrences unless even a reasonable adult would not have foreseen the consequences.

Thus the juvenile code might consist of relatively simple prohibitions on killing, raping, stealing, drug dealing, and trying to engage in these types of crimes, as well as a prohibition on engaging in conduct that endangered others, without the complicated mens rea terminology that sometimes accompanies these provisions in adult statutes. Juveniles would have a "defense" if such conduct was purely accidental and nonnegligent, or if they can prove self-defense or some other justification recognized in adult court. Otherwise, however, once the criminal act is proven to have been committed by the juvenile, the only remaining questions would be whether the offender posed a risk sufficient to warrant intervention and, if so, what type of intervention could reduce that risk.

Before discussing those issues, we want to emphasize that, in contrast to a culpability-based regime where proof of a crime should, at least in theory, mandate punishment of some kind, proof of an antisocial act does not and should not require intervention in a preventive system. If prevention is the goal, involvement in the adult system will often be the worst possible disposition, but entanglement with the juvenile justice system might well be the second worst. Many juveniles who have acted in an antisocial matter are unlikely to recidivate even if no intervention takes place, while others may not need any type of judicially-imposed disposition but rather can be handled through intelligent use of the educational system, social welfare programs, or community efforts that have no connection with government.[13] The juvenile justice system should be the last resort, not the first one, when prevention is the goal.

The Risk (Dangerousness) Requirement

Hendricks and most legal sources that address preventive interventions usually speak in terms of "dangerousness." We prefer the concept of "risk" because it connotes a focus on the probability of recidivism rather than a dichotomous, either-or decision. Risk assessments are probably no more prone to inaccuracy or arbitrariness than culpability assessments. But the difficulties inherent in predicting the future should not be taken lightly. Accordingly, we proffer two proposals, one quantitative (addressed here) and one qualitative (addressed in the next section), about how the preventive philosophy should be implemented in the juvenile context.

Derived directly from the principle enunciated in *Jackson v. Indiana*, the first, quantitative proposal is that the degree of risk posed, in terms of both probability and magnitude, must be proportionate to the nature of the intervention contemplated by the state. This proportionality rule is analogous to the just deserts principle governing retribution regimes, which grades punishment based on relative culpability. More important, it is a rule that is implicit throughout the legal system in situations involving assessments of risk. For instance, a brief patdown of the outer clothing requires only a reasonable suspicion of danger,[14] while a forty-eight-hour detention of a mentally ill person thought to be dangerous generally requires the higher standard of probable cause,[15] and full-term commitment of such a person requires clear and convincing evidence (quantified at about a 75 percent likelihood).[16] Commitment of a person as a sexual predator requires either clear and convincing evidence or proof beyond a reasonable doubt,[17] and the latter standard of proof is constitutionally required for proving dangerousness in a capital sentencing proceeding.[18] We seek merely to make explicit this already existing relationship between risk and intervention intrusiveness.

Consistent with the proportionality principle, proof requirements should be at their most stringent when physical confinement is sought. More specifically, a *high* degree of risk for *serious* crime in the *near* future must be shown to warrant confinement, regardless of its venue (jail, "reformatory," or prison);[19] prolonged confinement should be even more difficult to sustain, given the proportionate risk that would have to be proven. More specifically still, when the government seeks to confine an individual it should have to provide clear and convincing evidence that the juvenile poses a high risk of serious crime in the near future if not confined, and confinement beyond a certain period (perhaps six months or a year) should require proof beyond a reasonable doubt that the offender is not likely to respond successfully to community-based multisystemic intervention. An added justification for these strict requirements is the likelihood, corroborated by the research canvassed in Chapter 2, that the recidivism of youths who are institutionalized will be much higher than that of those who are not. The state's interest in preventing crime would hardly be met by increasing its likelihood, yet that may well be the result of relaxed proof requirements in confinement cases.

One might justifiably ask how these higher standards of proof can be met given the error rates associated with risk assessment. It must be admitted that the state will rarely, if ever, be able to show beyond a reasonable doubt (a 95%+ level of certainty) or even by clear and convincing evidence that a particular individual will commit a serious crime within a short period of time if not confined. One way of dealing with this practical reality, adopted in some jurisdictions, is to define the legal standard of risk as a particular probability, a quantification that at one time was merely symbolic but today can take on concrete meaning with the advent of actuarial instruments that provide specific probability estimates.[20] If "dangerousness" is defined as a "likelihood of violence" (with "likelihood" meaning more-likely-than-not), then, under the scheme described above requiring clear and convincing proof for initial confinement, the government would only be required to demonstrate roughly a 38 percent chance of violent crime being committed if the youth were instead treated in the community (the quotient of .75 × .51, on the assumption that clear and convincing evidence is equated with a 75% level of certainty and that more-likely-than-not is associated with a 51% chance of concurrence). If the government is seeking prolonged confinement beyond six months, it would be required to show roughly a 48 percent chance of recidivism for violent crime if treated in the community (the quotient of .95 × .51, on the assumption beyond a reasonable doubt is equated with a 95% level of certainty).

In other words, when seeking confinement, the government could be required to adduce "proof of a definite maybe," to use a phrase coined by John Monahan and David Wexler.[21] If this proof structure is considered insufficiently protective of the juvenile offender's interest in avoiding confinement, higher levels of certainty could be required.[22] But recall that culpability assessments are also subject to serious vagaries in proof, that mistakes about risk can be corrected through the periodic review process, and that confinement based on such proof should be pursued only if the predicted crime is serious in nature and only if it is *necessary* to reduce recidivism (compared, for instance, to community-based interventions which can often successfully manage even violent offenders). Note further that even if this relatively relaxed definition of risk is adopted, incapacitative intervention would be rare (probably involving less than 10% of all those juvenile offenders who have committed a serious crime and a much smaller percentage of juveniles who commit any crime),[23] and in any event should usually be of relatively short duration.

Proving Risk

The second proposal regarding the risk assessment stage of a preventive regime goes to the quality of evidence that government must produce to justify intervention. The evidence must be based on a thorough examination by a professional well acquainted with the risk-assessment and management literature and, when confinement is sought, should generally be statistical in nature. We elaborate on these propositions in some detail because much of the ferment over prevention-oriented regimes centers around controversies having to do with the feasibility and accuracy of risk assessment.

Examination Methodology. Some classic examples of improper risk testimony come courtesy of Dr. James Grigson, who for many years routinely testified for the state of Texas in death penalty cases, two of which were appealed to the United States Supreme Court. In one of these cases he purported to be able to address the offender's dangerousness, as well as his sanity at the time of the offense and his competency to stand trial, based solely on a ninety-minute "mental status examination" that the court order stated should be focused solely on the issue of competency.[24] Based on this examination, Dr. Grigson testified that the offender was "a very severe sociopath" who was untreatable and would "only get worse."[25] In the second case, *Barefoot v. Estelle*, Dr. Grigson did not even interview the defendant, but rather stated, based on a hypothetical question, that "there was a 100% chance" that a person with the defendant's criminal record and reputation would commit future acts of criminal violence.[26] He also admitted that he was unfamiliar with most of the literature regarding predictions of violence, but dismissed his ignorance as unimportant.[27]

Dr. Grigson's methodology, if it can be called that, was unscientific and unethical. It will be the rare case where a clinician can credibly state that the chances of recidivism are 100 percent, and no conclusions about risk should be attempted without interviewing the subject, gathering relevant third party information, and perusing the literature to discern pertinent risk factors.[28] In fact, in large part because of his sloppy evaluation procedures and testimony in capital cases, Dr. Grigson was eventually expelled from the American Psychiatric Association and retired as an expert witness.[29] But even had he continued to be available, he should not have been allowed to testify under the state analogue to Federal Rule of Evidence 703, which provides that experts may not present opinions unless they are based on information "of a type reasonably relied upon by experts in the particular field." Although the Supreme Court in *Barefoot* indicated that it saw no *constitutional* infirmity in Grigson's testimony in either case,[30] as an evidentiary matter it is simply not reasonable to testify about the risk posed by an individual based solely on a hypothetical question or a short evaluation that does not gather the relevant information.

Even when the dictates of Rule 703 are met, evaluation and testimony about risk should be subject to additional constraints when the government is seeking to *confine* the offender (whether for the first time or on a continuing basis). In these cases, experts should usually be limited to reports and testimony based on empirically derived and appropriately normed probability estimates, with only two exceptions: if such estimates are not available for the type of situation in question, the government should be able to rely on descriptions of previous criminal behavior, and if the juvenile opens the door to non-statistical, clinical prediction testimony by relying on it to prove he or she does not pose a significant risk, the state may respond in kind.

This proposal requires some elaboration on two issues: (1) Why prefer empirically driven probability estimates over other forms of risk assessment? (2) Why permit the offender to control when other forms of assessment will be heard? [31]

Confinement: The Argument for Probability Estimates. Several forms of risk assessment exist. For many years, such assessments were entirely *clinical* in nature, relying on the predilections of the individual examiner with respect to the factors that are relevant in making a prediction and the implications of those factors (this was Dr. Grigson's technique, although his implementation of it was far from ideal). More recently, researchers have touted *actuarial* approaches to risk assessment. An actuarial analysis relies on a finite number of pre-identified variables that statistically correlate to risk and that produce a definitive probability or probability range of risk (e.g., the individual belongs to a group that has a 38% to 45% chance of committing a violent act within a year if intervention does not take place). Splitting the difference is an assessment technique known as *adjusted actuarial* analysis, which begins with an actuarial assessment but then adjusts the risk calculation, based on individualized factors that are not incorporated into the actuarial instrument. A variation of the latter form of assessment is *structured professional judgment*, sometimes called *guided clinical assessment*. This technique, like the actuarial approach, relies on an evaluation of a finite number of pre-defined factors that have been associated with risk, but neither the factors nor the final conclusions about risk are mathematically obtained. Because they follow a particular format and can result in numerical scores, however, these protocols can generate results that in turn can be correlated with recidivism. Thus, for instance, the Psychopathy Checklist–Revised, which is a structured professional judgment instrument, can produce a score of up to 40, and follow-up research has indicated that over 75 percent of those with a score of 25 or higher recidivate within a three-year period.[32]

There has been considerable ferment over which of these approaches to risk assessment is optimal. Some researchers have argued that "actuarial methods are too good and clinical judgment too poor to risk contaminating the former with the latter."[33] On this view, even the adjusted actuarial assessment and structured clinical judgment techniques are suspect, because they rely in part on clinical analysis. Other researchers who tend to favor structured clinical judgment have argued that the error rates associated with actuarial instruments are unacceptably high when applied to individual cases because the samples used to validate the instruments were too small and thus not generalizable to most groups or individuals.[34] But the latter view has been challenged as insufficiently cognizant of the methodological precision employed in developing the best actuarial instruments.[35]

Members of the well-respected MacArthur Research Network on Risk Assessment, after considering an earlier iteration of this debate, concluded that "actuarial instruments . . . are best viewed as 'tools' for clinical assessment. This reliance on clinical judgment—aided by an empirical understanding of risk factors for violence and their interactions—reflects, and in our view should reflect, the standard of care at this juncture in the field's development."[36] In the specific context of crime prediction, other authors have endorsed a similar, *anamnestic* approach, which combines actuarial or base rate information with a detailed analysis of offense dynamics in an effort to discern the particular individual's offending patterns and their likely causes.[37]

Given the disagreement over the best method of assessing risk, other considerations besides science must come into play in determining how risk should be assessed. The rules of evidence make clear that to be admissible, evidence must have probative value—that is, indicia of reliability—and that expert reports and testimony, which is of course how risk-assessment information is presented, must meet additional reliability requirements.[38] The rules also provide that evidence should be excluded if its probative value is substantially outweighed by its prejudicial impact.[39]

Our application of these rules to risk-assessment evidence in the juvenile justice context starts with the observation that virtually all risk-assessment evidence has some probative value and probably also crosses any extra threshold required by the rules governing expert testimony. But some types of assessment evidence can also have a significant prejudicial impact. In particular, clinical risk assessments proffered by the government that are not associated with empirically based probability estimates are so prejudicial that they should be barred unless the defense decides to use such evidence itself.

Consider first the issue of probative value. Various commentators, including justices of the Supreme Court, have compared clinical risk assessment to coin-flipping, on the grounds that the experts are wrong at least as often as they are right.[40] But prediction science has improved, and the false positive rate (the rate at which people who do not recidivate are erroneously predicted to recidivate within the follow-up period) is probably well below 50 percent when modern risk assessment techniques are used, at least when assessing groups with a high base rate of crime.[41] More important, to be probative under the widely followed Federal Rules of Evidence, evidence only has to have "any tendency to make the existence of any fact that is of consequence to the determination of the action more probable or less probable than it would be without the evidence."[42] In the risk-assessment context, that definition requires only that a prediction has a better-than-chance likelihood of being accurate. Most testimony about risk, even when derived from clinical assessments, easily meets this threshold requirement. As one of us has written after examining the literature on risk assessment, "Today experts can correctly identify those who will be violent at an accuracy rate, ranging from 45 to 75 percent, that is considerably higher than the base rate for violence within the prediction group, usually in the 15 to 35 percent range. Thus, the coin-flipping analogy is specious and misleading."[43]

When evidence is presented by *experts*, it must not only be probative but, in most states, also clear an additional hurdle. Some states follow the "*Frye* test," which requires that the basis of expert evidence be "generally accepted" among the relevant field.[44] Assuming acceptable evaluation procedures are followed (accumulation of relevant information, use of adequately normed tests, etc.), this standard is easily met because most risk assessment techniques are widely used.

A more demanding, and arguably the more appropriate, evidentiary test comes from *Daubert v. United States*,[45] a Supreme Court opinion construing the Federal Rules of Evidence applied in federal court and followed in over half the states.[46] *Daubert* not only requires courts to look at whether expert testimony is based on generally accepted techniques or theories but also at whether those techniques or theories have been subjected to some type of scientific verification process, the extent to which their error rates are known, and the substance of peer review, if any. Some have argued that whatever the outcome should be under *Frye*, only actuarial assessment clears the *Daubert* hurdle,[47] and others have argued that given the error rates associated with prediction, *all* expert testimony about risk should flunk *Daubert*.[48]

These conclusions are erroneous, however. Many other types of expert testimony, including expert testimony about culpability, probably do fail the *Daubert* test, because their basis has not been subjected to a verification process.[49] In contrast, expert testimony on risk—even clinical prediction testimony—is based on techniques that have been continuously scrutinized through validation testing, testing that has generated specific error rates. Although the error rates are not low, the point of *Daubert* is to ensure that such rates can be presented to the fact finder, not to exclude testimony if it falls below a particular accuracy level.[50]

Meeting the probative value and *Frye* or *Daubert* tests is not a sufficient basis for admissibility, however. Evidence must also avoid having a significantly prejudicial impact, which in this context means that there must be reason to believe that the expert prediction evidence will be taken for what it is worth, rather than uncritically accepted as truth or used for some purpose other than assessing risk. Here, finally, there *is* a legally relevant difference between different types of risk-assessment techniques, at least when government experts use them. When risk testimony is based on a clinical evaluation, research strongly suggests that legal fact finders do not carefully consider the evidence, but rather use it merely to reconfirm their preconceived notion that a person who has just been convicted of an offense must present a high risk; in contrast, the same research indicates that statistically based assessments are treated with more skepticism.

For instance, one laboratory study found that "jurors weigh clinical opinion expert testimony more heavily than actuarial expert testimony" and that "adversarial procedures may be insufficient to remove this bias."[51] A second laboratory study conducted by the same researchers confirmed that whereas cross-examination of clinical testimony has little impact on dangerousness ratings, cross-examination of actuarial testimony does reduce those ratings.[52] A third simulation study, although not making the clinical-actuarial comparison, concluded that even strong cross-examination and an opposing expert could not shake the influence of a state expert when that testimony is clinical in nature.[53] A fourth study that provided experts with clinical information, actuarial information, or a mixture of the two concluded that relevant case history information leads to so much inflation of risk estimates that decision makers should be given only quantitative estimates of the likelihood of reoffending and should be prevented from receiving narrative information about a case.[54] Other observations of real-world effects have noted that agreement rates between a judge or jury and state experts are much higher when the expert relies on clinical assessment techniques than when the expert relies on techniques that are statistically based.[55] These findings make sense, because expert statements that a person is likely to be violent are much harder to rebut or put in perspective than statements using numerical estimates.

In light of this research, when the government seeks to confine a juvenile after an adjudication of guilt it should be limited to proving risk via either an actuarial risk assessment or an assessment based on a structured professional judgment instrument that has been empirically linked to recidivism probability. Although as recently as ten years ago relevant actuarial information was sparse, today probability estimates for juveniles who have committed violent acts—the offenders most likely to require confinement—are possible because a number of statistically based instruments have been developed for that purpose. For instance, the *Structured Assessment of Violence Risk in Youth* and the *Early Assessment Risk List* are structured professional judgment risk-assessment instruments that can provide relatively precise estimations of risk.[56] Other instruments that can aid in this endeavor are the *Youth Level of Service/Case Management Inventory*, the *Hare Psychopathy Checklist-Youth* and the *Risk, Sophistication-Maturity, and Treatment Amenability Inventory*.[57]

A recent review of a number of these instruments, conducted by Lorraine Johnstone, indicates that they have reasonable predictive validity, significantly superior to unstructured clinical judgment.[58] However, Johnstone also noted that, in contrast to adults, youths change rapidly. Thus, for instance, the "truism" that the best predictor of future behavior is past behavior, which informs many actuarial instruments, is probably *not* true with juveniles. About 80 percent of children who exhibit violence during teenage years desist by age twenty-one.[59] Randy Borum has stated that "a cross-sectional 'snapshot' of the personality, thinking, emotion, and behavioral functioning of a child—as opposed to an adult—has less predictive power and less likelihood of reflecting the child's typical patterns."[60] The same cognitive or volitional tendency at age eleven might manifest itself very differently at age sixteen, a process known as heterotypic (as opposed to homotypic) continuity.[61]

Furthermore, even with these caveats, relevant statistical information may not always exist. A given instrument may not have been normed on the relevant population, an appropriately normed instrument may nonetheless not take into account factors that are obviously relevant to risk (such as recent purchase of a gun or potential responsiveness to future intervention), or the instrument may only aid in predicting *some* type of crime rather than the serious crime that the proportionality principle requires before confinement may take place. In such cases, the government should be able to introduce lay evidence describing antisocial acts to prove its case on risk, but only recent ones, given the changeability of youth. Furthermore, when confinement is at issue (and thus when the government must show a high risk of serious crime) only evidence of similarly serious acts should be admissible for this purpose, unless other types of acts have been empirically correlated with serious crime by juveniles.

The Offender-First Approach. When a statistical assessment indicates they pose a high risk of serious crime, juvenile offenders may want to rebut the state's case not only with their own statistical evidence but also with "clinical" predictions that seek to individualize the evaluation. Even though the latter type of evidence is probably less probative than empirically derived estimates of risk, this defensive move should be allowed, for two reasons. First, such testimony is much less prejudicial when presented by the defense than by the government. Given the natural inclination to assume a person who has just been convicted poses a risk, legal fact finders are very likely to take any defense claim to the contrary with a grain of salt.

Second, precedent for this offender-first approach can be found in the character evidence rule, which has been adopted in every American jurisdiction.[62] As explained by the Supreme Court, the character evidence rule prohibits the prosecution from introducing evidence concerning an adult defendant's bad character at trial because (as is true of clinical prediction testimony) "the overriding policy of excluding such evidence, despite its admitted probative value,... tends to prevent confusion of issues, unfair surprise and undue prejudice."[63] However, as a bow to the defendant's constitutional right to introduce evidence on his or her behalf, the rule also permits defendants to present evidence of good character in an effort to undercut the state's assertion that the defendant committed the crime charged.[64] Thus, criminal defendants are permitted to proffer witnesses to prove the proposition that they are not the type of person who could commit or intend to commit a crime. The risk of doing so, of course, is that the prosecution can then introduce any evidence of bad character it is able to muster.

Analogous to the character evidence rule, the juvenile offender ought to be able to proffer clinical prediction testimony about protective risk factors such as responsiveness to community-based treatment whenever risk is an issue. Fairness to the state also requires that the government be allowed to respond in kind. Unless the defense opens the door on the issue, however, in cases involving potential confinement the state should be relegated to proving risk using empirically based risk assessments or, in the absence of relevant actuarial instruments, evidence of prior bad acts. Actuarial instruments that have been appropriately normed and that focus on the relevant types of harms more accurately reflect an offender's risk than vague clinical pronouncements that a person is or is not likely to reoffend, and are more likely to be given the appropriate weight by the fact finder. The offender-first approach "allows the government to prove dangerousness in the most accurate, least confounding manner, while permitting the offender-respondent to attack the state's attempt at preventive detention on the ground that the numbers do not accurately reflect his or her violence potential."[65]

It should be emphasized that this relatively complicated evidentiary regime is only necessary when the government wants to confine a juvenile offender in an institution. Otherwise, only the prerequisites of Rule 703 (requiring an adequate investigation) need be met. Interventions that take place in the community, while often coercive, do not result in the significant deprivation of liberty that incarceration does and work best if therapists are given flexibility. In cases where confinement is sought, however, the quantitative and qualitative limitations described in the previous pages need to be adopted to minimize the risk and cost of error associated with prediction. Recall that we would also require periodic reassessments of risk when confinement results, so that if errors do occur they are more likely to be caught. As a final protective mechanism, any intervention that takes place must be focused on reducing recidivism in the least drastic manner possible, a point that is emphasized below.

Untreatability and (the Abolition of) Transfer

To this point, we have analyzed the age jurisdiction of the juvenile court, the type of act that triggers that jurisdiction, and the manner in which risk should be conceptualized and proven. Another issue that has traditionally been a determinant of juvenile court jurisdiction is treatability. In many jurisdictions, retention of jurisdiction over juveniles above a certain age (usually 13 or 14) who have committed certain types of crime (usually violent felonies) depends upon whether the juvenile is amenable to treatment.[66]

In a preventive regime, however, treatability would not be relevant in determining whether a juvenile offender remains in juvenile court, for two reasons. First, the state should not be prohibited from incarcerating or in some other way coercively intervening against high-risk individuals just because they are not treatable. One of the arguments made against the statute at issue in *Hendricks* was that it did not premise the preventive confinement it authorized on a finding of treatability. But the Supreme Court rejected this contention, stating at one point that "incapacitation [alone] may be a legitimate end of the civil law"[67] and at another that "we have never held that the Constitution prevents a State from civilly detaining those for whom no treatment is available, but who nevertheless pose a danger to others."[68] Some have contended that because the Court believed Hendricks was receiving some sort of treatment, these statements are dicta.[69] It seems more likely, however, that the Court meant to approve purely incapacitative confinement. As the majority stated, "it would be of little value to require treatment as a precondition for civil confinement of the dangerously insane when no acceptable treatment existed."[70] This means that, in a preventive regime, the government would not need to demonstrate treatability to assert juvenile court jurisdiction over a juvenile offender.

A second reason the amenability to treatment issue would not be relevant in a preventive regime of the type we propose is simply that it would be rendered moot, because the ability to transfer juvenile offenders to adult court would not exist. Transfer jurisdiction is an artifact of a culpability-based approach to juvenile justice. When prevention is the focus, transfer becomes unnecessary. To help in understanding these points, we first discuss how transfer works today and then describe how it would work in an individual prevention regime.

Transfer Today. In a purely retributive regime, a juvenile offender's treatability would be irrelevant both at the front end and throughout disposition. A juvenile who commits murder, rape, or robbery is not rendered less culpable simply because he is treatable or more culpable because he is untreatable. This fact would seem to indicate that retribution is not driving the transfer decision under current laws that are based on a determination of amenability to treatment.

The manner in which the amenability concept is actually applied, however, suggests just the opposite. Courts tend to base transfer decisions predominantly on the seriousness of the offense, the number of prior offenses, and the length of time remaining for juvenile court jurisdiction,[71] factors that bear only a tangential relationship to treatability and a much more straightforward correlation with blameworthiness or dangerousness. Indeed, most state statutes are explicit about the matter.

Consider, for instance, the transfer criteria listed in the appendix to the Supreme Court's opinion in *Kent v. United States.*[72] Although neither endorsed nor relied upon by the Court (and rescinded in the jurisdiction from which it came before *Kent* was decided in 1966), the appendix's list of factors now appears in some version in most state transfer statutes,[73] probably because *Kent* is the Supreme Court's only decision dealing directly with the transfer decision. Minus two issues having to do with the strength of the state's case, those factors are

> (1) The seriousness of the alleged offense to the community and whether the protection of the community requires waiver; (2) Whether the alleged offense was committed in an aggressive, violent, premeditated or willful manner; (3) Whether the alleged offense was against persons or against property, greater weight being

> given to offenses against persons especially if personal injury resulted; (4) The record and previous history of the juvenile, including previous contacts with the Youth Aid Division, other law enforcement agencies, juvenile courts and other jurisdictions, prior periods of probation to this Court, or prior commitments to juvenile institutions; (5) The sophistication and maturity of the juvenile as determined by consideration of his home, environmental situation, emotional attitude and pattern of living; (6) The prospects for adequate protection of the public and the likelihood of reasonable rehabilitation of the juvenile by the use of procedures, services and facilities currently available to the Juvenile Court.

None of these factors, even (5) and (6) if interpreted as they are by modern courts, has much to do with whether a juvenile offender is treatable. Intuitively and empirically, the nature of the offense—factors (1), (2), and (3)—is at best tangentially related to treatability. Youths who commit homicide are not per se less amenable to treatment than youths who commit burglary or possess drugs. Thus, offense seriousness may well bear no relationship or even a negative relationship to treatability. Many courts that apply these criteria openly acknowledge this fact and base transfer largely on culpability or dangerousness determinations;[74] some even explicitly ignore the amenability to treatment issue entirely if the offense is serious enough.[75] In fairness, many other courts look at the youth's motives in committing the crime, the degree of maliciousness, whether it was part of a group action, and so on. However, even in these courts the rule of thumb is that the more serious the offense, the less likely a youth will be considered amenable to juvenile court disposition, which suggests that culpability, not treatability, is the focal point of the analysis.[76]

Similarly, most courts—at least most appellate courts—do not probe deeply into offense or treatment history (factor 4). The typical approach with respect to offense history is to list the number of prior offenses or to evaluate them relatively superficially, without investigating their precipitants.[77] That methodology makes sense if culpability is the issue, but not if measuring treatability is the goal; as with the current crime, past crimes can be helpful in determining whether and how treatment will succeed only if they are incisively analyzed for risk factors. Similar observations can be made about judicial assessment of past treatment attempts. While some courts are sensitive to whether any treatment efforts that took place were meaningful,[78] a number of cases suggest that the key issue with respect to this factor is simply the number of previous "contacts" with the juvenile system, with a higher number of contacts suggesting lesser treatability.[79] The problem with this shallow approach is that if past offenses did not trigger meaningful treatment or ended in diversion out of the system, then they should ordinarily not weigh heavily in the amenability determination. Even if treatment was administered in good faith, the reality is that the match between a youth's problems and treatment programs is not always felicitous and can often be improved upon; effective treatment often requires trial and error. To the extent that courts blink at that reality, they are once again treading more closely to the retributive model than a rehabilitative or preventive one.

Factor (5), which speaks of "the sophistication and maturity of the juvenile as determined by consideration of his home, environmental situation, emotional attitude and pattern of living," should be the crux of the amenability determination. Unfortunately, however, the way this factor is framed undercuts its relevance to that determination. While facts about "home, environmental situation, emotional attitude and pattern of living" are all highly useful in managing risk, several state statutes and judicial decisions make the first part of this language—the youth's "sophistication and maturity"—the focal point of the inquiry.[80] In these jurisdictions, sophistication and maturity trump environmental or psychological influences. Yet, as should be clear by now, the "street–hardened" youth, "old beyond his years," is not necessarily a bad candidate for treatment; he may still be impulsive or unable to empathize, or captive to a gang or bad family situation, features that may be responsive to intervention. Again, in these states culpability, as measured by maturity, seems to be the issue driving the inquiry.

Finally, factor (6)—"the prospects for adequate protection of the public and the likelihood of reasonable rehabilitation" in the juvenile system—seems to be based on two premises, neither of which, again, have to do with treatability, and both of which suggest that the entire concept of transfer needs to be rethought. The first premise is that the juvenile court system is not able to handle certain types of particularly dangerous juveniles, who must therefore be transferred to adult court. The second is that even juveniles who are not particularly dangerous and who are treatable may be transferred when the juvenile court system does not have the resources to provide the treatment. The first premise is discussed next, while the second premise is discussed in the following section.

Why Transfer Should Go. If the focus of juvenile justice is culpability, then transfer is probably a necessary corollary, since an offender who commits a serious crime, has a criminal history and is mature may require adult-like punishment even in a diminished retribution regime. But if the focus of juvenile justice is risk, then no offender, even offenders who are very high risk, needs to be transferred to adult court, because the juvenile system can handle such individuals on its own, with detention if necessary. Contrary to the insinuation of *Kent's* factors (1) and (6), both of which suggest that the public cannot be protected by the juvenile system, such a system should always be able to provide preventive detention of dangerous, untreatable juveniles through maintenance of secure detention facilities (although, under the proportionality rule, release would have to occur after a certain period—six months to a year was the period mentioned above—unless the probability of significant harm is very high, in which case it could last until the end of dispositional age jurisdiction).

Retaining juvenile court jurisdiction for all cases involving juvenile offenders makes good sense for at least three other reasons. First, research strongly suggests that detention of juveniles with other juveniles, although criminogenic, is much less so than incarceration within the adult system.[81] As Jeffrey Fagan, the leading researcher in this area, notes, "there is a consistent pattern of higher offending among adolescents punished as adults compared to adolescents punished as juveniles."[82] Second, the very existence of the transfer option gives rise to many difficult policy choices that can be avoided if it is abolished. As one recent analysis of the legal and empirical literature on transfer concluded:

> There may be some easy choices between alternative transfer policies but not many. Even assuming that the best choice for those accused of delinquency is always to minimize the number of transferred cases, it will often be quite difficult to determine which of a number of policy options will lead to the smallest number of transfers.[83]

Third, and most important, the existence of transfer authority undermines efforts to pressure courts and legislatures into providing the necessary treatment options. As it stands today, in many cases the transfer decision depends in large part on economics, or as *Kent's* factor (6) puts it, "the likelihood of reasonable rehabilitation of the juvenile by the use of procedures, services and facilities currently available to the Juvenile Court." A majority of state transfer statutes explicitly provide, consistent with *Kent's* appendix, that one factor to consider in determining whether transfer should occur is whether treatment programs are available within the jurisdiction.[84]

This language is often dispositive. Numerous decisions make clear that courts have transferred a juvenile to adult court solely because of a lack of accessible programs. For instance, one court waived juvenile court jurisdiction for a fourteen-year-old because the state's experts testified that they lacked adequate facilities to deal with a fourteen-year-old homicide offender.[85] Another court transferred a youth who became violent when he consumed alcohol because the jurisdiction offered no substance abuse programs.[86] In perhaps the most egregious case (now thankfully mooted by the Supreme Court's decision in *Roper v. Simmons*), a court rejected the argument that "the state has an obligation not to execute a juvenile who is deemed to be amenable to treatment but for whom the state offers no appropriate treatment program."[87] Courts also often routinely refuse to consider a juvenile offender treatable when the only pertinent programs are in another jurisdiction.[88]

If transfer were eliminated, courts would have to confront the problems caused by the current paucity of treatment programs and might become more willing to force legislatures to fund them. Furthermore, as discussed below, a prevention-oriented system provides courts with additional legal ammunition if they are inclined to be proactive in this way.

The Juvenile Court and Treatability

While *Hendricks* does not require a showing of treatability to trigger preventive intervention, it did strongly suggest that the state must provide treatment to those who end up being confined on the basis of risk and are treatable through currently available means.[89] And in the subsequent case of *Seling v. Young* the Court relied on *Jackson v. Indiana* in concluding that "due process requires that the conditions and duration of confinement . . . bear some reasonable relation to the purpose for which persons are committed."[90] This language supports an argument for a treatment obligation flowing from the idea that deprivation of a fundamental right such as liberty must take place in the least drastic manner possible.[91] Although the much earlier Court opinion in *Youngberg v. Romeo*[92] is commonly thought to have rejected that theory, it in fact explicitly states that involuntarily committed patients are entitled to the care necessary to prevent unnecessary restraint.[93] This holding could easily be parlayed into a robust right to any treatment necessary to reduce prolonged confinement.

Eric Janus and Wayne Logan have made the most comprehensive argument in this regard.[94] They contend that a correct interpretation of *Jackson*, *Seling*, and *Youngberg* requires that, as a matter of substantive due process, states may not simply "warehouse" individuals who are subject to preventive detention but must instead provide meaningful treatment, *especially* when the detention is not focused on people with serious mental disability (who perhaps can be subjected to detention without treatment on the ground that they are considered nonautonomous).[95] Professors Janus and Logan also canvass a number of lower court decisions that take this requirement seriously by carefully scrutinizing governmental claims that such treatment is being provided.[96]

Thus, juvenile courts not only must order treatment under appropriate circumstances but also should possess the authority to order the government to release a juvenile whose risk can be reduced by available modalities but who is not being provided such treatment. Note that this least-restrictive-alternative theory of treatment is much stronger when state intervention is preventive as opposed to retributive in nature. Under a purely retributive model, the length of sentence is set according to the nature of the offense and the offender's culpability. The fact that treatment might reduce the offender's dangerousness is irrelevant. Under a preventive model, by contrast, treatment may well determine the length of disposition and therefore must be provided by the state.

Indeed, one advantage of an individual prevention regime is that it provides a much stronger jurisprudential basis for establishing a right to treatment for juvenile offenders. Some courts have been willing to contemplate such an argument even under other approaches to juvenile justice. For instance, in the late 1960s when the rehabilitative model was just giving way to more retributive approaches, the District of Columbia Circuit Court of Appeals stated that while resource limitations were "undeniable," it could not "ignore the mockery of a benevolent statute unbacked by adequate facilities."[97] The court added: "To the extent that a juvenile with more affluent parents might avoid waiver because of the availability of privately–financed treatment and rehabilitation, constitutional issues may lurk . . . ."[98]

To date, however, most courts have rejected these kinds of arguments in all but the most egregious cases of government abuse or failure to provide fundamental services.[99] Their primary rationale for taking this position is that juveniles have no right to juvenile court disposition in the first place; rather, treatment entitlements are granted by the legislature and may be restricted or qualified in any "rational" way that it chooses.[100] That reasoning makes sense if the juvenile justice system is conceptualized as a retributive regime. When punishment is the primary goal, treatment can be viewed as a luxury and is certainly not an entitlement. If, however, the state is coercively intervening for the purpose of preventing harm to others and a specific treatment is the least drastic means of pursuing that goal, then *Jackson*, *Youngberg*, and *Seling* provide a solid basis for requiring such treatment.

Of course, for a host of prudential reasons, courts are naturally reluctant to force appropriation of public moneys. Moreover, the most pervasive risk factors (e.g., availability of drugs and guns; community poverty) are seldom susceptible to judicial control. These institutional infirmities make it likely that treatment advocates—armed with the strong social science evidence described in Chapter 2 showing the cost-effectiveness of various types of intervention programs—will ultimately have to depend upon the legislatures, not the courts, to provide the resources necessary for a viable prevention-oriented juvenile regime. But, as the history of the right to treatment for people with mental disability shows, the goal of nudging reluctant or myopic legislators along the right path can be aided immensely by court rulings establishing treatment rights.[101]

Another quite different legal issue concerning the juvenile courts' role in assuring that treatable juveniles receive treatment arises when treatment programs are available but the programs require the participation of individuals besides the offender. Some of the most effective treatment programs, involving "multisystemic" approaches, require participation of family, peers, schools, employers, and others to work properly. Yet the typical state statute grants the juvenile court specific power only to order the parents of a delinquent youth into therapy.[102] Even in that context the basis of the state's power to force participation in the treatment of another is not clear. One might argue, for instance, that before such coercive intervention may occur the state should have to adduce evidence that the third party not only was a "cause" of, but was also "responsible" for, the youth's problems.[103]

When the third party the court wishes to involve in the treatment plan is someone other than a family member (e.g., school classmates, gang members, other community members) the "responsibility" link is even more tenuous. At the least, without explicit legislative authorization, court–ordered intervention becomes progressively less viable as a legal matter the further it ventures from the individual–centered medical model of treatment. It also becomes increasingly less likely to generate enthusiastic support when parties beyond the immediate family are ensnared. Fortunately, experience with the various multisystemic programs suggests that third party participation is usually entirely voluntary or involves relatively trivial demands.

* * *

In sum, a juvenile court that attempts to implement the individual prevention model would have the following attributes: (1) age jurisdiction from infancy through age eighteen or so; (2) dispositional jurisdictional through age twenty-five or so; (3) act jurisdiction for conduct that would be criminal if committed by adults, minus mens rea requirements more demanding than negligence; dismissals for minor acts would be less frequent than in adult courts when the acts are empirically verified risk factors; (4) dispositions based on risk assessments, with residential placement requiring at least clear and convincing proof that serious crime is likely to be committed in the foreseeable future, based either on statistically obtained probability estimates or, if such evidence is not available, evidence of similarly serious past acts; (5) the abolition of transfer jurisdiction, including transfers based on the seriousness of the crime, prior criminal history, maturity, untreatability, or the unavailability of treatment resources; (6) the right to treatment that will reduce the duration of juvenile court intervention.

A final role the juvenile court must assume is monitoring any treatment that takes place. That topic is discussed in the next section, in the context of exploring in more detail how preventive intervention and treatment would work.

Juvenile Disposition: Risk Management and Social Ecological Interventions

An individual prevention-oriented juvenile justice system would be guided by social ecological research on the causes and consequences of juvenile crime as well as the empirical literature on risk assessment,[104] risk management,[105] evidence-based intervention,[106] and program evaluation.[107] A social ecological analysis of juvenile crime considers the type of psychological, biological, and contextual influences described in Chapter 2 in an effort to develop individualized intervention plans aimed at preventing recidivism. Such individualized intervention plans would utilize a variety of approaches, programs, and processes to enhance protective factors and reduce risk factors for antisocial behavior. While this approach resembles the juvenile court system's original goals, it would be markedly improved because it would be based on empirical evidence on how best to change and manage human behavior.[108]

The adoption of a social ecological perspective suggests that a rational thought process often is not the principal determinant of human behavior.[109] However, that does not mean that decision-making abilities and maturity of judgment, typically the primary focus of a "rational actor" analysis, would become irrelevant to judgments of juvenile responsibility. Such intrapersonal characteristics are important in the analysis of the individual's propensity to engage in antisocial behavior and should be considered as one among many relevant personal and contextual factors. Moreover, the adoption of a prevention-oriented system would not necessarily eliminate interventions—such as detention—associated with a retributive system. However, the reasons for these interventions would be different from those rooted in a backward-looking retributive system. In a prevention-oriented system, confinement connoting "punishment" would be an acceptable form of intervention only if it could be shown empirically to contribute to the instrumental goal of crime prevention.

Because the central task in constructing an intervention program in a preventive regime is prevention of reoffending, it must differentiate between three classes of people: those who will not reoffend, those who will reoffend if not treated, and those who will reoffend regardless of intervention. Theorists have described two methods of carrying out this task.[110] The *prediction* approach calls for a dichotomous, up-or-down decision as to whether a person is "dangerous" and treatable. The prediction ideally is based both on static predictor variables, such as gender and prior arrests, and on dynamic or changeable risk factors, such as current substance abuse, peer influences, or family problems, that may be subject to amelioration. The *risk-management* approach is more fluid, in that there is no single, final decision as to whether a person is or is not dangerous. Rather, an individual is continually assessed over time in an effort to gauge the ebb and flow of dynamic risk factors, and efforts are made to "manage" those factors in a way that minimizes recidivism.

In the individual prevention model we are proposing, the prediction model is necessary at the front end, to determine whether any type of intervention is necessary (which will often be the case) and, if so, whether confinement is necessary (which will seldom be the case). In this instance, an up-or-down decision is legally required. But in all other instances, including when the juvenile is confined, risk management is the proper approach. As detailed in the next two sections, both the initial risk assessment and risk management would be governed by three fundamental principles: (1) the use of the least restrictive intervention (2) to focus on dynamic (changeable) individual and contextual risk factors as intervention levers (3) in an effort to bring about the specific goal of recidivism reduction.

The Initial Risk Assessment—Risk Factors and Race

Following an adjudication of guilt in juvenile court (or perhaps even preceding it), a risk assessment would need to take place. This initial risk assessment could be based on the types of risk-assessment instruments described earlier in this chapter; if confinement is sought, such instruments, normed on the appropriate population, would be *required.* However conducted, the risk assessment would usually divide offenders into low-, moderate-, and high-risk offenders. Typically, about one-third of a given population of offenders is classified in each of the groups.[111]

Consistent with the three principles set out earlier, even higher risk juveniles would not necessarily be subject to residential placement. Indeed, there might be a general presumption that these offenders should be handled through some form of community-based multisystemic intervention (e.g., Multidimensional Treatment Foster Care [MTFC] or Multisystemic Therapy [MST]) even if the level of risk necessary to justify confinement can be proven. Only those whose propensity for violence cannot be managed safely in the community or who fail to benefit from a community intervention would be subject to detention. Individuals in the moderate risk category would most likely be offered regular sessions of family systems-oriented intervention such as Functional Family Therapy (FFT) and other individually and community-oriented interventions, based on an assessment of their needs and dynamic risk and protective factors. Finally, the low-risk offenders might be diverted out of the system or only required to make periodic contact with a case worker who is trained in principles of risk management.

The types of factors that might be considered in a typical risk assessment have already been discussed in Chapter 2. Those factors would include psychological, neurological, and environmental variables, both static and dynamic. It bears highlighting, however, that race has *not* been mentioned in connection with that discussion. Although certain static characteristics such as prior crimes and gender may be very relevant to calculations of risk in the absence of intervention, no proven correlation exists between a particular race and untreatability.[112] Even if such correlation existed, equal protection concerns would probably bar explicit reliance on this factor.[113]

At the same time, courts and clinicians evaluating risk and amenability should not ignore the possible effects of race and cultural attributes. Ethnic influences may help to explain antisocial behavior and point toward specific types of interventions.[114] They may also affect the assessment process itself. For example, experience with and beliefs about the traditional power structure might make minority males particularly cautious and reluctant to explain their behavior to those in authority.[115] If so, both the anamnestic approach and the assessment of willingness to undergo treatment will require that the professionals involved in assessing and managing these cases develop the relevant multicultural competencies.

Although race should not be an explicit factor in assessing risk, other risk factors, such as broken families and poor neighborhoods, might correlate with it. The research outlined in Chapter 2 firmly establishes that juvenile offenders from poorer neighborhoods are likely to have more risk factors than juveniles from upper- and middle-class neighborhoods. But that unfortunate reality should be squarely faced rather than ignored; ideally, it can also be managed, by dealing with the ecological variables that contribute to antisocial behavior. This forthright approach to recidivism reduction is preferable to the subterranean racism and classism that infects the retributive model. That model's focus on whether the individual "chooses" to commit crime rather than on the context in which crime is committed results in more intrusive interventions (as well as less effective interventions) because it fails to recognize that the choices of juveniles living in poverty are more constrained than the choices of those who are better off.

The Structure of Risk Management

Assume now that sufficient risk has been shown to require some type of intervention. What would a risk-management system and individual interventions within it look like? A preventive, performance-based, risk-management model of juvenile justice would include the following features or something like them.[116]

First, each juvenile offender would have an Individual Risk Management Plan (IRMP). This plan would focus on identifying and addressing dynamic risk and protective factors in the interconnected personal and social domains of the child's life. Again, these factors might include poor impulse control, social incompetence, parental deviance and incompetence, affiliation with deviant peers, and academic and vocational underperformance, depending upon the juvenile in question. In devising the plan, the offender's views on the appropriate approach ought to be taken into account to the extent possible consistent with protection of the public.[117] Likewise, the victim's views on the appropriate intervention should be considered, perhaps through "restorative justice" processes that involve offender-victim mediation.[118]

Second, each child's IRMP would be implemented by a risk-management team (RMT) headed by a caseworker, who would seek input from the child and other members of the team, which might include school authorities, juvenile justice officials, mental health experts, vocational counseling professionals, and family. The RMT would oversee the preparation, implementation, and ongoing evaluation of the IRMP, which would be subject to modification based on feedback and relevant empirical data on promising interventions that have been shown to work with juveniles with similar risk profiles. For example, as already noted, juveniles thought to be low risk might be diverted out of the system or require no more intervention than periodic contact with the caseworker heading the RMT, while the default option for moderate risk offenders might be some form of periodic Functional Family Therapy, and high-risk offenders might typically be assigned to comprehensive, multisystemic interventions. In each situation, the RMT would engage in periodic review and make recommendations for more or less intrusive intervention (including termination of juvenile justice jurisdiction) depending on the ongoing assessment of dynamic risk and protective factors in any given case.

Third, to aid in the feedback process, a juvenile justice record-keeping system would be established. This system should of course be capable of monitoring offender characteristics and risk profiles. But it should also be capable of tracking the efficacy of various intervention strategies to guide ongoing reform at the level of specific interventions and programs.

Finally, the juvenile court or some other organizational body with the competence to implement and evaluate juvenile justice policy would provide oversight of the Risk Management System and associated record keeping, with the goal of providing important information to guide reform at the policy level.[119] This organizational body might be a state-funded independent Institute for Juvenile Justice Program Evaluation and Policy Research or could be integrated into the core functions of the State Courts Administrator's Office. Its chief function would be to monitor process and outcomes at the systems level. For example, what programs work best for high-, moderate-, and low-risk offenders? How is recidivism reduction within a risk category or within a specific type of intervention affected or moderated by the age, gender, and socioeconomic background of the offender? What procedures are judged by offenders to be fair or unfair? Are perceptions of procedural fairness related to outcomes such as recidivism reduction? How much does it cost to treat low-, moderate-, and high-risk offenders? Does requiring some form of community or victim restitution affect recidivism reduction? Does it affect juvenile compliance? Public acceptance of a risk-management model? In short, the goal should be constantly to reexamine every substantive and procedural premise of the system.

Application of the Risk Management Approach

The following three cases illustrate how the risk-management approach would work in the juvenile context. These three cases are hypothetical, but all illustrate different aspects of prevention-oriented risk management and how it differs from other approaches.

> *Jimmy G.* Jimmy G. is fifteen. He is the oldest of four children and a good student in school. His mother, a homemaker throughout most of Jimmy's childhood, began working part-time as a cashier at the local supermarket about three years ago, when her husband began having difficulty holding a job as an auto mechanic because of drinking problems. Jimmy has never been in serious trouble with the law but lately he has been staying out all night with a group of rowdy friends. He has begun drinking heavily on the weekends because it makes him feel more confident and helps him forget about the horrific abuse that his father has leveled against him, his mother, and his younger siblings. When Jimmy was twelve, his father punched him in the mouth at the dinner table and knocked out his two front teeth because he spilled his glass of cola on the new light-colored carpet in the dining room. At home, Jimmy is always very edgy and anxious because he is never sure when he or some other family member will be beaten by his father during a drunken rage. Every member of the family has been beaten to the point of requiring medical treatment, but the causes of the injuries have always been covered up and hidden from the authorities because all family members fear that they will be assaulted even more severely if they tell on their father. Jimmy feels responsible for protecting his mother and siblings but is always hit himself if he tries to intervene during one of his father's rampages against another family member. Last week, Jimmy came home from school

> and saw his mother sitting on the couch, crying, with a badly broken nose and a split lip. He saw his father passed out on the easy chair with an emptied six-pack at his side. Without asking what happened, Jimmy walked calmly into his bedroom, grabbed a baseball bat from his closet, returned to the den, and bashed his father's head with the bat. His father died instantly. When the police arrived, he told the investigating officer that he had been trying to work up the nerve to confront his father over the past year or so. He is charged with first-degree murder.

Jimmy meets the age and act thresholds under the preventive regime proposed in this chapter: He is fifteen and he intentionally killed his father. Under the proposed regime, a third preliminary question is whether Jimmy presents a risk to others. Guided by the type of risk-assessment instruments described earlier, the RMT would gather information for the court and the IRMP on this issue. At a minimum it would ask Jimmy about his intentions regarding future violence, examine his school records for evidence of aggressive behavior, and interview family members about whether they or others are at risk if Jimmy is not sent to a secure facility.

If confinement is contemplated, a formal risk assessment, using an actuarial instrument or some other statistically oriented assessment methodology, would need to be performed. A hearing would be held at which a high degree of risk would need to be demonstrated. But because Jimmy has never been in any serious trouble with the law, and because his aggression to date has been directed solely at someone who had physically tormented him for several years and is now dead, such detention is probably not warranted.

Assuming that a secure placement is not necessary, Jimmy could probably be managed safely through probationary supervision by a caseworker. This supervision would decrease in frequency and intensity to the extent that he remains law abiding. Jimmy exhibits several psychosocial risk factors that would be addressed as part of his IRMP. He is highly anxious and fearful and may benefit from social skills training to help him develop nonviolent coping strategies for dealing with conflict. His excessive drinking and potential familial risk for alcoholism may be targets of intervention to the extent that alcohol abuse is judged to be a risk factor for future aggressive behavior. Likewise, behavioral contracting to avoid socializing with rowdy and aggressive peers may be an integral component of his IRMP. Jimmy's success at dealing with these factors, his functioning in the family, school, peer, and neighborhood contexts, and his compliance with the law would be assessed on a periodic basis and his IRMP would be updated and modified accordingly. If he remained law abiding, juvenile justice jurisdiction might expire within a few years or even after several months. If, on the other hand, Jimmy reoffended, his IRMP would be modified and tailored to ensure he received the most appropriate intervention at the most appropriate level of supervision to minimize future recidivism risk.

Note that unlike a rehabilitation-oriented system that would look to improving Jimmy's psychological well-being in general, the individual prevention model would focus on dynamic risk factors (both psychological and contextual) that are empirically linked to reduced recidivism risk. Once the level of risk is managed and minimized, Jimmy would no longer be under the jurisdiction of the juvenile justice system. He and his family would of course be free to choose whether to pursue psychotherapy and other sources of assistance aimed at enhancing his general well-being, but these programs would not be offered as part of a prevention-based juvenile justice system.

Even more dramatic is the contrast between Jimmy's treatment under a preventive risk-management system and the disposition of Jimmy's case under a retributive regime. The latter system would focus on establishing Jimmy's culpability for his father's death and calibrating the appropriate punishment. Conviction would probably result in imprisonment for a fairly long term. In today's world, that incarceration would probably take place in an adult institution, where Jimmy's recidivism risk would be enhanced and his chances for developing a stake in his own future would be obliterated. Even diminished retribution advocates might push for incarceration in such cases. For instance, in discussing the well-publicized case of Lionel Tate, the twelve-year-old boy who killed a six-year-old girl while simulating wrestling, Scott and Steinberg suggest that Tate should have been detained in a secure facility (albeit within the juvenile system).[120] We think detention of such a young person could be counterproductive and would certainly not be as effective as multisystemic therapy in reducing the risk of this sort of person.

> *Charles M.* Charles M. is sixteen years old and has been arrested repeatedly for auto theft. His mother is a single parent who works as a nurse's aide and who always stands by her son when he gets into trouble. She says and truly believes that he is basically a good kid who is just a little "mixed up." Charles has been subject to detention on a number of occasions and has been in and out of court-ordered treatment programs for years. He was eventually placed in a group home but "escaped" from the premises on two separate occasions, each time eventually being apprehended by police, but not before he had stolen several vehicles on each outing, usually in league with members of a gang to which he belongs. The prosecutor is presently petitioning to have him tried as an adult due to his habitual offending.

Charles M. is a repeat offender whose recidivism risk is very high. That fact, combined with his previous "escapes" from group homes, makes Charles a potential candidate for secure detention for an indeterminate period. But if he has no record of serious violence, the initial intervention under a risk-management model might still be a community-based, multisystemic intervention. He would be placed in a residential setting only if the program staff deemed him inappropriate for a community-based intervention. Furthermore, that placement would be limited in duration, as mandated by the proportionality and least drastic means principles.

Regardless of the type of intervention, Charles's RMT would conduct a comprehensive ongoing risk assessment. It would look at the nature of his criminal history (e.g., is he joyriding, vandalizing, or selling the cars he steals?), his mother's past attempts to monitor his behavior (has she ever attempted to set appropriate limits for him?), and the nature and appropriateness of past treatment programs (is there any evidence that such treatment programs are effective with young car thieves?). It would also assess whether there are positive male role models in Charles's family, school, or neighborhood, and the extent to which Charles's car thefts have been tied to his association with delinquent peers.

The RMT's overall goal would be the reintegration of Charles into his community, either with his family or on his own, equipped with the vocational or educational skills necessary to develop a stake in his own future. Toward that goal, the RMT would assess Charles's recidivism risk on a periodic basis, both while he is in confinement and once he is out. If his behavior is gang related, particular emphasis would be placed on weaning him away from that influence. Even if Charles showed complete unwillingness to respond positively to these efforts, he would remain in the juvenile justice system, in contrast to the likely outcome under a retributive system, which would probably treat him like an adult from the outset or at least after the second or third offense.[121] Again, the emphasis would be on crime prevention and recidivism risk reduction rather than on more general rehabilitation aimed at enhancing his psychological well-being and improving his personality—worthy goals he may or may not decide to pursue on his own.

> *Billy B.* Billy B. is nine years old and has been a difficult child from birth. He cried incessantly as an infant and was especially difficult to console. His parents like him least of their three children. He never listens to his parents' reprimands and is usually a bully toward smaller and younger children. He is very unpopular at school because of his bullying and has no friends his own age. For the past week he has been skipping school and taking his BB gun into the woods near his house, shooting at birds, frogs, and other small animals. He would like to shoot his neighbors' cat, but they never let it out of their yard. The school principal calls Billy's mother and informs her that Billy has not been attending school.

Because he has committed only a minor criminal offense, Billy B. would probably not be prosecuted under a retribution-oriented regime. Even if he were, he would probably receive only the proverbial slap on the wrist. Further, in a retributive regime the assessment would be backward looking, focusing on whether Billy intended to harm the other children or the animals and whether he has the mental capacity to be held accountable for his acts.

Whatever the outcome of this assessment, the nature and duration of the punishment would be aimed primarily at punishment and only secondarily, if at all, at attacking the conditions that are prompting this behavior.

Under an individual prevention approach, in contrast, Billy would almost certainly be subject to juvenile justice jurisdiction, so long as his bullying or his cruelty to animals were codified as criminal acts under the relevant code. That is because both types of acts are risk factors for later criminal behavior. Indeed, for professionals, alarm bells would probably go off in a case like this because Billy's difficult temperament, bullying, peer rejection, cruelty to animals, and truancy, when combined, are highly predictive of an intractable, life course of delinquency, especially if left untreated. As we have noted, considerable empirical evidence indicates that early intervention with such high-risk youngsters may have a significant impact on reducing risk for later juvenile delinquency and even adult crime. Thus, this case presents the greatest contrast between the two systems. A preventive risk-management regime would invest considerable resources in children like Billy B., whereas a punishment regime would be relatively unconcerned with him.

Note also that the reasons for this investment of resources would be different from those underlying a traditional rehabilitation-oriented juvenile justice system. Under the risk-management approach, resource allocation would be concentrated toward those risk factors whose reduction has been empirically linked to crime prevention. Under a more traditional rehabilitation-oriented system, Billy might be subjected to a wider range of paternalistic interventions and more intrusive measures deemed beneficial for his general psychological well-being (at least some of which are not likely to be supported by the empirical evidence). Crime prevention would be an incidental benefit.

A sense of how risk management might work can also be gained from considering its application to the three broad categories of troubling youth identified in Frank Zimring's work for the Twentieth Century Fund.[122] The first category consists of youth who under modern statutes are sometimes called "persons in need of supervision."[123] These children might be runaways, violate curfews, drink heavily, routinely miss school, or routinely disobey their parents or foster parents. For reasons developed in Chapter 3, the juvenile court should not have jurisdiction over these youths. They have not engaged in conduct that would be criminal if they were adults. That does not mean that the state would not exercise some control in these situations. Dependency court might assert jurisdiction if these children are neglected, and primary and secondary prevention programs administered through schools or welfare agencies might come into play for truant or disobedient youths. And, of course, these types of conduct often lead to more serious misbehavior like Billy B.'s, which would trigger juvenile court jurisdiction in a preventive regime.

The next category of troubling youth Zimring identified comprises those who commit offenses against property or, as in Billy's case, violent offenses that are not directed at persons. Writing from a diminished retributive perspective, Zimring proposes a "three strikes and you may be out" formula that would preclude detention until the third property offense and instead permit only "intermediate" sanctions such as restitution and community-based treatment programs for offenders who have not met this threshold.[124] As Zimring admits, however, these types of responses "are not, strictly speaking, penal measures."[125] As the case of Charles M. illustrates, Zimring's proposal comes much closer to the approach that would be taken in a risk-management regime, with the difference that detention might not occur even after the third offense. Zimring acknowledges that even after three strikes, "resort to secure confinement as a kind of punishment for contempt of court is expensive and difficult to justify,"[126] presumably in part because incarceration might actually increase criminal propensities. Programs like MST should be given the maximum chance for success. Only if they clearly are a failure should more serious interventions take place.

The final category of youth consists of those who commit a violent crime. As Zimring points out, several subcategories exist here. Youths who, like Jimmy G., react disproportionately to a threat, youths who respond to taunts with violence, and youths who are accomplices to a serious crime only in the sense that they follow a group differ from those who coldly plan out a killing or an armed robbery, not only in terms of desert but as a matter of risk. The latter type of offender is much more likely to reoffend and is most likely to be a bad candidate for community-oriented treatment. But, in contrast to Zimring, who concludes that detention and perhaps even waiver to adult court is necessary in such cases (albeit perhaps with some dispositional discount because of the offender's immaturity[127]), a risk-management approach would counsel that even the very serious offender should be considered for community treatment in a program like MST, at least after a first offense when risk is not considered substantial. Even if this type of disposition triggered significant outrage from the community, authorities should pursue it; community angst often dissipates quickly, while the damage to youth caused by adult-like incarceration is much longer term.

A final subcategory of violent crime is the chronic violent offender (youths with three or more violent offenses). Some research indicates that these juveniles are responsible for a huge percentage of overall crime. For instance, the National Youth Survey data indicate that in 1980 this group accounted for 79 percent of all felony theft, 66 percent of all illegal transactions (primarily drug selling), and 50 percent of all self-reported crime.[128] In a study of delinquency in Philadelphia, 15 percent of youthful offenders accounted for 75 percent of all official crime.[129] In an individual prevention regime, offenders in this group (which, if the thesis of this book is correct, should be much smaller than it is today because of early interventions) would often be subject to detention if community treatment fails. Furthermore, that detention might be prolonged, with a maximum disposition lasting until age twenty-five and the (very slim) possibility of even longer detention for those who are extremely dangerous and not responsive to treatment. But, contrary to Zimring's scheme, the juvenile would always remain in the juvenile justice system.

Conclusion

As this chapter has demonstrated, an ecologically focused risk-management regime would be quite different from either a system based on retribution or one based on rehabilitation in the broad sense. The driving force behind it would be evidence-based assessments of risk and of interventions that reduce risk. Culpability assessments would be irrelevant once adjudication has occurred. Treatments designed to make the juvenile a "better person" would be eschewed in favor of interventions focused on minimizing risk factors, enhancing protective factors, and preventing delinquent conduct.

We have alluded several times to the "administrative" nature of this risk-management system. The individual risk-management plan and the risk-management team are essential components of that system. But we have yet to flesh out the precise role of the legal system in facilitating risk management. The next chapter does so.

5

The Procedural Implications of Social Science Research

This chapter presents a framework for reconceptualizing due process in juvenile justice with the ultimate aim of striking an optimal balance between fairness, accuracy, and efficiency in handling delinquency cases. Rather than mechanically turning to adult criminal procedure as the gold standard of due process, we propose the adoption of a performance-based management system that draws on both modern trends in administrative law and recent advances in social science research concerning procedural justice and decision making and program evaluation research. While we believe that the procedural framework we present can and should effectively be linked to the rejuvenation of rehabilitative and preventive goals of the juvenile justice system, the merits of our procedural framework also should appeal to those committed to more punitive and retributivist regimes.

Proponents of the original juvenile court thought that procedural informality would best serve the court's substantive objective of individualized care. Thus, for more than half a century, the juvenile justice system functioned largely in the absence of the procedural rules found in adult court and beyond the oversight and review of the regular judicial system. Juveniles were subject to "adjudication" and "disposition," not trial and sentencing. Juvenile delinquency proceedings often consisted of conversations between judge and the suspect, in the absence of juries, witnesses, and often even counsel.

Over time, however, it became apparent that the juvenile justice system was not living up either to its rehabilitative goal or to the expectation that relaxed procedures would facilitate that goal. Among legal scholars, courts, and other policy makers, the belief grew that procedural formality had been sacrificed for a rehabilitative agenda that never materialized.[1] The culmination of this criticism came in Justice Fortas's famous speculation in *Kent v. United States* that those enmeshed in the juvenile justice system were receiving "the worst of both worlds: . . . neither the protections accorded to adults nor the solicitous care and regenerative treatment postulated for children."[2]

Given the Court's long-standing reticence about using substantive due process to order change in state practices, the "world" the justices decided to alter was the procedural one. And the way they sought to heal the systemic wound perceived in *Kent* was to transplant adult procedures to the juvenile context. Subsequent Court decisions provided juveniles with the rights to counsel, silence, confrontation, and almost all of the remaining adult procedural armamentarium.

Important to note, however, is that this procedural revolution was based in large part on the general language of the Due Process Clause, not the specific adversarial guarantees in the Sixth Amendment providing for notice, public jury trial, confrontation, compulsory process, and counsel in "all criminal prosecutions." In other words, the Court imposed the adult model on the juvenile court not because the language of the Constitution required it but because the adult model was considered necessary to avoid deprivations of liberty without "due process of law." That interpretive approach means that if it turns out other procedural mechanisms can be shown to be just as "fair" as the adversarial model, those mechanisms might satisfy the Constitution.

Much legal scholarship on the juvenile justice system, however, has assumed just the opposite. Most scholars seem to think it obvious that the Sixth Amendment, as well as the Fifth Amendment's right to silence, should apply to juveniles, and that juvenile procedures should be the same as or even more adversarial than those in adult court.[3] Indeed, some commentators have proposed the abolition of the juvenile justice system as a separate procedural entity.[4] Consistent with Justice Fortas's observation, abolitionists remain skeptical about the reality and potential for rehabilitation but are much more sanguine about the benefits of traditional adult procedural guarantees. In effect, they assume that adult criminal procedural requirements are the epitome of "due process." Yet the pinnacle of procedural due process is not necessarily synonymous with adult criminal procedure requirements, and youngsters can be afforded comparable or even enhanced procedural due process in other ways.

The first part of this chapter recaps the procedural history of the juvenile court. Its primary message is that the Supreme Court's procedural reform of the juvenile justice system was based on the Due Process Clause and general principles of fundamental fairness, which leaves the door open to flexible approaches to juvenile justice procedure. The second part then plumbs developments in the broader constitutional jurisprudence of procedure, particularly in the administrative and civil law arenas, which enthusiastically endorse a flexible view of due process. With the legal groundwork laid for the proposition that juvenile justice procedure can be rethought, the third part summarizes research on "procedural justice," which suggests that the adversarial model of procedure is not necessarily the most "just," whether viewed from a subjective or objective perspective. The chapter closes with a discussion of the implications of this research, and a proposal that due process in juvenile justice be reconceptualized in a way that allows empirical research and a performance-based management system to identify those procedures that best promote fairness, accuracy, and efficiency. It bears repeating that although our proposal fits best with the individual prevention model we endorse in this book, the points we make could apply to other models as well.

A Procedural History of Juvenile Court

In the original juvenile court, the rehabilitative focus was accompanied by procedural informality—the near total absence, as one commentary put it, of "law, lawyers, reporters, and the usual paraphernalia of courts."[5] Recounted in Chapter 1 was Judge Mack's idyllic image of how the court should function: "Seated at a desk, with the child at his side, where he can on occasion put his arm around his shoulder and draw the lad to him, the judge, while losing none of his judicial dignity, will gain immensely in the effectiveness of his work."[6] As this statement suggests, the logic behind the relaxation of procedure was that judicial understanding of the child's character, lifestyle, and underlying problems, and thus of the appropriate treatment, could be obtained only through an informal, relaxed process. The adult adversarial process was thought to be counterproductive for children; it was seen as stigmatizing, traumatizing, and above all else irrelevant, given that the primary role of the court was to encourage rehabilitation, not to determine beyond a reasonable doubt whether the child had committed a bad act.

Although this informal process was a far cry from the procedures available in adult court, and thus seemed ripe for challenge, as late as 1966 the Supreme Court had not decided a single case involving juvenile court issues. In part, this judicial abstinence had to do with the Court's changing view of its role as a national guardian of liberties. Only in the early 1960s had the Court begun looking seriously at the *adult* criminal process: the Sixth Amendment's right to trial counsel was not imposed on the states until 1963,[7] while the Fifth Amendment's privilege against self-incrimination and the Sixth Amendment right to confront and cross-examine witnesses did not apply nationally until 1964 and 1965, respectively.[8] But part of the Court's silence on juvenile court issues was also due to the aforementioned lack of judicial oversight, even by the lower courts, over this separate system of justice.

Once the Supreme Court commenced its scrutiny of the juvenile courts in 1966, however, it did so with alacrity. Its first decision addressing a juvenile justice issue, *Kent v. United States*,[9] involved a sixteen-year-old boy who was summarily transferred from juvenile to adult court once he admitted to the police that he had participated in housebreaking, robbery, and rape. The Court held, unanimously, that the failure to convene a transfer hearing to determine whether Kent should have been tried as an adult violated the Constitution. The era of unbridled discretion in juvenile justice was suddenly over.

The year after *Kent*, the Supreme Court considered another case with even more important ramifications for juvenile justice procedure. In *In re Gault*,[10] a fifteen-year-old boy was committed by a juvenile court to a state industrial school for a maximum of almost six years (the remainder of his minority status), simply for making an obscene phone call to a neighbor. Had Gault been an adult he would have faced no more than a $50 fine or a maximum of two months in jail. Furthermore, of course, he would have been entitled to the full panoply of procedural safeguards guaranteed to adults.

Instead, Gault received virtually no procedural protections. Neither Gault nor his parents ever received formal notice of the charge. At the initial hearing the day after his arrest, with no lawyer and in the absence of *Miranda* warnings (which the Supreme Court had required in adult proceedings the year before), Gault was questioned by the judge about whether he made lewd calls. He was then detained, without explanation as far as the record showed, in a children's detention home for three or four days pending his adjudicatory hearing. At that hearing the probation officer, testifying without being sworn, described un-*Mirandized* statements made by Gault while he was in the detention home, and also presented a "referral report" to the judge, which the Gaults were not allowed to see. Nor was the complaining neighbor present at the hearing. Had she been there, Gault or his parents would have had to conduct cross-examination themselves, because his family had not retained a lawyer, and had never been told they could do so.

The Arizona Supreme Court concluded that this bare-bones procedure, one replicated every day in juvenile courts around the country, did not offend the requirements of the "due process concept." But the United States Supreme Court reversed, holding that when a delinquency proceeding might lead to confinement in a state institution the state must provide (1) written notice to the child and to the child's parents of the charges against the child, provided far enough in advance to allow for preparation for the hearing; (2) a right to counsel, including the right to have counsel appointed free of charge if the child or family is unable to afford one; (3) the right to confront and cross-examine witnesses, who are required to testify under oath; and (4) the privilege against self-incrimination. In short, juveniles were now to receive most of the procedural protections accorded adults under the Sixth and Fifth Amendments.

Three years later, in *In re Winship*,[11] the Supreme Court administered the final touch to its "adultification" of the juvenile delinquency process.[12] The Court first held that adults may not be convicted of a criminal offense unless its essential elements are proven beyond a reasonable doubt. It then applied that holding to the adjudication phase of a delinquency proceeding. With this decision, and within a five-year period, the Court had imposed virtually all of the adult criminal procedure guarantees on the juvenile process.

An important aspect of these three Supreme Court decisions that is often ignored, however, is their legal basis. Adult criminal procedures flow primarily from the Sixth Amendment. *Kent, Gault,* and *Winship*, on the other hand, relied almost exclusively on the Due Process Clause. That difference affords a much greater degree of flexibility in constructing a procedural framework.

The Court recognized this fact in all three decisions. For instance, in *Kent*, in the sentence immediately following his "worst of both worlds" observation, Justice Fortas stated that "this concern, however, does not induce us . . . to accept the invitation to rule that constitutional guaranties which would be applicable to adults charged with . . . serious offenses . . . must be applied in juvenile court proceedings."[13] Thus, Fortas stated, while juveniles in Kent's situation were entitled to counsel, access to relevant records, and a statement of reasons for the transfer decision, the transfer hearing could still be "informal" and need not "conform with all of the requirements of a criminal trial or even of the usual administrative hearing."[14] In short, the procedural adequacy of the hearing granted in *Kent* was to be measured not by the extent to which it copied or incorporated all of the requirements of a criminal trial but rather by whether it functioned in accordance with principles of fundamental fairness.

In *Gault* as well, the Supreme Court anchored its requirements regarding notice, counsel, and confrontation in what it called "due process standards," which it cautioned should be "intelligently and not ruthlessly administered" in the juvenile context;[15] only the right to silence, found in the Fifth Amendment, was derived from a more specific Bill of Rights guarantee. In essence, Justice Fortas's majority opinion adopted a hybrid approach. The majority's result was identical to that reached by Justice Black in his concurring opinion, which argued that the procedural safeguards the Court adopted were tied to the explicit text of the Fifth and Sixth Amendments, but its rationale was closer to Justice Harlan's concurring and dissenting opinion, which contended that all of the constitutionally mandated procedural safeguards in the delinquency context should stem from the Due Process Clause and derive from basic concerns about "fundamental fairness."

For this reason, Harlan's framework for analyzing procedures is worth a closer look. He argued that the process due in juvenile proceedings should depend on three criteria:

> First, no more restrictions should be imposed than are imperative to assure the proceeding's fundamental fairness; second, the restrictions which are imposed should be those which preserve, so far as possible, the essential elements of the State's purpose; and finally, restrictions should be chosen which will later permit the orderly selection of any additional protections which may ultimately prove necessary. In this way, the Court may guarantee the fundamental fairness of the proceeding, and yet permit the State to continue development of an effective response to the problems of juvenile crime.[16]

Applying these criteria, Harlan would have required that those subjected to juvenile delinquency proceedings be afforded only the rights to notice, state-paid counsel if institutionalization was possible, and a written record maintained by the court. Although the majority obviously believed that these prescriptions were not enough, its reliance on the Due Process Clause at least did not unalterably foreclose use of Harlan's more flexible analysis.

In *Winship*, the Supreme Court relied on the same hybrid formula it adopted in *Gault*. As in *Gault*, the Court equated the adult and juvenile standards, but the basis of the decision was the Due Process Clause (as it had to be, given the absence of any specific constitutional language supporting the reasonable doubt standard). The Court also emphasized that its holding with respect to juveniles would not have "any effect on the informality, flexibility, or speed of the hearing at which the factfinding takes place," nor would it affect the informality of the pre-hearing or dispositional phases of the juvenile process.[17] Justice Harlan wrote a concurring opinion agreeing that any lesser standard of proof "offends the requirement of fundamental fairness embodied in the Due Process Clause of the Fourteenth Amendment" but emphasizing the minimal impact that holding would have on the rest of the juvenile system.[18]

None of this should obscure the fact that these three decisions made the juvenile court look very similar to adult criminal court. In his dissent in *Winship*, Chief Justice Burger was not persuaded by the assurances to the contrary in the majority and concurring opinions in that case. He warned:

> What the juvenile court system needs is not more but less of the trappings of legal procedure and judicial formalism; the juvenile court system requires breathing room and flexibility in order to survive... . I cannot regard it as a manifestation of progress to transform juvenile courts into criminal courts, which is what we are well on the way to accomplishing. We can only hope the legislative response will not reflect our own by having these courts abolished.[19]

At the time, this last comment could have been read as somewhat hyperbolic. But, as we have documented in earlier chapters, a number of factors, including the Court's case law, have brought Justice Burger's forecast close to fruition; for older adolescents at least, juvenile courts are now so much like adult courts, substantively and procedurally, that abolition would not occasion a significant change.

At the same time, the conceptual difference between the two procedural systems is real. That much Burger helped make clear in joining *McKeiver v. Pennsylvania*,[20] the decision that provided the strongest signal yet that the Supreme Court is serious about differentiating the legal bases for the adult and juvenile systems. Decided one year after *Winship*, *McKeiver* held that in contrast to adults, juveniles do not have a constitutional right to a jury trial. As in *Kent*, *Gault*, and *Winship*, instead of grounding its analysis in the constitutional text of the Sixth Amendment—which guarantees the right to a public, jury trial in all criminal prosecutions—the Court framed the issue in due process terms. The difference between *McKeiver* and the Court's other juvenile justice decisions is the extent to which it emphasized this point.

Justice Blackmun's plurality opinion began by stressing that *Kent, Gault,* and *Winship* had consciously refrained from equating juvenile delinquency with adult criminal proceedings. Then, in a more definitive tone than it had in the past, the Court asserted that the adequacy of procedural requirements in the context of delinquency adjudications should be assessed solely according to whether they "'measure[d] up to the essentials of due process and fair treatment.'"[21] Using this metric, the Court reasoned that because a jury is not necessary to obtain "accurate" results,[22] and because of the need to maintain the "intima[cy]" of the juvenile proceeding and avoid the "clamor" of the adversarial process, the failure to provide juries to juveniles would not be fundamentally unfair.[23] In language that sums up application of the due process model to juvenile court, the Court added: "We are reluctant to disallow the States to experiment further and to seek in new and different ways the elusive answers to the problems of the young, and we feel that we would be impeding that experimentation by imposing the jury trial."[24]

This crowning decision of the due process era in juvenile justice made clear that despite the "adultification" of the juvenile court, Justice Harlan's fundamental fairness theory had taken root. Yet legal scholars who claim that *Gault* ushered in an era in which juvenile offenders secured the procedural safeguards afforded adult criminal defendants tend to gloss over the fact that, with the exception of the right to silence, these safeguards were derived from the Due Process Clause of the Fourteenth Amendment.[25] Behind this nonchalant attitude toward the legal basis of the Court's decision seems to be an assumption that the Court's fundamental fairness theory is merely an artifact of its decision to exclude the juvenile justice system from the ambit of the "criminal prosecutions" mentioned in the Sixth Amendment. In fact, however, this theory is entirely consistent with the Court's adoption of a more flexible approach to procedural questions in other settings.

Other Visions of Procedural Due Process

> The Supreme Court has yielded too readily to the notions that the adversary system is the only appropriate model and that there is only one acceptable solution to any problem, and consequently has been too prone to indulge in constitutional codification. There is a need for experimentation, particularly for the use of the investigative model, for empirical studies, and for avoiding absolutes.[26]

Although these comments, made by Judge Friendly in an article published in 1975, were foreshadowed by *McKeiver* four years earlier and could be seen as critical of *Gault,* they were not prompted by the Court's juvenile justice decisions but rather were a reaction to developments in administrative law in the early 1970s. In particular, Friendly's criticism was aimed at *Goldberg v. Kelly,*[27] a 1970 Supreme Court decision about procedure in welfare cases that could be called the *Gault* of administrative law because of its preference for the traditional adversarial model of dispute resolution. Unlike *Gault*, however, *Goldberg's* influence was short-lived. In 1976, the year after Judge Friendly's article was published, the Court decided *Mathews v. Eldridge*,[28] a case that has come to define modern trends toward administrative, as opposed to judicial, models of procedural justice.

The due process revolution in juvenile justice is usefully compared to these parallel developments in the administrative/civil realm because the latter developments reinforce the case for a fundamental fairness approach to juvenile justice that is not wedded to adult criminal procedures. In its due process decisions involving adult administrative settings, the post-*Mathews* Court has definitively rejected a one-size-fits-all procedural model and instead seems to be following Judge Friendly's injunction to experiment with different approaches. Even in situations that involve significant deprivations of liberty and property, application of *Mathews*'s framework has produced decisions that resonate with Harlan's and Friendly's flexible approach rather than with *Gault*'s equation of procedural due process and the adult criminal trial.

Due Process in the Administrative Setting

Before the 1970s, administrative decision making, like decision making in the juvenile process before 1966, was not a major concern of the Supreme Court.[29] On those few occasions when the Court held that the Constitution required any process in such proceedings, it demanded only a mini-trial, "however brief" and "however informal."[30] Above all, the Court saw the due process inquiry as a flexible one, immortalized in Justice Frankfurter's concurring opinion in *Joint Anti-Fascist Refugee Committee v. McGrath*:

> Expressing as it does in its ultimate analysis respect enforced by law for that feeling of just treatment which has been evolved through centuries of Anglo-American constitutional history and civilization, "due process" cannot be imprisoned within the treacherous limits of any formula... . Due process is not a mechanical instrument. It is not a yardstick. It is a process. It is a delicate process of adjustment inescapably involving the exercise of judgment by those whom the Constitution entrusted with the unfolding of the process... . The precise nature of the interest that has been adversely affected, the manner in which this was done, the reasons for doing it, the available alternatives to the procedure that was followed, the protection implicit in the office of the functionary whose conduct is challenged, the balance of hurt complained of and good accomplished—these are some of the considerations that must enter into the judicial judgment.[31]

This context-dependent due process analysis was seriously challenged, albeit only briefly and indirectly, with the Court's decision in *Goldberg*. In

Goldberg—decided three years after *Gault*, the same term as *Winship*, and one year before *McKeiver*—the Supreme Court addressed the procedure for terminating a mother's welfare benefits under the Aid to Families with Dependent Children program. The Court began somewhat ambivalently. It agreed with the petitioner that some sort of pre-termination hearing was required because loss of benefits would put her in an "immediately desperate" situation.[32] But it also stated that the hearing "need not take the form of a judicial or quasi-judicial trial." Rather it need merely meet "minimum procedural safeguards, adapted to the particular characteristics of welfare recipients, and to the limited nature of the controversies to be resolved."[33] To this point, the opinion sounded like something Justice Harlan or Justice Frankfurter might have written.

But it soon became *Gault*-like. The Court held that the "minimum" procedural requirements for carrying out benefits terminations were (1) timely and adequate notice detailing the reasons for termination; (2) the opportunity to appear personally before the decision maker and make oral arguments and present evidence (entitlements the Court thought necessary given the likely difficulty many welfare recipients would have with written submissions and the usefulness of "mold[ing one's] argument to the issues the decision maker appears to regard as important"); (3) the opportunity to confront and cross-examine adverse witnesses; (4) the right to retain an attorney at personal expense; (5) an impartial decision maker who was not involved in making the decision under review; and (6) a statement by the decision maker indicating the reasons for the determination and the evidence relied on.[34] The only adult criminal procedural safeguards missing from this list were the right to counsel at state expense and the right to a jury.

Goldberg was roundly criticized, both within the Court and without, for imposing costly procedures on a simple decision. Yet the case led to what some commentators called a "due process explosion"[35] throughout the early 1970s, lasting until the decision in *Mathews*. During this period courts tended to "judicialize" administrative decision-making procedures in any setting where individuals faced the potential loss of liberty or property, broadly defined, at the hands of a government actor.[36] In essence, the courts treated due process more like a "mechanical instrument" than the "delicate process of adjustment" envisioned by Justice Frankfurter.

In the midst of this due process explosion, it was often forgotten that the *Goldberg* Court had, in theory at least, agreed with Justice Frankfurter about the need for due process to be context dependent. The Supreme Court's decision in *Mathews* six years later recognized as much, and took the principle very seriously. Its emphasis on the flexible nature of due process ultimately put the brakes on the constitutional codification of traditional adversarial safeguards outside the adult criminal setting.

The issue in *Mathews* was whether Social Security disability benefits, as distinguished from the welfare benefits at issue in *Goldberg*, could be terminated without an evidentiary hearing. Seven members of the Court concluded that no hearing is required in such situations. Justice Powell's opinion for the

Court first established that due process analysis requires consideration of the following three distinct factors:

> First, the private interest that will be affected by the official action; second, the risk of an erroneous deprivation of such interest through the procedures used, and the probable value, if any, of additional or substitute procedural safeguards; and finally, the Government's interest, including the function involved and the fiscal and administrative burdens that the additional or substitute procedural requirement would entail.[37]

Applying this test, the Court found that termination of disability benefits was not as significant a hardship as the termination of welfare benefits involved in *Goldberg* (because people with disabilities often have other sources of income); that adversarial procedures were not as important when the focus of the decision is objective medical evidence, as is the case with disability determinations; and that the costs of elaborate hearings "may in the end come out of the pockets of the deserving."[38]

Mathews's three-part test, often described as requiring a balancing of fairness, accuracy, and efficiency considerations,[39] has provided the framework for most of the Supreme Court's due process cases since the mid-1970s. The framework provides considerable latitude for informality and flexibility, and it has now been applied to a wide variety of contexts. The contexts most relevant for our purposes are those involving juveniles.

Juvenile Due Process in Nondelinquency Settings

A precursor to *Mathews* by one year, but completely consistent with its approach, is the Supreme Court's decision in *Goss v. Lopez*.[40] There the Court held that a hearing is required before schools may subject students to suspensions of ten days or more, because without a hearing the chance of an erroneous deprivation of the student's entitlement to a public education is too high. However, the Court went on to conclude that the due process "hearing" need only consist of an informal meeting between the student and the relevant school official, at which the student is informed of the charge and is permitted to tell his or her side of the story; a judicial hearing, the Court noted, "might well overwhelm administrative facilities in many places and, by diverting resources, cost more than it would save in educational effectiveness."[41] Despite its finding that the suspension involved a nontrivial property deprivation (suspension from school), the Court did not refer to *Gault* or any other juvenile justice decision.

Of course, a ten-day suspension from school is not comparable to the six-year commitment that faced Gerald Gault. Outside the delinquency context, the Supreme Court decision involving the situation most closely analogous to *Gault* is *Parham v. J.R.*,[42] decided three years after *Mathews*. There, the Supreme Court addressed the issue of whether an adversarial proceeding was required prior to a juvenile's civil commitment to a state psychiatric facility pursuant to a petition brought by the juvenile's parents or guardians. The three-judge federal district court, relying on *Gault*, held that due process in the juvenile commitment context required adequate notice and an adversary-type pre-deprivation hearing before an impartial judicial or quasi-judicial body. But the Supreme Court reversed, holding that due process was satisfied simply by an evaluation from a neutral fact finder, who could be the admitting psychiatrist. Thus, Chief Justice Burger concluded for six members of the Court, if the parents or guardian seek admission and the neutral evaluator determines that evidence of mental illness exists and that the child is suitable for treatment, the child may be admitted to a psychiatric facility.

In justifying this decision, the Court used *Mathews*'s three-factor balancing test, looking at the first and third factors (the private interest at stake and efficiency) before examining the second, risk of error, factor. The Court conceded that civil commitment of a minor implicates the juvenile's constitutionally protected liberty interest. However, the Court reasoned that this liberty interest was qualified by and coupled with the parental interest in the child's well-being. While recognizing that parents do not always act in their child's best interests, the Court was willing to assume that they normally do, an assumption that weighed against highly formal procedures when parents seek care for their children. The Court also agreed with the state's argument that adversarial proceedings were an inefficient means of meeting its goals, by noting the benefits of speedy care, the need to minimize the time mental health professionals spend in admission proceedings, and the concern that the costs of "hundreds—or even thousands—of hearings each year . . . would come from the public moneys the legislature intended for mental health care."[43]

Finally, the Court was not convinced that adversarial procedures were needed to reduce the risk of erroneous commitment and even suggested it might increase it. The commitment decision, the Court reasoned, is primarily a medical, not a legal, judgment and thus less in need of adversarial testing. The majority even went so far as to suggest that the benefits of using adversary proceedings to assure decision-making accuracy in this setting were "more illusory than real."[44] Furthermore, such proceedings might pit parent against child, or the child against his or her eventual therapist, which would bode ill for both relationships. Thus, the Court was "satisfied that an independent medical decisionmaking process, which includes [a] thorough psychiatric investigation . . . followed by additional periodic review of a child's condition, will protect children who should not be admitted." The Court saw no need for either a judge or a lawyer to be involved in the process, because it did not "believe the risks of error in that process would be significantly reduced by a more formal, judicial-type hearing."[45]

Although *Goss* and *Parham* are often characterized by critics as cases that deny due process protections to juveniles, both decisions did in fact address issues at the heart of due process doctrine: truth seeking and fairness. For example, the comprehensive evaluation required in *Parham*, which the Court stated should "carefully probe the child's background using all available sources, including, but not limited to, parents, schools, and other social agencies [and] an interview with the child," is clearly aimed at promoting decision-making accuracy.[46] Moreover, although the child subject to commitment does not have the right to call or cross-examine witnesses, he or she is provided with some "opportunity to be heard" through the required face-to-face interview, a procedure that *Goss* also mandates for students subject to possible suspension. At the same time, consistent with the framework outlined in *Mathews*, in neither case was the Court concerned solely with issues of accuracy and fairness of decision making; it also explicitly addressed the government's interest in the efficient use of public resources. Thus, as noted above, in *Goss* the Court was worried about a "diversion of resources" if it required more elaborate procedures, and in *Parham* it likewise favored an investigative model over a legal adversary process in part to ensure that mental health professionals spend most of their time treating youngsters in need rather than testifying in legal proceedings.

Parham is a particularly important decision for this discussion about juvenile justice because it dealt with civil commitment. Civil commitment can result in a serious deprivation of liberty that can often be as intrusive and as long in duration as the detention experienced by juveniles charged with felony offenses,[47] yet the procedure outlined in *Parham* is a far cry from that endorsed in *Gault*.[48] That observation raises what, for us, is a central question. Which procedural approach makes the most sense from the standpoint of promoting fair and accurate decision making, public safety, and the well-being of children under the jurisdiction of the juvenile justice system: the adversarial procedural framework outlined in *Gault*, or the investigative framework outlined in *Parham* and inspired by *Mathews*?

We believe that whatever the merits of *Gault* at the time it was decided, today the investigative model informed by the Supreme Court's analysis in *Parham* and *Mathews* holds the greater promise for promoting these goals. We are *not* suggesting that the specific procedures permitted in *Parham* (much less in *Goss*) be mechanically transplanted to the context of delinquency adjudications. But we are arguing that the *Mathews*-derived investigative approach in *Parham* and *Goss* is far more promising as a means of achieving a fundamentally fair system. To live up to that promise, the procedural framework guiding the juvenile justice system must be informed by modern social psychological research aimed at understanding and promoting fairness, accuracy, and efficiency.

Social Psychological Research on Procedural Justice

Recent due process cases have insisted on a multifactor balancing analysis that places as much emphasis on the risk of reducing error, the "value" of procedural safeguards, and systemic efficiency as it does on liberty and property interests. Although some due process traditionalists find this trend alarming, social and behavioral scientists, many of them with legal training, are producing social psychological research that suggests this type of balancing analysis may come closer to achieving "just" procedures than a rigid adherence to the adversarial model. In particular, research on procedural justice points to several ways in which nonadversarial methods may be superior to the traditional adult criminal procedural safeguards in certain settings.

The study of procedural justice in the social sciences largely traces its roots to the pioneering work of John Thibaut, Laurens Walker, and their colleagues in the 1970s. This group coined the "procedural justice" term to refer to the social psychological effects of varying decision-making procedures, particularly with respect to the effects these procedural variations have on fairness judgments.[49] In their groundbreaking work, *Procedural Justice: A Psychological Analysis*,[50] Thibaut and Walker used empirical methods to explore differences between the adversary model followed by American courts (where the parties are responsible for producing evidence) and the inquisitorial model employed by courts in many European countries (where the judge or a judicial delegate takes on the investigative role).

In carrying out this research, Thibaut and Walker addressed both "objective" and "subjective" aspects of procedural justice. As defined by Allan Lind (a sometime colleague of Thibaut and Walker) and Tom Tyler, objective procedural justice is concerned with "the capacity of a procedure to conform to the normative standards of justice, to make either the decisions themselves or the decision-making process more fair by, for example, reducing some clearly unacceptable bias or prejudice."[51] Thus, objective aspects of procedural justice include accuracy of outcome and the collection and use of available information. Subjective procedural justice, in contrast, concerns the "capacity of each procedure to enhance the fairness judgments of those who encounter the procedures."[52] Here the perceptions of the participants are the important focal point. Because the relevant data are the most robust, the following discussion begins with a description of findings from Thibaut and Walker and others concerning subjective procedural justice. It then examines empirical findings relevant to objective procedural justice. These two aspects of social science research roughly correspond to the fairness and accuracy considerations identified in *Mathews*. The discussion ends with a brief comment on how social science can also address the efficiency prong of the *Mathews* analysis.

Subjective Procedural Justice/Fairness

One of the most significant findings of Thibaut and Walker's early research was that satisfaction with dispute outcomes is substantially affected by factors other than winning or losing the dispute.[53] Thus, even those who fail to prevail on their claim nonetheless exhibit greater outcome satisfaction and express greater willingness to accept the decision when the procedures used to reach the decision are perceived as fair. "This finding," Lind and Tyler have noted, "showed that it is possible, by judicious choice and design of procedures, to enhance the quality of social life without increasing the outcomes available for distribution under the procedures."[54] As Thibaut and Walker themselves explained, subjective justice is "crucial because one of the major aims of the legal process is to resolve conflicts in such a way as to bind up the social fabric and encourage the continuation of productive exchange between individuals."[55] In short, subjective procedural justice is an important means of getting both litigants and society at large to buy into the decisions that resolve disputes.

Thibaut and Walker's early work, reported in the mid-1970s, suggested that both disputants and the public preferred the adversary system to the inquisitorial system because they perceived the former system's procedures to be fairer. More specifically, Thibaut and Walker found that their research participants felt the adversarial mode gave them more decision control (ability to "unilaterally determine the outcome" of the case) and process control (ability to determine "the development and selection of information"), and particularly more of the latter.[56] These perceptions of fairness, in turn, led to a greater willingness to accept verdicts arrived at through adversary procedures than those that resulted from an inquisitorial process,[57] a preference shared even by individuals from countries with inquisitorial systems.[58]

Thibaut and Walker's findings in this regard were compromised, however, by the fact that they generally tested only "pure" models of adversarial and inquisitorial systems. As they described these models, "in a pure adversary system, openly biased advocates urge their clients' cases before a passive decisionmaker," while a "pure inquisitorial system" involves "an expert decisionmaker [who] actively investigates the claims of unrepresented litigants."[59] In other words, Thibaut and Walker's pure inquisitorial model prevented disputants from presenting their own view of the facts unencumbered by interference from the decision maker.[60]

Subsequent research, often using less rigid depictions of the two models, called into question Thibaut and Walker's conclusions about adversarial and inquisitorial procedures. For instance, more recent research directly contradicted their finding that culture does not affect preferences for certain procedures.[61] Furthermore, a number of studies have challenged the finding that Americans prefer the adversarial process. Based on this second generation of research, Lind and Tyler concluded that "pure" adversarial and inquisitorial procedures both have something to offer in terms of subjective procedural justice, and that policy makers "should be able to design a variety of hybrid procedures that engender high[er] levels of perceived fairness."[62]

A brief accounting of some of this newer research demonstrates the type of hybrid procedures that might be perceived as fairer than either of the pure forms. For example, Blair Sheppard conducted two studies in which participants were offered four, rather than two, procedural options: an inquisitorial procedure that involved a single investigator; an inquisitorial procedure that involved two investigators (one for each side of the dispute); a pure adversary procedure; and a hybrid procedure that allowed the disputants to present their evidence and arguments but also allowed the judge to ask questions and seek clarification.[63] He found that while the subjects preferred the adversary procedure to the two inquisitorial procedures, the great majority preferred the fourth, hybrid procedure above any of the other three, apparently because they perceived it as the most fair.[64]

A similar study, conducted by Norman Poythress and his colleagues, asked mental health professionals to compare the adversarial process to a number of hybrid alternatives in the context of a simulated medical malpractice scenario.[65] One hybrid involved the exclusive use of court-appointed medical experts subject to cross-examination by the parties. A second hybrid hypothesized a court-appointed research psychologist who surveyed experts in the field as to their evaluation of various diagnoses and treatments relevant to the facts of the case. The adversarial model, in contrast, relied on the parties to find and examine the experts. Participants evaluated these alternatives in terms of their preference for the procedure and its perceived fairness, among other variables.

Results revealed that each of the hybrid procedures compared favorably with the adversarial procedures in almost all respects. The hybrids fared significantly better in terms of perceived accuracy, process control, fairness, satisfaction regardless of outcome, control of outcome, and overall preference. The adversarial model was rated most favorably only with respect to "voice" (involvement in the process). As Poythress and his colleagues noted, while this latter finding reflected "the relatively unbridled control over case presentation [that the adversarial model provides], subjects' consistent assignment of more favorable ratings to hybrid models on other dimensions suggests a willingness to relinquish some of that control in return for the enhancement of other procedural justice attributes."[66] Accordingly, the authors concluded, the results suggested that "there are variations in the standard adversarial trial procedures that will permit us to optimize all criteria for a just system and escape the dilemma of a system that purchases fairness at the expense of (objective and subjective) accuracy."[67]

Donna Shestowsky's research regarding preferences for dispute resolution methods arrived at similar results.[68] Noting that, due to the growth of alternative dispute resolution mechanisms such as mediation, the "legal landscape has changed remarkably" since Thibaut and Walker's work in the 1970s, Shestowsky conducted three experiments designed to investigate preferences for "nonadjudicative" as well as "adjudicative" procedures. All three experiments involved a claim for damages. In order, they investigated whether preferences for a given procedural model were influenced by (1) the relative status of the disputants (in terms of age and standing in the community); (2) the party's role in a dispute (plaintiff or defendant) where the facts favored one side; and (3) the party's role in a dispute in which the facts were equally favorable to both the defendant and plaintiff.

Shestowsky found that participants' preferences for procedures were consistent across all the three experiments. Of particular interest here, she found that, regardless of condition, fewer than 10 percent of the participants rated adjudicative procedures (involving a judge as decision maker and lawyers for both sides) as their preferred method of dispute resolution. She also found that across all conditions, disputants preferred "direct control over the presentation of evidence (rather than using a representative to do so)."[69] Again, these results, which are representative of a considerable body of research,[70] contrast with the early findings of Thibaut and Walker, who found, using "pure" adversarial and inquisitorial models, that participants are partial to adversarial procedures and lawyers.

These three studies concluding that hybrid procedures are preferred to the pure adversarial and inquisitorial models are all subject to methodological criticism. For instance, the participants in Shestowsky's study were Stanford students, who might have felt more comfortable representing themselves than would many others. And in all three studies, the stakes involved were minimal, meaning their results might not be generalizable to criminal prosecutions and similar types of disputes.[71] Finally, all three studies were conducted in the "laboratory," using mock scenarios, not disputants involved in actual cases (an external validity complaint that is also true, it should be noted, of Thibaut and Walker's work). At the least, however, this type of research calls into question the latter's findings that adversarial procedures are superior from a subjective procedural justice perspective.

Surveys of those who have actually experienced differing types of dispute resolution in the criminal process also challenge that conclusion. A "meta-analysis" of such surveys, some of which involved offenders charged with very serious crimes, found that victim–offender mediation and family conferencing (often with no judges or lawyers involved) were consistently more successful than traditional criminal justice in fostering defendants' perceptions of fairness (with 91% of offenders whose cases were handled in mediation finding the process fair, versus 78% of those whose cases were handled by a court).[72] Similar differences were found in terms of defendants' satisfaction with the handling of their cases (84% to 73%); their perception that they had an opportunity to tell their stories (88% versus 64%); their perception that their opinions were adequately considered (72% versus 55%); their assessment of the decision maker's fairness (91% versus 63%); and their satisfaction with the outcome (77% versus 67%).[73] The differential in victims' reaction to nonadjudicative and adjudicative procedures was generally even more marked, again in favor of the former.[74]

In sum, both experimental research and participant surveys suggest that alternatives to the traditional adversarial procedure are often perceived as more fair and more accurate. Whether the latter perception is correct has also been the subject of empirical study.

Objective Procedural Justice/Accuracy

Objective procedural justice aims at constructing procedures that promote accurate decision making. A major challenge to evaluating objective justice, of course, is the criterion variable: when is a decision accurate? As Lind and Tyler asked, "How is one to know which defendants are truly guilty or innocent?"[75] Perhaps because of these methodological difficulties, the research on objective procedural justice is decidedly less robust, and thus less definitive, than the research on subjective procedural justice. Even Thibaut and Walker conceded, however, that what they called "autocratic" procedure, in which both process and decision control is delegated to a third party, "is most likely to produce truth."[76] Their continued preference for the adversary model stemmed from their belief that "the fundamental objective of the legal process" is not "the discovery of truth" or "the realization of the most accurate view of reality," but rather "the attainment of distributive justice," which they asserted the adversary system, with its requirement that the parties present their own view of the evidence, is most likely to achieve.[77]

These conclusions were derived primarily from examinations of the ability of adversarial and inquisitorial procedures to reduce bias and increase the amount and accuracy of information used by the decision maker. Thibaut and Walker produced the groundbreaking research in this area as well, and much of it did appear to favor the adversarial process. For instance, one of their studies found that subjects who were exposed to new evidence using adversarial procedures relied less on their existing biases than participants in the inquisitorial condition.[78] In another study, this time with Lind, they found that, while law students acting as attorneys usually gathered about the same number of facts regardless of whether they were placed in an adversarial or inquisitorial role, attorneys in the adversarial condition engaged in a more thorough investigation of the facts when the evidence was unfavorable to the student-attorneys' clients.[79]

This early research did not all point in one direction, however. First, Lind and Tyler have noted that contrary to the conclusion one might draw from the finding reported just above, "there is no real evidence in the original experiment that inquisitorial procedures suffer from premature cessation of investigation."[80] More important, a third Thibaut, Walker, and Lind study, which used the same methodology as the latter study but examined the accuracy of the facts presented, produced results that were not supportive of the adversarial process.[81] This study found that when the evidence favored the client or was balanced, attorneys in both conditions presented evidence that reflected the facts of the case. When the facts weighed against the client, however, the adversarial attorneys were much more likely to present biased evidence, creating the impression that the facts were more evenly balanced than they were.

This research suggested that inquisitorial procedures may result in the presentation of more accurate and less biased information. To test these propositions further, Sheppard and Vidmar studied the effect of adversarial and inquisitorial procedures on the preparation of witnesses and their impact on the decision maker, using students as lawyers, witnesses, and judges.[82] They found that, while witness biasing did not occur in the inquisitorial condition, "adversary procedures create lawyer role demands that in turn may result in the biasing of witness testimony."[83] Additionally, the data suggested that the biased testimony influenced the decision maker. A second study by Vidmar and Laird found that bias may be produced simply by labeling a witness the plaintiff's or the defendant's. This research found that witnesses subtly varied phrasing of their testimony depending on whether the plaintiff, the defendant, or the court called them, enough so that a three-judge panel, while stating that they perceived the witness appointed by the court to be "neutral," were more likely to find for the plaintiff when the witness testified for the plaintiff, and for the defendant when the witness was called by the defendant.[84]

As with much of the research on subjective procedural justice, the generalizability of this experimental work can be questioned. But impressionistic evidence from observers of our legal system supports the surmise that the adversarial process obstructs access to evidence and produces biased information, especially as it operates in the criminal justice system. American prosecutors are routinely blamed for failing to disclose exculpatory evidence or information that could be used to challenge the credibility of witnesses.[85] Defense attorneys commonly raise obstructionist objections and introduce questionable evidence in an effort to create reasonable doubt.[86] In contrast, in more inquisitorial systems such as those in many European countries, the practice of judicial investigation substantially reduces the pressure on the parties to produce or withhold evidence to win a case.[87] Coaching of witnesses is unethical,[88] and the evidence produced does not depend on prosecutorial whim or the energy or resources of the defense.[89] On objective measures as well, the adversarial system may not provide the optimal procedure.

Efficiency

Research providing statistical information is likely to have its most conspicuous impact in connection with this third prong of the *Mathews* test. The costs of certain procedures, both in terms of direct expenditures on the process and in terms of the monies thereby diverted from other parts of the system are, in theory at least, more quantifiable than either subjective or objective justice. Social science can therefore make contributions here as well.

Unfortunately, to date, there appear to be no studies directly comparing the costs of inquisitorial, adversarial, and hybrid procedures in a given legal setting. But the Supreme Court's assumption, in cases like *Mathews* and *Parham*, that adversarial procedures are more expensive is not unreasonable, especially if such procedures include the jury trial. Indeed, it may be because of its expense that the American criminal process rarely actually uses the adversarial process[90] and instead relies primarily on plea bargaining, which is itself inquisitorial in nature.[91]

Another cost that should be factored into the efficiency calculus is the extent to which parties to the dispute can afford the process. Privately financed evidence collection, which is the hallmark of the adversarial system, may discriminate against the poor. In an inquisitorial system, on the other hand, the judge/decision maker is responsible for developing the evidence and can be of significant assistance to an indigent defendant. As Professor Stephanos Bibas has noted, "appointed defense counsel are often chronically underfunded, overworked, and of uneven competence… . Thus, [indigent defendants might] prefer a quasi-inquisitorial system, with a neutral magistrate who is charged with digging up the truth."[92]

All of this is speculative. But, as with the research on subjective and objective justice, these comments about efficiency call into question the superiority of the adversarial process.

Toward a Performance-Based System of Juvenile Justice

The upshot of the procedural justice research is that the automatic equation of adversarial procedures and fairness or accuracy is not warranted. It may well be that, in some settings, alternatives to a process in which parties represented by counsel are responsible for providing and challenging evidence better promote both subjective and objective justice, and they will often cost less as well. The central question raised in this chapter is whether the juvenile delinquency proceeding is one of those settings.

Unfortunately, we cannot answer that question here. Although the research we have briefly surveyed suggests that the procedures that many consider the gold standard of due process do not deserve that status, it only begins to answer the inquiry. Since very little empirical work focusing on the juvenile justice setting exists, we would be foolish to suggest otherwise.

The point we can make, one that is a predicate for answering the above question, is that decisions about fundamental fairness should be performance based and management oriented. By that we mean to endorse the following basic tenets:

1. Consistent with *Mathews*, procedures should be constructed so as to promote individual and public perceptions of fairness, accurate decision making, and the efficient use of available resources in a way that optimizes fairness and accuracy.
2. The best method of determining whether specific procedures meet this goal is through ongoing feedback, evaluation, and reform, both in individual cases and systemically, in the experimental spirit endorsed by Judge Friendly.
3. An administrative mechanism that can manage this evaluation process must exist.

The application of these tenets to juvenile justice requires, first and foremost, that questions about appropriate procedure be recast into empirical hypotheses rather than framed, as they have been up to now, by reference to adult criminal procedure requirements. The scope of a juvenile offender's rights, the identity of the juvenile court decision maker, the role of the attorneys, and even whether attorneys are involved at all should depend on an empirical assessment of the extent to which these procedural attributes enhance perceptions of fairness, accuracy, and efficiency. Only if empirical answers are not available should formalistic considerations, such as the language of a particular constitutional provision, be given weight.

Second, a performance-based approach requires, as Justices Harlan and Frankfurter emphasized, that any special attributes of the individuals involved in the process be taken into account. In the juvenile justice context, these special aspects might include the facts that juveniles tend to be dependent on and under the authority of others, are less likely than adults to be competent to make the types of decisions that arise in the legal arena, and are less willing than adults to reveal their thoughts and feelings to attorneys or adults generally.[93] They may also be particularly sensitive to any failure on the part of legal actors to listen to their story and treat them with dignity.[94]

Finally, a performance-based approach must look at the extent to which a particular procedural framework helps or hinders the achievement of substantive goals. For example, effective implementation of the individual prevention vision of juvenile justice that we have endorsed throughout this book might call for quite different procedures from those required by a retributive system. Indeed, the latter system may be inherently much more resistant to the type of procedural flexibility we are advocating. Because it requires proof that a crime has been committed with the requisite degree of culpability and results in punishment commensurate with blameworthiness, a retributive regime is very similar, if not identical, to the "criminal prosecution" referenced in the Sixth Amendment, which requires *Gault*-type rights.

Thus, although nominally governed by the Due Process Clause in juvenile cases, a retributive regime may have more difficulty departing from adult procedures in the absence of clear empirical proof supporting a different approach. For instance, the Kansas Supreme Court recently decided that once the legislature required juvenile court judges to abide by adult-like determinate sentencing guidelines, the Sixth Amendment applies with full force to juvenile proceedings and jury trials are required.[95] In contrast, because the individual prevention vision of juvenile justice is not punishment oriented, "criminal prosecution" is not involved. Thus, as a legal matter, the adult template is more easily discarded in such a regime, if doing so appears to enhance accuracy, fairness, and efficiency.

With these considerations in mind, next we explore some possible alternatives to the adult procedural model. It may be that various rules that are taken for granted in adult court make little legal or empirical sense in juvenile court, especially if the court adopts an individual prevention model of justice.

Adjudicative and Decisional Competency

In adult court, defendants must be competent to stand trial, competent to plead guilty, competent to waive the right to counsel, and competent to make other decisions during the process.[96] Richard Bonnie has helpfully organized these various types of competencies into two categories: *adjudicative competence*, or the ability to understand the criminal process and communicate relevant information to the attorney, and *decisional competence*, or the ability to make decisions about rights and other legal matters.[97] Under Bonnie's schema, adjudicative competence is an important means of assuring the reliability of the adjudication because an accused who does not understand the process, has trouble understanding others, or cannot communicate pertinent facts cannot attend to and confront his or her accusers. Decisional competence is important as a means of assuring that individual autonomy is given its due.

A number of studies have assessed the adjudicative and decisional competence of juveniles as a group.[98] The findings indicate that juveniles ages eight through thirteen are somewhat less likely than adults to demonstrate the ability to understand legal matters associated with adjudicative competence, and *much* less likely to demonstrate the judgment associated with decisional competency. Juveniles who are fourteen and over are significantly better on both counts, although the younger juveniles in this group still fall below adult standards in terms of decisional competency.

These deficiencies in adjudicative and decisional competence can cause real problems in a juvenile justice system modeled on the adult process (which, as noted above, is more likely to occur under the retributive approach). In that sort of system, juveniles cannot be tried if they lack adjudicative competence; moreover, if the impairment causing the incompetency is simply immaturity (as opposed to, say, mental disability), they may *never* be triable, at least until the aging process works its magic. A lack of decisional competency can also seriously thwart the process if juveniles are to be given the rights of adults, which include the right to (waive) counsel, the right to (waive) a jury, and the privilege against self-incrimination, which can be waived through a guilty plea or during the interrogation process.

In contrast, in a juvenile justice system governed by due process principles—one that easily coincides with the individual prevention approach—adult competency requirements would apply only if necessary to assure reliability and fairness. To meet the due process standard of adjudicative competence, the juvenile offender would still need to be able to provide and follow factual accounts well enough to be able to challenge erroneous information about the triggering act and the relevant risk factors. But more elaborate cognitive abilities may not be necessary, at least if an attorney is also present. Thus, a demonstration that the child is competent to testify (which courts have been willing to attribute to witnesses well under ten[99]), along with assurance that the youth's attorney knows how to deal with young, often reticent, clients, may suffice for adjudicative competence.

The degree of decisional competence required as a matter of due process depends upon whether fairness concerns demand that juveniles be given adult-level decision-making authority, despite the possibility that reliability and efficiency might thereby be reduced. If juveniles in fact have less autonomy than adults and thus need or are perceived to need more paternalistic oversight, then perhaps juvenile offenders should not have complete control of the decisions in their case. If the individual prevention model of juvenile justice were adopted, decisional competency would be much less important in any event. As explained below, that regime's goal of effective risk assessment and management, based on evaluations by experts, would render certain adult-style entitlements, such as the right to jury, the right to silence, and the "right" to a reduced charge in exchange for a guilty plea, irrelevant or meaningless. Furthermore, the adult right to self-representation, which stems from the Sixth Amendment,[100] need not apply in the juvenile context and thus could be deemed unwaivable, making decisional competence concerning this issue irrelevant as well.[101]

The Right to Remain Silent

Gault decided that the Fifth Amendment applies in the juvenile court setting, which means that juveniles, like adults, are entitled to *Miranda* warnings before custodial interrogation and can refuse to testify at trial without fear of adverse comment about the failure to take the stand.[102] Had the Supreme Court evaluated the right to silence in terms of its effect on fairness, accuracy, and efficiency, it might have decided differently. Permitting a juvenile to remain silent during interrogation or trial could easily reduce reliability and efficiency in the typical case, concerns that arguably trump the lesser autonomy interests at stake in the juvenile context.

That is not to say the special protections for juveniles are not warranted during interrogation or trial. Allison Redlich and Saul Kassin have argued that juveniles are particularly likely to confess falsely, in light of research on adult interrogations indicating that such confessions have been correlated with suggestible personalities, lack of criminal justice experience, and "evasive" behavior during interrogations (e.g., lack of eye contact; slouching), all of which are likely to be associated with youth.[103] Research focused on juveniles tends to confirm that, compared to adults, children under fourteen are more likely to yield to suggestions of wrongdoing and older adolescents are more likely to shift their stories in response to negative feedback.[104] Yet police do not seem to alter their interrogation techniques when interrogating young suspects.[105]

These findings suggest certain policies designed to avoid false confessions, which could range from an unwaivable right to counsel during interrogation of juveniles, to exclusion of statements obtained using techniques that take advantage of adolescent vulnerability, to training of police officers to sensitize them to the greater suggestibility of youth. At the same time, this research does not indicate that *Miranda* warnings, which obviously can hinder accumulation of useful information, are a necessary means of preventing juveniles from confessing to crimes they did not commit; if other means of avoiding false or coerced confessions are available and more efficient than the warnings, due process analysis would not require them.[106] Similarly, analogous to arguments made in the adult context,[107] adherence to the right to silence at trial may not make sense from a due process perspective. If juvenile defendants have the assistance of counsel to help them prepare and are not subject to impeachment using prior offenses, requiring their testimony at trial will *enhance* the reliability of the proceedings and probably also make those proceedings appear more fair to a public that is likely to think defendants should have to tell their side of the story. As discussed in more detail below, juveniles themselves might consider a process in which they are encouraged or cajoled into talking more fair than one in which their attorneys routinely refuse to put them on the stand in deference to common wisdom about strategic use of the Fifth Amendment.

Given *Gault's* application of the Fifth Amendment to juvenile proceedings, is any of this possible? The answer is yes, at least in an individual prevention regime. While a retributive regime is "criminal" in nature and thus would probably find the Fifth Amendment's prohibition of compelled testimony "in any criminal case" hard to ignore, *Hendricks* indicates that regimes that focus on prevention are "civil" in nature. Indeed, in *Allen v. Illinois*[108] the Supreme Court explicitly held that where the purpose of state intervention is something other than "punishment" the privilege against self-incrimination does not apply. This position is bolstered by research suggesting that promotion of the right to silence inhibits prospects for rehabilitation.[109] As a practical matter, application of *Allen* to juvenile justice would mean that the many technical rules that have developed around *Miranda* would not need to be followed by law enforcement officials. It would also mean that, as occurs in Europe (in adult as well as juvenile cases),[110] juveniles who refuse to talk could be told their silence may be used against them as a way of cajoling information from them that might be useful during adjudication and disposition.

Sixth Amendment Trial Rights

The typical components of adult criminal court, stemming from the Sixth Amendment, include the right to confront one's accusers, the right to jury trial, and the right to assistance of counsel. In short, these rights dictate an adversarial process, run by the parties rather than the judge, aimed at convincing a group of laypeople who are otherwise uninvolved in the case that their story is the correct one. Due process might demand the same procedures. But a performance-based approach would be open to any number of permutations or combinations of adversarial and inquisitorial procedures as viable candidates for achieving optimal reliability, fairness, and efficiency. Given the scantiness of research on the topic, we can only suggest the spectrum of options.

For instance, Judge Sciolino has proposed a process in which the judge (1) speaks directly to the defendant rather than defense counsel; (2) works collaboratively with a treatment team; (3) is a proactive participant in a nonadversarial process; (4) applies a direct, immediate, and personal approach to each offender; and (5) recognizes success with praise, applause, rewards, or a graduation ceremony in the courtroom.[111] As this list and the previous review of the procedural justice literature suggests, we should be willing to contemplate the possibility that time-honored adversarial procedures do not promote accuracy or fairness. We have already noted the research indicating that party control of evidence may obfuscate rather than clarify.[112] Similarly, rigorous cross-examination by opposing sides may not be, as Dean Wigmore claimed, the "greatest legal engine ever invented for the discovery of truth."[113] As one well-known evidence expert has noted, cross-examiners rarely ask questions to which they don't know the answer, meaning that the fact finder may not always get the information it needs from the questioning process. Thus, he suggests, the fact finder should be able to ask follow-up questions, a procedure that is, at the least, quasi-inquisitorial.[114] It may also be the case that juries are more likely than judges to give into biases when it comes to evaluating guilt; the available research suggests that factors such as gender, race, empathy, and perceived dangerousness heavily influence individual juror conclusions about juvenile culpability, conclusions that deliberations with other jury members rarely budge.[115]

Finally, although the presence of counsel is undoubtedly an important attribute of procedural justice in most cases, their traditional adversarial role might not survive an empirically based assessment of how it affects fairness, accuracy, and efficiency. Research indicates that juveniles familiar with the justice system often distrust or are cynical about defense attorneys.[116] Furthermore, experience in so-called problem-solving courts, such as drug courts and mental health courts, has challenged the notion that the best defense lawyer is one who acts as the sole conduit of information from the criminal defendant. Rather than an advocate standing between the client and the system who rarely interacts with other actors in the system unless a "deal" can be struck, the defense attorney in problem-solving courts is often more open to cooperation and networking. Because the goal of these courts is more therapeutic than punitive, the adversarial stance is deemphasized. As one commentator put it,

> Unlike the traditional criminal process, in which the actors are bound together largely through conflict, the problem-solving court community is sustained by a more complementary and constructive ethos... . The defense lawyer is better able to communicate with and advocate for the client because of her rapport with other community members, and the client is better able to take advantage of the lawyer's advice because of reduced dependence upon it. The fluid, more organic nature of this process offers the promise of avoiding the stultifying routinization that has plagued criminal courts and prompted the creation of this alternative model in the first place.[117]

As this passage suggests, the possibility that unfamiliar defense counsel and rules of evidence curb a juvenile defendant's ability to tell his or her story should be considered. Juveniles often have a very difficult time conversing with adults. Unlike adult offenders, who may malinger by claiming mental problems in the hopes of achieving a better disposition, adolescents are far more likely to "clam up" or present themselves as streetwise "tough guys," because the label of "delinquent" or "troublemaker" is much less threatening to their self-esteem and reputation than being considered "crazy" or in need of help.[118]

Juveniles may also be unwilling to cooperate because they don't trust the system. Perhaps they have been through "youth programs" before and found them lacking in benefit. Or perhaps they feel abused by a system that doesn't treat them with dignity.[119] Allowing juveniles to hide behind their lawyer's words or formal rules of evidence may only exacerbate these tendencies. Perhaps instead, informal "face–saving" mechanisms should be developed to facilitate a youth's admission that help is needed.

More generally, the procedural justice literature canvassed in this chapter makes clear that participation in the process is an important component of fairness, subjectively if not objectively. When a lawyer functions as the juvenile's mouthpiece, that sense of participation may be diminished. Relying on these insights, Emily Buss suggests that "adolescents should play a far greater and more direct role in the proceeding, and . . . judges should more actively and clearly speak to the adolescent throughout."[120] That experience may not only improve juveniles' perception of how fair their particular adjudication was but also enhance "their attitudes about themselves, their government and society, and their own relationship with that government and society."[121]

Procedure and Substance

The reassessment of whether adult rules should apply in the juvenile context that we are proposing must also pay close attention to the procedure's ability to promote substantive policy objectives, such as rehabilitation, crime prevention, and retribution. Thus, if the juvenile justice system were focused on individual prevention, challenges to adult-type trial procedures might be particularly powerful. For example, as *Mathews* itself suggested,[122] inquisitorial methods might be perceived as fairer and more accurate when the inquiry is "scientific," and thus might be preferable when the decision is a clinical judgment about whether a juvenile needs treatment to prevent recidivism (the principal goal of a preventive system) rather than a moral judgment about blameworthiness and punishment. Research on "teen courts" likewise suggests that an adjudicative process that mimics aspects of the European inquisitorial model might be more "therapeutic" for juveniles and more effective at curbing their antisocial behavior than the traditional adversarial model.[123] Copying another European practice, victims might play a much bigger role in an individual prevention regime for two reasons. First, research from the burgeoning restorative justice movement suggests that victim-offender conferencing aimed at mending victims and reintegrating offenders reduces recidivism (and also increases both defendant and victim satisfaction with the process).[124] Second, public acceptance of an individual prevention approach is more likely if victims are perceived to be involved with and endorse the system.

Another likely distinguishing characteristic of an individual prevention regime is that trials, however constructed, would be more frequent than in a retributive regime, or at least more frequent than they are in the adult process as it operates today. As noted earlier, plea bargaining, which is both necessitated by and responsible for nullifying the effect of the many trial rights afforded criminal defendants, is endemic in the adult system. But private deals between the defense and the prosecution would not be possible in an individual prevention regime, since experts, monitored by a judge, would have to be involved in the risk-assessment and management process. While some efficiency would thereby be sacrificed, the slimmed-down trial process, together with the elimination of the right to silence, might more than make up for this loss (and, given its openness relative to the bargaining process, would also improve perceived fairness, if not reliability).

Even if, however, the juvenile justice system continues its trend toward the punishment model, a preference for the traditional adversarial regime over a more investigative approach is not a foregone conclusion, as the European example illustrates. The procedural choice should not be based, as it has largely been up to now, on whether the juvenile justice system is genuinely therapeutic (and therefore does not require more "protective" adversarial procedures[125]), but rather should be driven primarily by an empirical assessment of which procedural mix best achieves the goals of the system, whatever they are. The important point is that data should be collected in an ongoing manner to assess the extent to which specified and adopted policy objectives are being met at the individual-child level and with respect to the system as a whole.

With these possibilities in mind, Gerald Gault's "trial" may not have been the egregious violation of procedural rights it is often said to be. Neither the failure to give *Miranda* warnings nor the direct questioning by the judge in that case necessarily infringed due process. While Gault should have been told his charges and been allowed to see the "referral report" against him, the relevant information was presumably communicated to him by the judge. The absence of the complaining neighbor may have been irrelevant if Gault fully confessed to the "crime." Even the absence of a lawyer may not have been prejudicial, given the simplicity of the charge and the presence of his parents (although, as implied above, we think lawyers can be very helpful at various stages of the process and are probably essential in challenging expert testimony about risk). We are not willing to say that Gault's trial was a model of due process (nor do we think that the six-year detention he received makes any sense from either a desert or a preventive perspective). But we do think that its failure to abide by adult-like procedures did not automatically mean it either violated the Constitution or failed to provide a fair and reliable adjudicatory process.

Conclusion

Justice Fortas was correct when he proclaimed that juvenile offenders prior to the *Kent* decision experienced the worst of both worlds, because they received neither adequate due process protection nor effective rehabilitation. For several decades, juvenile justice reforms, instigated by lawyers and assisted by advocacy-oriented social scientists, sought to fix the juvenile justice system by focusing on providing children with adult procedural "safeguards." The reformers' hope was that children would at least get the best of one world: adult criminal due process protections.

We have seen, however, that these modern procedural reforms rest on the misguided assumption that adult criminal procedures necessarily provide the ultimate in due process protections. When procedural due process is instead conceptualized in terms of maximizing accuracy, fairness, and efficiency in decision making, its implementation becomes an empirical question open to feedback and based on particular contextual demands. Procedural justice research to date casts serious doubt on the reformers' premise. We are not calling for a blind return to kangaroo juvenile courts or advocating, under the once popular quid pro quo theory, that juveniles receive lesser process in return for rehabilitative services.[126] But we do believe that if the juvenile justice system reorients itself toward an empirically based process *and* adopts preventive goals, juveniles will truly receive the best of both worlds: procedural safeguards that have a demonstrated impact on the fairness and accuracy of decision making, and intervention programs focused on principles of least restrictive intervention and crime prevention.

6

The Future of (Juvenile) Justice

The perspective presented in this book reflects an integration of developing trends in the fields of both law and psychology. In the legal realm, recent efforts to conceptualize and implement due process in various contexts, ranging from drug and mental health courts to sexually violent offender commitment schemes, have moved toward more administrative models.[1] In comparison to the traditional backward-looking adjudicative model associated with criminal justice, these administrative models take a forward-looking approach to decision making that is more open to nonlegal expertise and empirical data and more focused on problem solving. Whereas traditional approaches depend upon divining moral culpability for past acts, administrative models offer the flexibility to implement a wide range of policy objectives,[2] ranging from rehabilitation to individual crime prevention, and even to "punishment" (qua confinement) when it can be shown to have a positive instrumental effect on crime prevention.

In the realm of psychology, efforts to understand and change human behavior have become increasingly ecological in nature. Research conducted in the past several decades makes clear that contextual, neurobiological, and emotional factors, often outside individual awareness, are at least as important as rational thought processes in explaining human behavior, especially the behavior of children and adolescents. Moreover, the newer research suggests, these contextual factors, which include dynamic risk and protective factors in the realm of family, peer, school, and community life, can be used as levers for effective intervention, risk management, and prevention. Just as administrative models of due process have become more managerial in nature, effective treatment and preventive interventions have become increasingly focused on risk management.

The confluence of these legal and psychological trends suggests the possibility and desirability of a juvenile justice system focused on individual prevention for youth at risk. Throughout this book, we have drawn on normative arguments and empirical evidence in making the claim that this model of juvenile justice offers the most likely prospect for bringing about the best of both worlds for youth and for society, primarily because it is the best means of reducing the likelihood that juveniles will engage in criminal behavior. As a framework for making this point, in Chapters 1 and 3 we introduced and critically analyzed four distinct but interrelated models of juvenile justice based on their policy objectives: rehabilitation, adult retribution, diminished retribution, and individual prevention.

The rehabilitation model provided the guiding philosophy for the juvenile justice movement that took hold in the United States at the beginning of the twentieth century. This movement was rooted in both idealism and paternalism. The expectation was that juveniles would not be treated as evildoers deserving of punishment but as misguided children who needed assistance from the state in helping to shape their developing personalities in ways that would make them good citizens. The tools to accomplish this task were borrowed from the worlds of psychotherapy and social work. Proponents of this new approach to troubled youth believed that the traditional substantive and procedural legal rules were counterproductive to their rehabilitative enterprise.

The major accomplishments of the rehabilitative approach were largely aspirational. Introduction of the rehabilitative ethos instilled in the legal system the desire to change troublesome children in ways that would make them more law abiding. The major shortcomings of this model were threefold. First, the scope of expected psychological transformation was overly broad. It was assumed that almost any intervention that made the child into a better person was permissible, with the consequence that the juvenile court could and often did deprive juveniles of liberty for trivial misconduct such as disobedience or truancy. The second major shortcoming of the rehabilitative approach was its failure to deliver concrete success, due in large part to its intrapsychic approach to therapy. Any reduction of recidivism that occurred was largely an incidental benefit that flowed from the improved personality of rehabilitated youngsters; as a result juvenile crime rates remained unchanged or even increased. These two shortcomings in the scope and effectiveness of intervention were coupled with a third significant legal flaw—procedural safeguards so lax that the Supreme Court had to step in and declare them unconstitutional.

By the last third of the twentieth century, these deficiencies in the rehabilitation model contributed to calls for the abolition of a separate juvenile justice system or at least a system more oriented toward the adult brand of criminal justice. Substantively, adult criminal justice has many goals, but for at least the past quarter century it has been firmly rooted in notions of retribution and proportionate punishment. Procedurally, the adult criminal justice system has long been anchored in the explicit texts of the Fifth and Sixth Amendments of the U.S. Constitution. The retribution model of juvenile justice, therefore, aims principally to make juvenile offenders pay their just deserts for past crimes through a process that is ideally adversarial in nature. The adult retribution variant of this approach equates youths, or at least older adolescents, with adults in terms of desert. The diminished retribution model, in contrast, views juveniles as "works in progress" who have not yet reached the level of psychological development necessary for mature autonomous decision making; thus youthful offenders should pay for their past criminal behavior, but usually at a discount rate.

From the perspective of the new managerial perspectives in law and psychology, both variants of the retributive model have several drawbacks. The adult retribution model fails to recognize that youths are less developed in terms of cognitive capacities and managing themselves. The diminished retribution model recognizes this fact but makes too much of it; adults with similar deficiencies rarely receive the type of significant reductions in punishment that the diminished retribution model envisions for youths. Furthermore, under both models disposition is supposed to fit the culpability of the offender. Thus, reduction of recidivism is accomplished only indirectly, if at all; indeed, to the extent they view incarceration as the sanction demanded by proportionality, these models probably exacerbate criminal propensities. Concerns about negative instrumental outcomes—like the social, economic, educational, and personal costs of punitive intervention for its own sake—take a back seat to insuring that culpability assessments are properly adjusted within a retribution framework.

Most important, neither retributive model takes sufficient account of modern behavioral science research on the causes and consequences of criminal conduct. Modern efforts to understand and change human behavior have become increasingly ecological and multisystemic in nature. As Chapter 2 demonstrated, behavioral scientists have identified a number of psychological, neurobiological, and contextual risk and protective factors which, alone or in combination, increase or decrease the likelihood that a juvenile will engage in delinquent behavior. These risk factors span multiple levels of analysis and domains, including social skill deficits, harsh parenting, association with delinquent peers, substance abuse, and impoverished neighborhoods and communities.

These findings appear to be of no interest to those who want to treat juvenile offenders like adult offenders. And while the most recent advocates for the diminished responsibility model are aware of this research and vaguely suggest that it should be relevant to the dispositional calculus, in the end they too are unable to take full advantage of this empirical work because their model is still essentially backward looking. In contrast, the individual prevention model relies heavily on this empirical work both in its legal analysis and its implementation.

As a legal matter, Chapter 3 explained, the research findings of the past few decades concerning juveniles generally and juvenile offending specifically provide a strong basis for a separate juvenile system, *if* it is aimed at reducing recidivism. Most important, the research establishes the proposition that adolescents are more impulsive and reckless than adults. Lesser deterrability is precisely the rationale the Supreme Court has endorsed in holding that not all antisocial behavior needs to be handled through a punishment-oriented system. Instead, a forward-looking administrative regime aimed at prevention is constitutionally permissible if it makes a good faith effort at achieving that goal through treatment.

This good faith effort would be the purpose of the separate juvenile system we described in Chapters 4 and 5. That system would depend upon recent advances in behavioral science that push toward proactive, managerial, systemic approaches to problem solving. More specifically, behavioral science research that pinpoints dynamic risk factors and that evaluates community-based programs that can minimize those factors would be the linchpin of the system, not, as under the retributive models, an ignored or tangential consideration. Further, because the system would be administrative in nature, research in procedural justice would help shape the best manner of assuring both objective and subjective fairness. To us the new "Gault" is a system that constantly experiments with process and monitors its operation in a way that assures feedback on the optimal method of achieving procedural justice.

As this discussion suggests, the framework for juvenile justice presented in this book is, and by its nature, always will be, a work in progress. A performance-based individual prevention model of juvenile justice can facilitate and perhaps even vastly accelerate this progress by turning the juvenile court system into what Michael Dorf and Charles Sabel have called an "experimentalist" court.[3] Indeed, the most significant contribution of the preventive model could well be that the juvenile court is structured to serve as a natural laboratory for ongoing basic and applied research on adolescent development, individual crime prevention, and procedural justice.

For example, a preventive, performance-based risk management system would allow for comparison of retributive and risk-management strategies on such criteria as cost and effectiveness. Whether alternatives to traditional punitive interventions are cheaper and better at reducing recidivism of offenders without decreasing the law's credibility is an empirical question that can be addressed within the preventive juvenile justice system itself. Within the realm of individual preventive interventions, numerous other practical and theoretical questions can be addressed. For example, what kinds of family-based interventions work best with what types of children? Do physically abused children respond to the family component of multisystemic intervention in the same ways as children who were not abused, as children whose parents have a criminal record, or as children whose parents have experienced mental illness? In the procedural realm, do juveniles have better outcomes when they are represented by adversarial or by "problem-solving" counsel?

Does allowing juveniles to have input and voice in the intervention process influence their likelihood of complying with intervention requirements? The list of potential questions is limited only by the creativity and imagination of those responsible for the administration of justice under a preventive, performance-based, risk-management model of juvenile justice.

The experimentalist juvenile court would also enable research about systems and entities outside the criminal/administrative constellation, guided by the fifth principle of the preventive model of juvenile justice we introduced in Chapter 4 (providing that those who work in the juvenile justice system "must have ongoing and mutually informative relationships with other youth-socializing institutions such as families, schools, communities, and the child welfare, health care, and adult criminal justice systems"). A connection with schools and other entities will facilitate research and intervention aimed at preventing younger children from crossing the threshold of overt behavior that places them within the jurisdiction of the juvenile justice system. Coordinated research efforts with these institutions will also help establish how kids who get into trouble with the law are different from (and similar to) youngsters who stay out of trouble.

To sum up, then, the individual prevention approach to juvenile justice that we advocate in this book provides the following advantages over other models of juvenile justice: (1) a more coherent legal rationale for maintaining a separate juvenile justice system; (2) a more persuasive political rationale for such a system, focused neither on "punishment" nor on "treatment" but on "prevention," a concept which both liberals and conservatives ought to be able to support; (3) a stronger legal platform for taking advantage of recent advances in treatment designed to reduce recidivism; (4) a stronger legal argument for a right to treatment for juvenile offenders; (5) a greater likelihood of fairer, more accurate procedures in juvenile court; (6) a greater likelihood that evidence-based practices will be incorporated into the juvenile justice system; and (7) a system better equipped to generate data about the success of programs and processes that are established.

These advantages need to be emphasized for two reasons. First, inertia is a powerful force. Even those who are very concerned about the current state of the juvenile court system might be anxious about advancing a new theoretical rationale for its existence. After all, the juvenile court is in no danger of disappearing in the near future and the current hybrid system—mixing together determinate punishment, treatment, general deterrence, and a general goal of keeping kids out of harm's way—serves a number of ends. The best "reform," it might be argued, is simply to make sure the various community treatment programs described in these pages are added into the mix, and trust that things will get better. A bit more ambitiously, reformers could attempt to narrow transfer jurisdiction and reduce sentences.

This attitude is short-sighted. The reason no state is interested in abolishing the juvenile court at present is because it is much easier to *broaden* transfer and act jurisdiction and *extend* the duration of juvenile court detentions.

Arguments that juveniles are less culpable or more treatable than adults will not reverse these legislative tendencies unless they can be coupled with proof that adult-like dispositions are more costly both financially and in terms of public safety. In the meantime, the impetus for diligently pursuing community-based crime-reduction programs is nonexistent. In the current system, there is no legally enforceable least-drastic means requirement, right to treatment, or proportionality limit on confinement duration.[4]

A second, related reason to emphasize the advantages of the individual prevention model is the need to counter unfounded fears about it. Based on past experiences with insufficiently conceptualized rehabilitation and preventive regimes, some have worried that the prevention model is unavoidably associated with a number of problems, most prominently an inability to channel the moral preferences of the community, a reliance on suspect assessments of risk prone to disparate and discriminatory outcomes, and a tendency toward lax procedures. We countered the objections that stem from these perceptions in Chapters 3, 4, and 5. Under the individual prevention model we endorse, both accountability for illegal behavior and long-term dispositions (sometimes involving confinement) will still occur, the impact of risk assessments will be better cabined than the guesses associated with culpability assessments, and adult-like procedures will continue to govern when they produce more reliable, fair, and efficient results than alternatives. To the extent that these types of responses do not dissipate angst about the proposal, we trust that the advantages listed above do so.

It is possible that the benefits of an individual prevention regime could occasion rethinking of the adult criminal system as well.[5] Outside of a growing body of work on prisoner reentry,[6] however, the research base in the adult setting is quite thin compared to the empirical information we currently possess on the causes and prevention of juvenile crime. That differential exists in part because of the assumption that juveniles are more malleable than adults and are thus more responsive to contextual influences, including rehabilitative interventions.[7] It also exists because of the assumption that absent insanity, adult offenders freely choose whether or not to obey the law, thus making contextual influences largely irrelevant. Perhaps success with juvenile offenders will encourage greater experimentation and evaluation of contextually based interventions with adults, which in turn will lead to challenges to both of these assumptions. That development, however, would require a rethinking of the fundamental premises and constitutional requirements of the adult criminal justice system, a topic well beyond the scope of this book.

In the meantime, juvenile justice programs and policies aimed at helping juveniles at risk and preventing crime must continually strive to draw on and integrate the very best cutting-edge scholarship, research, and practices the legal and behavioral science communities have to offer. A prevention-oriented, administrative approach is the best way to achieve this aim. Only if society is willing to rely on evidence-based dispositions and procedures do we have a chance at creating a first-class system of justice for our children.

APPENDIX

Four Recidivism-Reduction Programs for Youth

Functional Family Therapy (FFT)

From The Center for the Study and Prevention of Violence (CSPV)
http://www.colorado.edu/cspv/blueprints/modelprograms.html

Program Summary

Functional Family Therapy (FFT) is an outcome-driven prevention/intervention program for youth who have demonstrated the entire range of maladaptive, acting out behaviors and related syndromes.

Program Targets:

Youth, aged 11–18, at risk for and/or presenting with delinquency, violence, substance use, Conduct Disorder, Oppositional Defiant Disorder, or Disruptive Behavior Disorder. Often these youth present with additional comorbid challenges such as depression.

Program Content:

FFT requires as few as 8–15 sessions of direct service time for commonly referred youth and their families, and generally no more than 26 total sessions of direct service for the most severe problem situations.

Delivery modes: Flexible delivery of service by one and (rarely) two person teams to clients in-home, clinic, school, juvenile court, community based programs, and at time of re-entry from institutional placement.

Implementation: Wide range of interventionists, including trained probation officers, mental health technicians, degreed mental health professionals (e.g., M.S.W., Ph.D., M.D., R.N., M.F.T., L.C.P.).

FFT effectiveness derives from emphasizing factors which enhance protective factors and reduce risk, including the risk of treatment termination. In order to accomplish these changes in the most effective manner, FFT is a phasic program with steps which build upon each other. These phases consist of:

- *Engagement*, designed to emphasize within youth and family factors that protect youth and families from early program dropout;
- *Motivation*, designed to change maladaptive emotional reactions and beliefs, and increase alliance, trust, hope, and motivation for lasting change;
- *Assessment*, designed to clarify individual, family system, and larger system relationships, especially the interpersonal functions of behavior and how they relate to change techniques;
- *Behavior Change*, which consists of communication training, specific tasks and technical aids, basic parenting skills, problem solving and conflict management skills, contracting and response-cost techniques; and
- *Generalization*, during which family case management is guided by individualized family functional needs, their interface with community based environmental constraints and resources, and the alliance with the FFT therapist/Family Case Manager.

Program Outcomes:

Clinical trials have demonstrated that FFT is capable of:

- Effectively treating adolescents with Conduct Disorder, Oppositional Defiant Disorder, Disruptive Behavior Disorder, alcohol and other drug abuse disorders, and who are delinquent and/or violent;
- Interrupting the matriculation of these adolescents into more restrictive, higher cost services;
- Reducing the access and penetration of other social services by these adolescents;
- Generating positive outcomes with the entire spectrum of intervention personnel;
- Preventing further incidence of the presenting problem;
- Preventing younger children in the family from penetrating the system of care;
- Preventing adolescents from penetrating the adult criminal system; and
- Effectively transferring treatment effects across treatment systems.

Program Costs:

The 90-day costs range between $1,600 and $5,000 for an average of 12 home visits per family. Current costs vary and are highly dependent on cost of labor.

Program Background

Many therapies are named to reflect a theoretical perspective (e.g., behavioral, object relations) or a primary focus (e.g., multiple systems, cognitive). Functional Family Therapy (FFT) is named to reflect a set of core theoretical principles which represents the primary focus (family), and an overriding allegiance to positive outcome in a model that understands both positive and negative behavior as representations of family relational systems (functional). Thus, Functional Family Therapy has adopted an integrative stance that stresses functionality of the family, the therapy, and the clinical model.

The developers and replicators of Functional Family Therapy have recognized that solutions require an integration of high quality science, tested theoretical principles, and extensive clinical experience in pursuit of specific functional goals of:

1. Effectively changing the maladaptive behaviors of youth and families, especially those who at the outset may not be motivated or may not believe they can change;
2. Reducing the personal, societal, and economic devastation that results from the continuation or exacerbation of the various disruptive behavior disorders of youth; and
3. Doing so with less cost, in terms of time and money, than so many of the more expensive (but not necessarily effective) treatments currently available.

Unlike other therapies, FFT was not developed on college students, neurotic individuals, or inpatient adults. Instead, FFT grew out of a need to serve a population of at-risk adolescents and families that were under served, had few resources, were difficult to treat, and were often perceived by helping professions to be treatment resistant. In many cases these families entered the "system" angry, resistant, and unmotivated to change. Essentially the "helping professions" did not know how to treat this population. FFT developed out of the awareness that to be successful in treatment of this population we needed to be culturally competent, and understand why this group was so treatment resistant. Thus, FFT attempted to develop ways to engage these families in order to help them achieve obtainable change and become more adaptable and productive. Over the last 30 years, FFT has learned that it is important to do more than simply stopping bad behaviors. We know that it is important to motivate families to change in a positive way by uncovering and developing the unique strengths of the family in ways that enhance the families' self-respect while providing specific ways to improve.

Since its inception in 1969, FFT has accomplished its primary goals by integrating the most promising theoretical perspectives, the empirical data available, and hours and hours of direct clinical experience with the troubled youth we wanted to help. FFT is designed to increase efficiency, decrease costs, and enhance our ability to provide service to more youth by:

1. Targeting risk and protective factors that we can, in fact, change and then programmatically changing them;
2. Engaging and motivating the families and youth so they participate more in the change process;
3. Entering each session and phase of intervention with a clear plan and by using proven techniques for implementation;
4. Constantly monitoring process and outcome so we don't fool ourselves or make excuses for failure; and
5. Believing in the families we see and then believing in ourselves.

At the time of the inception of Functional Family Therapy, the major theoretical perspectives and services available for treating troubled youth in a family context were rudimentary, though promising. Early on, FFT represented an integration of systems perspectives and behavioral techniques. The systemic background of FFT emphasized dynamic and reciprocal processes which needed to be identified in referred families. This led to early observational research on the interactions of delinquent and nondelinquent families using a systemic framework. The behavioral background of FFT provided not only specific, manualizeable interventions such as contracting, but it also featured an urgent awareness of the need for rigorous treatment development—a scientific imperative to systematically examine the effects of intervention and develop strategies for identifying positive change processes. These origins led to a continuing series of studies involving controlled outcome evaluations and additional replications. During the mid-1970s, FFT also began addressing issues of therapist characteristics and in-session processes from an integrated clinical/research perspective, both reflecting and contributing to the training of therapists for subsequent interventions. In the late 1990s FFT further articulated the clinical change model, adding a comprehensive system of client, process, and outcome assessment implemented through a computer-based client tracking and monitoring system (FFT-CSS).

Throughout its development FFT has insisted on step by step descriptions of the clinical change process as well as rigorous evaluation of both the process and outcomes of this work. FFT has also insisted on integrating high quality science (in regard to evaluation and research) with sound clinical judgment and experience and comprehensive theoretical principles. Thus, over the last 30 years FFT has been a dynamic and evolving clinical system that retains its core principles while adding clinical features that further enhance successful outcomes. In its most recent iteration, FFT has developed a functional family assessment system to aid FFT therapists in targeting and implementing therapeutic change goals in a way that leads to accountability through process and outcome evaluation. Thus, FFT has matured into a clinical intervention model with systematic training, supervision, and process and outcome assessment components all directed at enhancing the delivery of FFT in local communities (see Figure A.1).

Brief Description of Intervention

Functional Family Therapy (FFT) is a well documented family prevention and intervention program which has been applied successfully to a wide range of problem youth and their families in various contexts. While commonly employed as an intervention program, FFT has demonstrated its effectiveness as a method for the prevention of many of the problems of at-risk adolescents and their families. Functional Family Therapy is an empirically grounded intervention program that targets youth between the ages of 11 and 18, although younger siblings of referred adolescents are also treated. FFT is a short-term intervention with, on average, 8 to 12 one-hour sessions for mild cases and up to 26 to 30 hours of direct service for more difficult situations. In most programs sessions are spread over a three-month period of time. Target populations range from at-risk preadolescents to youth with very serious problems such as conduct disorder. The data from numerous outcome studies suggests that when applied as intended, FFT can reduce recidivism between 25% and 60%. Additional studies suggest that FFT is a cost-effective intervention that

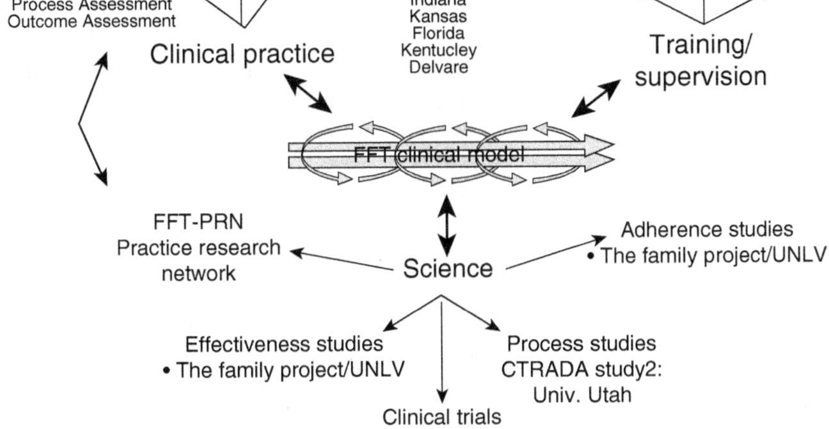

Figure A.1. Mature Clinical Model

can, when appropriately implemented, reduce treatment costs well below that of traditional services and other family-based interventions.

As it developed, FFT has been readily adopted in many contexts due to its clear identification of specific phases, each of which includes descriptions of goals, requisite therapist characteristics, and techniques. The phases of intervention, and their component activities, have developed in the context of many clinical hours with many families of various characteristics, coupled with intensive supervision and clinical case discussion. As a result, each phase involves clinically rich and successful interventions that are organized in a coherent manner and allow clinicians to maintain focus in the context of considerable family and individual disruption. The phases consist of:

1. Phase 1: Engagement and Motivation. During these initial phases, FFT applies reattribution (e.g., reframing) and related techniques to impact maladaptive perceptions, beliefs, and emotions. This produces increasing hope and expectation of change, decreasing resistance, increasing alliance and trust, reducing the oppressive negativity within family and between family and community, and increasing respect for individual differences and values.
2. Phase 2: Behavior Change. This phase applies individualized and developmentally appropriate techniques such as communication training, specific tasks and technical aids, basic parenting skills, and contracting and response-cost techniques.
3. Phase 3: Generalization. In this phase, Family Case Management is guided by individualized family functional needs, their interaction with environmental constraints and resources, and the alliance with the therapist.

Each of these phases involves both assessment and intervention components. Family assessment focuses on characteristics of the individual family members, family relational dynamics, and the multisystemic context in which the family operates. The family relational system is described in regard to interpersonal functions and their impact on promoting and maintaining problem behavior. Intervention is directed at accomplishing the goals of the relevant treatment phase. For example, in the engagement and motivation phase, assessment is focused on determining the degree to which the family or its members are negative and blaming. The corresponding intervention would target the reduction of negativity and blaming. In behavior change, assessment would focus on targeting the skills necessary for more adaptive family functioning. Intervention would be aimed at helping the family develop those skills in a way that matched their relational patterns. In generalization, the assessment focuses on the degree to which the family can apply the new behavior in broader contexts. Interventions would focus on helping generalize the family behavior change into such contexts.

As a clinical model, FFT has been conducted in varied clinical settings and as a home-based model. The fidelity of the FFT model is achieved by a specific training model and a sophisticated client assessment, tracking, and monitoring system that provides for specific clinical assessment and outcome accountability (FFT-CSS). The FFT Practice Research Network (FFT-PRN) allows clinical sites to participate in the development and dissemination of FFT model information.

Evidence of Program Effectiveness

To date, thirteen studies in referenced journals (plus one in preparation) demonstrate dramatic and significant positive treatment effects, including follow-up periods of up to five years. Rates of offending and foster care or institutional placement have been reduced at least 25 percent and as much as 60 percent in comparison to the randomly assigned or matched alternative treatments, or base rates. One study also demonstrated a positive three year follow-up effect on siblings. Additional formal program reports (e.g., county and federal funded projects) from completed and ongoing replications reflect similar positive outcomes, and five currently funded trials (National Institute of Drug Abuse, National Institute of Alcohol Abuse and Alcoholism, Government of Sweden) promise additional data regarding generalization of effects for FFT across more contexts and populations. Studies have also identified specific FFT based interventions and direct changes in family functioning which relate to the outcome findings.

One major factor in the successful evolution of FFT has been the continuous (29 year) involvement of its progenitors and many of its co-contributors in various university settings. This context has not only maintained a standard of scientific scrutiny, but has also contributed to the conceptual integrity of the major constructs and techniques. The prime example of this impact is the extensive work on reframing in FFT, informed by other well-developed theoretical perspectives such as information processing theory, social cognition, and the psychology of emotion. Laboratory based research has identified specific components of this critical technique, which in turn has led to applied research on cognitive set and attributional processes in referred adolescent families. Further, investigations have identified in-session therapist characteristics and family interaction processes relevant to the phases of FFT which are predictive of positive change. Most notable process changes appear to be in family communication patterns, and especially negative/blaming communications and "withholding" types of silence. With respect to therapist characteristics, process and outcome data demonstrate that FFT therapists must be first relationally sensitive and focused, then capable of clear structuring and teaching, in order to produce significantly fewer dropouts during treatment and lower recidivism.

More recently, FFT has been widely adopted because it has evolved an increasingly multicultural perspective, and has added effective home-based intervention. In the home-based Clark County, Nevada, Youth and Family Services program, for example, referred adolescents are roughly 30 percent

African American, 20 percent Hispanic/Latino (mostly Mexican American), and just under 50 percent European American with a few American Indian and Asian American youth. Preliminary data on the first year of FFT involvement indicate no difference in reoffense rate among the different ethnic/racial groups, supporting the generalizability of FFT effects across cultural/racial groups. The Fayetteville, North Carolina, program has involved primarily White and African American families and therapists, including a significant number of mixed race relationships and offspring. The two clinical trials being conducted in New Mexico involve Hispanic/Latino and White youth, and the home-based program in urban Willow Run, Michigan, involves a large proportion of African American and mixed families… . As the model has been increasingly adopted in multicultural contexts, focus is being placed on issues of culture and ethnicity, with much of this recent work undertaken in the context of the multi-site National Institute of Drug Abuse (NIDA) funded Center for Research on Adolescent Drug Abuse (CTRADA, Howard Liddle, P.I.).

Taken together, 28 years of data and clinical experience with FFT involving hundreds of therapists and thousands of families have provided strong empirical support for this family-based intervention with adolescents. In addition, the research has demonstrated that intervention must include a major focus on changing emotional and attributional, especially blaming, components of family interaction, then provide a program of specific behavior change techniques that are culturally appropriate, family appropriate, and consistent with the capabilities of each family member.

The Above Information was Excerpted From:

Alexander, J., Barton, C., Gordon, D., Grotpeter, J., Hansson, K., Harrison, R., Mears, S., Mihalic, S., Parsons, B., Pugh, C., Schulman, S., Waldron, H., & Sexton, T. (1998). Blueprints for Violence Prevention, Book Three: Functional Family Therapy. Boulder, CO: Center for the Study and Prevention of Violence.

Multisystemic Therapy (MST)

From The Center for the Study and Prevention of Violence
http://www.colorado.edu/cspv/blueprints/modelprograms.html

Program Summary

Multisystemic Therapy (MST) is an intensive family- and community-based treatment that addresses the multiple determinants of serious antisocial behavior in juvenile offenders. The multisystemic approach views individuals as being nested within a complex network of interconnected systems that encompass individual, family, and extrafamilial (peer, school, neighborhood) factors. Intervention may be necessary in any one or a combination of these systems.

Program Targets:

MST targets chronic, violent, or substance abusing male or female juvenile offenders, ages 12 to 17, at high risk of out-of-home placement, and the offenders' families.

Program Content:

MST addresses the multiple factors known to be related to delinquency across the key settings, or systems, within which youth are embedded. MST strives to promote behavior change in the youth's natural environment, using the strengths of each system (e.g., family, peers, school, neighborhood, indigenous support network) to facilitate change.

The major goal of MST is to empower parents with the skills and resources needed to independently address the difficulties that arise in raising teenagers and to empower youth to cope with family, peer, school, and neighborhood problems. Within a context of support and skill building, the therapist places developmentally appropriate demands on the adolescent and family for responsible behavior. Intervention strategies are integrated into a social ecological context and include strategic family therapy, structural family therapy, behavioral parent training, and cognitive behavior therapies.

MST is provided using a home-based model of services delivery. This model helps to overcome barriers to service access, increases family retention in treatment, allows for the provision of intensive services (i.e., therapists have low caseloads), and enhances the maintenance of treatment gains. The usual duration of MST treatment is approximately 60 hours of contact over four months, but frequency and duration of sessions are determined by family need.

Program Outcomes:

Evaluations of MST have demonstrated for serious juvenile offenders:

- reductions of 25–70% in long-term rates of rearrest,
- reductions of 47–64% in out-of-home placements,
- extensive improvements in family functioning, and
- decreased mental health problems for serious juvenile offenders.

Program Costs:

MST has achieved favorable outcomes at cost saving in comparison with usual mental health and juvenile justice services, such as incarceration and residential treatment. At a cost of $4,500 per youth, a recent policy report concluded that MST was the most cost-effective of a wide range of intervention programs aimed at serious juvenile offenders.

Program Background

Multisystemic Therapy (MST) was developed in the late 1970s. It addresses several limitations of existing mental health services for serious juvenile offenders which include minimal effectiveness, low accountability of service providers for outcomes, and high cost.

Treatment efforts, in general, have failed to address the complexity of youth needs, being individually-oriented, narrowly focused, and delivered in settings that bear little relation to the problems being addressed (e.g., residential treatment centers, outpatient clinics). Given overwhelming empirical evidence that serious antisocial behavior is determined by the interplay of individual, family, peer, school, and neighborhood factors, it is not surprising that treatments of serious antisocial behavior have been largely ineffective. Restrictive out-of-home placements, such as residential treatment, psychiatric hospitalization, and incarceration, fail to address the known determinants of serious antisocial behavior and fail to alter the natural ecology to which the youth will eventually return. Furthermore, mental health and juvenile justice authorities have had virtually no accountability for outcome, a situation that does not enhance performance. The ineffectiveness of out-of-home placement, coupled with extremely high costs, have led many youth advocates to search for viable alternatives. MST is one treatment model that has a well-documented capacity to address the aforementioned difficulties in providing effective services for juvenile offenders.

Theoretical Rationale/Conceptual Framework

Consistent with social-ecological models of behavior and findings from causal modeling studies of delinquency and drug use, MST posits that youth antisocial behavior is multidetermined and linked with characteristics of the individual youth and his or her family, peer group, school, and community contexts. As such, MST interventions aim to attenuate risk factors by building youth and family strengths (protective factors) on a highly individualized and comprehensive basis. The provision of home-based services circumvents barriers to service access that often characterize families of serious juvenile offenders. An emphasis on parental empowerment to modify the natural social network of their children facilitates the maintenance and generalization of treatment gains.

Brief Description of Intervention

MST is a pragmatic and goal-oriented treatment that specifically targets those factors in each youth's social network that are contributing to his or her antisocial behavior. Thus, MST interventions typically aim to:

- improve caregiver discipline practices;
- enhance family affective relations;
- decrease youth association with deviant peers;

- increase youth association with prosocial peers;
- improve youth school or vocational performance;
- engage youth in prosocial recreational outlets; and
- develop an indigenous support network of extended family, neighbors, and friends to help caregivers achieve and maintain such changes.

Specific treatment techniques used to facilitate these gains are integrated from those therapies that have the most empirical support, including cognitive behavioral, behavioral, and the pragmatic family therapies.

MST services are delivered in the natural environment (e.g., home, school, and community). The treatment plan is designed in collaboration with family members and is, therefore, family driven rather than therapist driven. The ultimate goal of MST is to empower families to build an environment, through the mobilization of indigenous child, family, and community resources, that promotes health. The typical duration of home-based MST services is approximately four months, with multiple therapist-family contacts occurring each week, determined by family need.

Although MST is a family-based treatment model that has similarities with other family therapy approaches, several substantive differences are evident:

1. MST places considerable attention on factors in the adolescent and family's social networks that are linked with antisocial behavior. Hence, for example, MST priorities include removing offenders from deviant peer groups, enhancing school or vocational performance, and developing an indigenous support network for the family to maintain therapeutic gains. MST programs have an extremely strong commitment to removing barriers to service access (e.g., the home-based model of service delivery).
2. MST services are more intensive than traditional family therapies (e.g., several hours of treatment per week vs. 50 minutes).
3. Most importantly, MST has well-documented long-term outcomes with adolescents presenting serious antisocial behavior and the adolescents' families.

The strongest and most consistent support for the effectiveness of MST comes from controlled studies that focused on violent and chronic juvenile offenders. Importantly, results from these studies showed that MST outcomes were similar for youth across the adolescent age range (i.e., 12–17 years), for males and females, and for African American as well as White youth and families.

Evidence of Program Effectiveness

The first controlled study of MST with juvenile offenders was published in 1986, and three randomized clinical trials with violent and chronic juvenile offenders have been conducted since then. In these trials, MST has demonstrated long-term reductions in criminal activity, drug-related arrests, violent offenses, and incarceration. This success has led to several randomized trials and quasi-experimental studies aimed at extending the effectiveness of MST to other populations of youth presenting serious clinical problems and their families. [For results, see above.]

The Above Information was Excerpted From:

Henggeler, S.W., Mihalic, S.F., Rone, L.,Thomas, C., & Timmons-Mitchell, J. (1998). Blueprints for Violence Prevention, Book Six: Multisystemic Therapy. Boulder, CO: Center for the Study and Prevention of Violence.

Multidimensional Treatment Foster Care (MTFC)

From The Center for the Study and Prevention of Violence
http://www.colorado.edu/cspv/blueprints/modelprograms.html

Program Summary

Multidimensional Treatment Foster Care (MTFC) is a cost effective alternative to group or residential treatment, incarceration, and hospitalization for adolescents who have problems with chronic antisocial behavior, emotional disturbance, and delinquency. Community families are recruited, trained, and closely supervised to provide MTFC-placed adolescents with treatment and intensive supervision at home, in school, and in the community; clear and consistent limits with follow-through on consequences; positive reinforcement for appropriate behavior; a relationship with a mentoring adult; and separation from delinquent peers.

Program Targets:

MTFC targets Teenagers with histories of chronic and severe criminal behavior at risk of incarceration and those with severe mental health problems at risk for psychiatric hospitalization.

Program Content:

MTFC Training for Community Foster Families emphasizes behavior management methods to provide youth with a structured and therapeutic living environment. After completing a pre-service training and placement of the youth, MTFC parents attend a weekly group meeting run by a program supervisor where ongoing support and supervision are provided. Foster parents are contacted daily during telephone calls to check on youth progress and problems. MTFC staff are available for consultation and crisis intervention 24/7.

Services to the Youth's Family occur throughout the placement. Family therapy is provided for the biological (or adoptive) family, with the goal of returning the youth back to the home. The parents are supported and taught to use behavior management methods that are used in the MTFC foster home. Closely supervised home visits are conducted throughout the youth's placement in MTFC. Parents are encouraged to have frequent contact with the MTFC program supervisor to get information about their child's progress in the program.

Coordination and Community Liaison. Frequent contact is maintained between the MTFC program supervisor and the youth's case workers, parole/probation officer, teachers, work supervisors, and other involved adults.

Program Outcomes:

Evaluations of MTFC have demonstrated that program youth compared to control group youth:

- Spent 60% fewer days incarcerated at 12 month follow-up;
- Had significantly fewer subsequent arrests;
- Ran away from their programs, on average, three time less often;
- Had significantly less hard drug use in the follow-up period;
- Had quicker community placement from more restrictive settings (e.g., hospital, detention); and
- Had better school attendance and homework completion at 24 months follow-up.

Program Costs:

The cost per youth is from one-half to one-third less in MTFC than in residential, group or hospital placements and averages approximately $3,900 per month. The average length of stay is seven months.

Program Background

Violent juvenile crime is a growing concern in most communities. Citizens are reaching for solutions. Getting youth who commit crimes off the streets has become a high priority. This is especially true for violent and sexual offenders. Increased capacity for incarceration is an option that many states have taken. However, long-term incarceration is costly and has other disadvantages. Alternatives to incarceration typically involve placement and treatment of youth in congregate care settings.

The Oregon Social Learning Center (OSLC) Multidimensional Treatment Foster Care (MTFC) Program was developed as an alternative to institutional, residential, and group care placement for teenagers with histories of chronic and severe criminal behavior. In most communities, such juveniles are placed in out-of-home care settings prior to being sent to closed custody incarceration. Typically, these settings include some type of group home or cottage on a larger institutional campus where youngsters reside with others who have similar problems and histories of offending. On a continuum of care, MTFC is a relatively non-restrictive community-based placement that can be used in lieu of residential or group care or that can be used for youth transitioning back to the community from such settings. MTFC is less expensive than placement in group, residential care, or institutional settings.

Theoretical Rationale/Conceptual Framework

Many adults, including some policy makers and treatment providers, accept the notion that adolescents are beyond adult influence. From the popular literature on adolescence and from personal experiences "we know" that the influence of peers takes on enormous proportions during the teenage years, especially in relation to the influence of parents. In the scholarly literature on the development and maintenance of delinquency, there has been consistent empirical support for the powerful role of negative (or deviant) peer relations. Therefore, it seems logical that treatment approaches must abandon or at least not rely on parental efforts to supervise and discipline youngsters in the face of the emerging power of the peer group.

Association with deviant peers has been shown to be a strong predictor of involvement in and escalation of aggressive and delinquent behavior. For example, peer support for aggressive behavior in the classroom increases aggression. Interaction with negative peers predicts substance use. Research in sociology and developmental psychology over the past 25 years has clearly shown that youngsters who have strong bonds with delinquent peers are at far greater risk for becoming delinquent in the first place and for escalating delinquency over time than those who associate with nondelinquent peers.

It is ironic then that most delinquency treatment programs put youngsters with criminal histories together in groups that can potentially facilitate further bonding and development of common social identities among group members. These treatments run the risk of actually contributing to the maintenance and enhancement of delinquent friendship cliques.

Most widely used treatments for delinquency, such as Positive Peer Culture, attempt to use the "group process" to gain a therapeutic effect. The assumption is that the peer group can best motivate and influence youth to change their behaviors and attitudes. However, it seems unreasonable to expect youngsters with histories of serious delinquent behaviors to function as a group and somehow become good influences on each other or establish prosocial norms or values. It may be that these approaches vastly underestimate the influence that adult-initiated norms and rules of conduct can have in the face of day-to-day involvement in a peer-dominated culture. A more sensible intervention would involve minimizing the influence of peers and immersing the youngster in a nondelinquent culture.

A number of studies have shown that parents play a key role in the support and socialization of their adolescents. Specifically, adolescent adjustment can be enhanced by the extent to which parents are able to effectively supervise their teenager, to follow through with consequences when necessary, and to promote positive involvement in school and other normative activities.

Conversely, the development of adolescent antisocial behavior leads not only to escalating problems with delinquency and drug use, but the behavior itself wears down and neutralizes what normative socialization forces exist that could potentially guide the adolescent into more prosocial patterns of adjustment. As the conflict between parents and youth increases, parents' capacity to provide a supportive or corrective influence decreases, and the youngster becomes increasingly committed to and influenced by delinquent peers who, in turn, reinforce the teenager's alienation from adult influence. If delinquency escalates, the youngster's behavior finally begins to compromise community safety to the point where courts intervene and require that the youth be held accountable. At this point in the youth's development, where close parental supervision and guidance are absolutely critical, parents are typically distressed, demoralized, defeated, and cynical. The challenge is to come up with an intervention to provide corrective or therapeutic parenting for antisocial adolescents whose parents, for one reason or another, are unable to rise to the occasion.

Social Learning Theory underpins the MTFC model. Social Learning Theory describes the mechanisms by which individuals learn to behave in social contexts. In family settings, daily interactions between family members shape and influence both prosocial and antisocial patterns of behavior that children develop and carry with them into their interactions with others outside of the family (e.g., peers, teachers, coaches). A number of studies at the Oregon Social Learning Center and elsewhere have identified specific family processes or interaction patterns that predict the development of antisocial behavior patterns in children and adolescents. Parents in these families inadvertently reinforce their child for being negative or coercive as a means of getting their own way or avoiding tasks or minding. Typically these parents will make repeated requests and demands, the child will whine, yell, and otherwise noncomply, and the parent will respond by giving in. In this manner the child is actually reinforced for coercive behavior and has "learned" that negative coercive responses such as crying are an effective way to get parents to back off. Thousands of these interactions are embedded in family life and because they may "work" in the short term, both parents and children are gradually shaped to use more negative control strategies over time. Unfortunately, there are damaging long term effects. For example, observational studies in family homes have shown that not only do families with antisocial youngsters have more negative interactions, parents also do not notice when their child is behaving appropriately. The child is not only "taught" to be coercive, they do not develop the skills necessary to have positive behaviors that could be of use in making friends or in relating positively to teachers, coaches, or other adults.

By the time an antisocial child has reached school age, three processes are well underway. Parents are responding to him/her negatively; the child uses coercive tactics as his/her main strategy for getting what s/he wants and avoiding what s/he does not want (e.g., chores, homework); and s/he has deficits in prosocial behavior, having failed to learn the skills necessary to cooperate in the classroom, on teams, or in clubs. There is substantial evidence that aggressive children are likely to be rejected by their peers and that rejected children are more likely to associate with other aggressive, rejected children who tend to reward negative behavior in their interactions with each other. Antisocial aggressive children are also at risk for school failure. The "coercive training" that they received in their families reduces their behavioral and social competencies which sets them up for social and academic failure at school.

Over time, without effective intervention, these processes continue and become amplified. The youth's experience of early failure in school, parental negativity, rejection by peers, and exclusion from clubs and sports activities all set the stage for association with delinquent peers, school drop-out, drug use, and delinquency in adolescence.

Brief Description of Intervention

In Multidimensional Treatment Foster Care, adolescents are placed, usually singly or at most in twos, in a family setting for six to nine months. Community families are recruited, trained, and supported to provide well-supervised placements and treatment. MTFC parents are part of the treatment team along with program staff. They are paid a monthly salary and a small stipend to cover extra expenses. MTFC parents implement a structured, individualized program for each youth that is designed to simultaneously build on the youngster's strengths and to set clear rules, expectations, and limits. MTFC parents are contacted daily (Monday through Friday) by telephone, and data are collected on the youth's behavior during the past 24 hours. During this call, potential problems are discussed, and plans for the coming day are reviewed. MTFC parents are supported by a case manager who coordinates all aspects of the youngsters' treatment program. Additional components of the program include weekly supervision and support meetings for MTFC parents; skill-focused individual treatment for youth; weekly family therapy for biological parents (adoptive or other aftercare resource); frequent contact between participating youth and their biological/adoptive family members, including home visits; close monitoring of the youngsters' progress in school; coordination with probation/parole officers; and psychiatric consultation/ medication management, as needed.

Weekly meetings with MTFC parents are run by the case manager and attended by other involved program staff. During these meetings, telephone data collected during the prior week are reviewed and discussed, and the youths' individualized programs are adjusted as needed. Each individualized program is structured to give the youth a clear picture of what is expected of him/her throughout the day and evening. During the placement period, individualized programs are readjusted to fit youths' changing needs, to reflect progress, and to target new problem behaviors that emerge. The individualized programs help guide MTFC parents to be specific in the way they reinforce progress and to consistently set limits and consequences. Individualized programs give youth a concrete way to measure their success. The individualized programs also are used by biological/adoptive parents or relatives during home visits and when youth return home after placement.

Because youth who participate in the program have committed several delinquent acts (i.e., an average of thirteen previous arrests in our most recent sample), the level of supervision required is high. Youth are not permitted to have unsupervised free time in the community, and their peer relationships are closely monitored. Over the course of the placement, levels of supervision and discipline are adjusted, depending on the youth's level of progress or lack thereof. Close monitoring of youngsters at home and at school is a hallmark of the MTFC model. There is heavy emphasis placed on teaching interpersonal skills and on participation in positive social activities, including sports, hobbies, and other forms of recreation.

The MTFC model uses a specific and structured multi-modal treatment approach. Multi-modal treatment includes behavioral skills training across settings (e.g., home, school, with peers). The success of the program depends on the group of adults, including the MTFC parents and the MTFC program staff (i.e., case manager, family therapist, individual therapist), that work intensively with the youth and his/her parents (or other relatives) and that surround the youngsters with positive role models and mentors. The youth is taught how to do well in a family setting and at school and is intensively supervised, consistently disciplined, and isolated from other delinquent peers. Both the youth and his/her parents participate in a structured program where the rules and limits are clear, as are the consequences for failing to comply with the program rules. By the time youth return home, their parents have improved their ability to provide a successful home environment. They are practiced in keeping youth from associating with delinquent peers. They know how to set limits and follow through with discipline. They understand the importance of helping the youth succeed in school and on the job. The MTFC placement is an opportunity for youth and their families to experience a turning point towards positive and productive relationships and activities.

Throughout the MTFC placement, the youth's biological family (or adoptive family or other aftercare resource) participates in the treatment. Parents attend weekly treatment sessions and have on-call access to MTFC staff. During weekly sessions, effective methods for supervising, disciplining, and encouraging the youth are discussed. Biological parents and youth have a number of opportunities to practice these skills during home visits that are scheduled throughout the youth's placement. During home visits, parents run the youth's individualized program which is similar to the one used in the MTFC home. Home visits start out being short, one to two hours in length, and as the youth and his/her parents progress through the program, eventually overnight visits are scheduled. Following each home visit, the family therapist debriefs the biological parents and the youth regarding problems and progress.

Evidence of Program Effectiveness

Researchers and policy makers agree that development of effective interventions for youngsters with severe conduct problems should take advantage of the substantial body of basic research that addresses the life course development of aggression and antisocial behaviors. Further, to be most useful, expensive intervention trials need to provide experimental tests of their underlying theoretical model of change. Thus, an efficient intervention study should ideally serve two purposes: evaluate the effectiveness of the intervention and provide specific information that can guide the development of better interventions in the future. Therefore, the goals of our program of research have been:

- to systematically evaluate the immediate and longer-term outcomes of the interventions, and
- to evaluate the contribution of the intervention's key variables to changes in outcomes.

The MTFC model has been tested in two studies where the feasibility of using this model in lieu of incarceration for adolescents referred for delinquency was explored. The first study of 32 youth used a matched control group. Results from this study showed that MTFC was not only feasible but, compared to alternative residential treatment models, it was cost effective and the outcomes for children and families were better. For example, during a two-year follow-up period, the number of days delinquent youngsters were incarcerated in the state training school were lower for participants in MTFC than for a comparison group of youngsters placed in group care programs. The savings in incarceration costs alone were $122,000… . The boys and girls in this study had all been committed to the state training school and due to overcrowding were being diverted to placement in community-based programs. All youngsters came into the program from juvenile detention. Three-quarters of the youth in both the MTFC and the matched groups had previously spent some time during the last year in the state training school (an average of 23 days for MTFC youth and 15 days for youth in the comparison group).

These initial findings encouraged us to apply for federal funding to conduct a full-scale clinical trial on the efficacy of MTFC for adolescents with serious and chronic delinquency. When designing the study, in addition to looking at the relative effectiveness of the treatment models, we were interested in the broader issue of understanding the factors or key treatment components which led to success or failure for individual participants.

In 1991, a study to compare the effectiveness of two treatment models for male adolescents who had histories of chronic delinquency was initiated… . The two models used very different approaches to exposure to delinquent peers. One attempted to use peer group interactions therapeutically, and the other attempted to maximize the influence of mentoring adults and prosocial peers and to isolate boys from their delinquent peers. Seventy-nine boys, who were mandated into out-of-home care by the juvenile court, were randomly assigned to placement in Group Care (GC) or Multidimensional Treatment Foster Care (MTFC). In GC, boys lived with six to fifteen others who had similar histories of delinquency. In MTFC, a boy was placed in a home with a family who had been recruited from the community. MTFC parents were trained in the use of behavior management skills and were closely supervised throughout the boy's placement. In both conditions, treatment lasted for an average of seven months.

Boys who participated were from 12 to 17 years old (average age, 14.3), had an average of thirteen previous arrests and 4.6 prior felonies, and half had committed at least one crime against a person. All participants had extensive previous contacts with the juvenile justice system, had been supervised by parole or probation officers, and were labeled by the Department of Youth Services as chronic offenders. On average, study boys had spent 76 days during the previous year in juvenile detention. Their offenses included both misdemeanors and felonies; parole violations and status offenses were not included in the boy's offense counts. All boys were on parole or probation, depending on whether they had previously been committed to the state training school (in which case they were on parole), and were supervised by a parole/probation officer throughout the course of their placement and in aftercare. The period of time that parole/probation supervision lasted after treatment varied depending on the length of the jurisdiction, the boy's age, and whether he had completed restitution. There was no difference in parole/probation supervision for the two groups.

Data was collected on official arrests, including each boy's arrest history prior to entering the study. In addition, confidential self-reports of criminal activity were collected from each boy. The number of days each boy was incarcerated and/or "on the run" was tracked, as was information on school attendance and academic advancement. Mental health outcomes were also assessed. To measure outcomes, boys were assessed at baseline, three months after placement, and then every six months throughout a two-year follow-up period. To assess the contribution of key treatment components, variables were identified that were thought likely to influence a boy's success or failure in treatment. This was done by reviewing the research literature on the development of aggression and delinquency. Problems with adult supervision and discipline practices, as well as adult attachment and involvement with the child, were indicated as powerful predictors of child conduct problems. As discussed, the influence of negative peers appeared to play a key role, especially in escalation of delinquency, and especially if problems already existed. To examine the relative contribution of these variables to individual outcomes, the boy and his caretaker (i.e., line staff in GC, MTFC parent in MTFC) were assessed in the placement setting after he had been there for three months. The relationship between scores on these in-program variables and case outcomes were then examined.

Summary of Results

At one-year after treatment exit, boys in MTFC had less than half the number of arrests as boys in GC (i.e., an average of 2.6 offenses for MTFC boys and 5.4 offenses for GC boys; see Figure 2). Boys in MTFC had an 83 percent higher rate of desistance from arrest than did boys in GC. Nearly three times as many

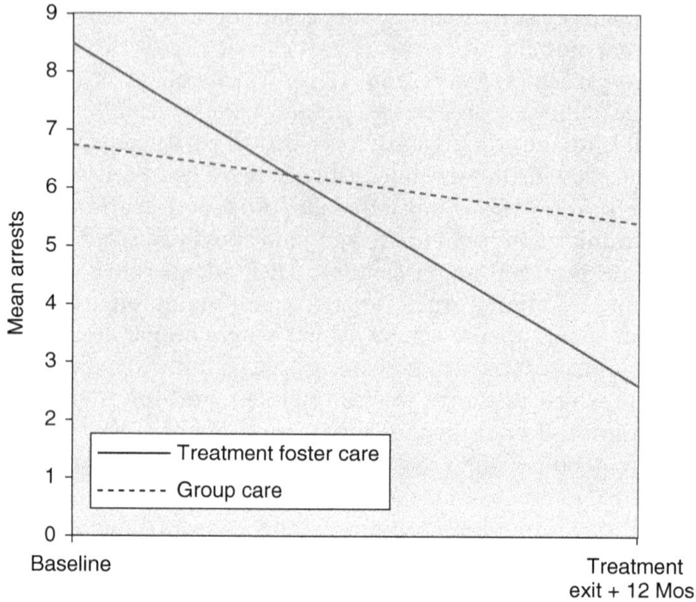

Figure A.2. Mean Number of Arrests

boys ran away or were expelled from their programs in GC than in MTFC (5 out of 36 MTFC boys, and 15 out of 38 GC boys). Boys in MTFC spent about twice as many days living with parents or relatives in follow-up than did boys in GC.

A series of analyses were conducted to control for factors that commonly affect rates of delinquency. These included boy's age, age of first offense, and number of previous arrests. In a multiple regression analysis we found that where the boys were placed (in MTFC or GC) was the only factor that reliably predicted further arrests even given consideration of the control variables (i.e., age, age at first offense, number of previous offenses); placement in MTFC predicted significantly fewer arrests than placement in GC.

In addition to looking at official arrest rates, rates of boy's self-reported delinquency was examined. Boys were asked in a confidential self-report interview to tell how many criminal acts they had committed during the past six months. Boys in MTFC reported committing significantly fewer criminal acts than GC boys at 6, 12 and 18 months post-enrollment in the study.

Next, we looked at whether the variables that we thought would mediate the effectiveness of treatment related to arrest rates during the time that boys were in the program and in follow-up. It was found that regardless of placement setting (i.e., MTFC or GC), the mediating variables examined (i.e., supervision, discipline, deviant peers) predicted arrests one year after boys had completed treatment. In other words, boys in either MTFC or GC who got good supervision; consistent, predictable discipline; and had less association with delinquent peers had fewer arrests in follow-up that those who did not. However, the structure of the GC programs (i.e., boys lived with other delinquent youth) promoted association with delinquent peers. Because of this, for GC boys, scores on the association with delinquent peers measure were higher (more negative), but the scores for effective supervision and discipline were lower than the scores for boys in MTFC. The evidence supports the theoretical rationale to the extent that the risk factors are impacted, the behavioral outcome (i.e., arrests) will be impacted. This set of findings has implications for all programs which aim to reduce rates of criminal offending in juveniles.

The Above Information was Excerpted From:

Chamberlain, P., & Mihalic, S.F. (1998). Blueprints for Violence Prevention, Book Eight: Multidimensional Treatment Foster Care. Boulder, CO: Center for the Study and Prevention of Violence.

Chamberlain, P., Leve, L., & DeGarmo, D. (2007). Multidimensional Treatment Foster Care for Girls in the Juvenile Justice System: Two Year Follow-up of a Randomized Clinical Trial. *Journal of Consulting and Clinical Psychology*, *75*(1), 187–193.

Fast Track Program

http://www.fasttrackproject.org/fasttrackoverview.htm

Design of the Fast Track Project

Fast Track is a comprehensive 10-year intervention project designed to prevent serious antisocial behavior and related adolescent problems in three successive cohorts of children selected at being at high risk when entering first grade. The intervention is guided by a developmental theory positing the interaction of multiple influences on the development of antisocial behavior. Low-income, high crime communities place stressors and influences on children and families that increase their risk levels. In such contexts, families characterized by marital conflict and instability make consistent and effective parenting difficult to achieve, particularly with children who are impulsive and of difficult temperament. These children usually enter school poorly prepared for the social, emotional, and cognitive demands of this setting. Their parents often are unprepared to relate effectively with school staff and a poor home-school bond often exacerbates the child's adjustment problems. Often the child attends a school with a high density of other children who are similarly unprepared, and who are negatively influenced by disruptive classroom contexts and punitive teacher practices. Over time, aggressive and disruptive children are rejected by families and peers, and tend to receive less support from teachers—further exacerbating aggressive exchanges and academic difficulties. The process of escalating risk extends from elementary school years into adolescence, where peer influences, academic difficulties, and dysfunctional personal identity development can contribute to serious conduct problems and related risky behaviors. The Fast Track prevention program is thus based on the hypothesis that improving child competencies, parenting effectiveness, school context, and school-home communications will, over time, contribute to preventing antisocial behavior across the period from early childhood through adolescence.

The Study Sample

Fast Track identified a sample of high-risk children in kindergarten by their conduct problems at home and at school through multistaged screening of nearly 10,000 children. At each of four sites across the United States, sets of schools were matched on size, ethnic composition, and poverty, and randomly assigned to intervention and control conditions. Within the schools, teacher and parent ratings of aggressive, disruptive, and oppositional behavior were used to identify children at high risk for chronic conduct problems. In this manner, three successive cohorts were recruited in 1991, 1992, and 1993 to yield a sample of 891 children (445 in the intervention group, and 446 in the control group). Attrition throughout the study has been low, with participation rates for year eleven of the study at eighty percent for the control group, and eighty five percent for the intervention group.

Prevention Program

The developmental model guiding this project indicates that an effective prevention program would address classroom, school risk, and family risk factors, including communication between parents and schools. The program extends from first through the tenth grade, with particularly intensive interventions during the transitions at school entry and from elementary to middle school. The most intense phase of intervention took place in the first grade year for each of three successive cohorts. The six components of the *elementary school phase of the intervention* (grades 1 –5) include:

- Teacher-led classroom curricula (called PATHS) as a universal intervention directed toward the development of emotional concepts, social understanding, and self-control (including weekly teacher consultation about classroom management); and the following five programs administered to the high-risk intervention subjects:
- Parent training groups designed to promote the development of positive family-school relationships and to teach parents behavior management skills, particularly in the use of praise, time-out, and self-restraint;
- Home visits for the purpose of fostering parents' problem-solving skills, self-efficacy, and life management;

- Child social skill training groups (called Friendship Groups);
- Child tutoring in reading; and Child friendship enhancement in the classroom (called Peer Pairing).

The adolescent phase of the intervention program (grades 6–10) included standard and individualized activities for high-risk youth and families. Group-based interventions were de-emphasized, in order to avoid promoting engagement with deviant peers. However, curriculum-based parent and youth group meetings were included in the intervention, to support children in their transition into middle school (grades 5–7). The focus of this phase of the intervention was primarily on individualized prevention planning, according to criterion-based assessment. Individualized services, designed to strengthen protective factors and reduce risk factors in areas of particular need for each youth, include: academic tutoring, mentoring, support for positive peer-group involvement, home visiting and family problem-solving, and liaisons with school and community agencies.

Evaluation of the Fast Track Program

The efficacy of the Fast Track prevention program is tested periodically, by comparing the group of children receiving intervention services to children in the control group, with regard to a wide range of problem-behavior outcomes and their development over time. The findings are modest to moderate in a positive direction, but statistically robust and indicative of the important impact of Fast Track as a set of preventive interventions.

Significant progress was made toward the goal of improving competencies of the children receiving intervention services and their parents. Compared to the control group, the intervention children improved their social-cognitive and academic skills, and their parents reduced their use of harsh discipline. These group differences also were reflected in behavioral improvements during the elementary school years and beyond. Compared with children in the control group, children in the intervention group displayed significantly less aggressive behavior at home, in the classroom, and on the playground. By the end of third grade, 37 percent of the intervention group had become free of conduct problems, in contrast with 27 percent of the control group. By the end of elementary school, 33 percent of the intervention group had a developmental trajectory of decreasing conduct problems, as compared with 27 percent of the control group. Furthermore, placement in special education by the end of elementary school was about one-fourth lower in the intervention group than in the control group.

Group differences continued through adolescence. Court records indicate that by eighth grade, 38 percent of the intervention group boys had been arrested, in contrast with 42 percent of the control group. Finally, psychiatric interviews after ninth grade indicate that The Fast Track program intervention has reduced serious conduct disorder by over a third, from 27 percent to 17 percent. These effects generalized across gender and ethnic groups, and across the wide range of child and family characteristics measured by Fast Track.

The success of the Fast Track program has led to its implementation in several school systems across the country, as well as in several schools in Great Britain, Australia, and Canada. Fast Track is one of several chronic violence prevention programs, but it is one of the most rigorously evaluated.

Notes

Chapter 1: Juvenile Justice in Flux

1. These three cases are taken from Amicus Brief of Former Juvenile Offenders, in Graham v. Florida & Sullivan v. Florida, Nos. 08–7412 and 08–76 July 21, 23, 2009.
2. Edward Humes, No Matter How Loud I Shout: A Year in the Life of Juvenile Court 33 (1996).
3. Id. at 29–30.
4. William Ayers, A Kind and Just Parent: The Children of Juvenile Court 28 (1997).
5. Id. at 152.
6. Anthony M. Platt, The Child Savers: The Invention of Delinquency 9–10 (2d ed. 1977) (stating that by 1917, all but three states had a separate juvenile court, and by 1932, over 600 juvenile courts existed nationwide).
7. *See* Janet E. Ainsworth, *Re-Imagining Childhood and Reconstructing the Legal Order: The Case for Abolishing the Juvenile Court,* 69 N.C. L. Rev. 1083 (1991); Robert O. Dawson, *The Future of Juvenile Justice: Is It Time to Abolish the System?* 81 J. Crim. L. & Criminol. 136 (1990); Katherine Hunt Federle, *The Abolition of the Juvenile Court: A Proposal for the Preservation of Children's Legal Rights,* 16 J. Contemp. L. 23 (1990); Barry C. Feld, *Abolish the Juvenile Court: Youthfulness, Criminal Responsibility, and Sentencing Policy,* 88 J. Crim. L. & Criminol. 68 (1997).
8. "Convictions" have numerous negative consequences, including potential sentence enhancements and employment prohibitions. As a result, most state juvenile systems avoid use of that term, although the punitive trend in recent years has reduced protections against post-adolescence use of juvenile records. See Robert E. Shepherd, *Collateral Consequences of Juvenile Proceedings: Part II,* 15 Crim. Just. 41 (2000).
9. Jane Addams, My Friend Julia Lathrop 137 (1935).

10. Ben Lindsey & H. O'Higgins, The Beast 133 (1970) (Reprint of 1909 edition).
11. Martin R. Gardner, *The Right of Juvenile Offenders to Be Punished: Some Implications of Treating Kids as Persons,* 68 Neb. L. Rev. 182, 191 (1989).
12. David S. Tanenhaus, *The Evolution of Transfer Out of the Juvenile Court,* in The Changing Borders of Juvenile Justice: Transfers of Adolescents to Adult Court 13, 18 (Jeffrey Fagan & Franklin E. Zimring eds, 2000) (hereafter Changing Borders).
13. Id.
14. Platt, The Child Savers 141.
15. *See* also Julian W. Mack, *The Juvenile Court,* 23 Harv. L. Rev. 104, 107 (1909).
16. Tanenhaus, *The Evolution of Transfer,* at 40–41, n. 17.
17. *See,* e.g., Kolender v. Lawson, 461 U.S. 32 (1983); Papachristou v. City of Jacksonville, 405 U.S. 156 (1972).
18. Platt, The Child Savers, at 54.
19. Id.
20. Youth Violence: A Report of the Surgeon General 118–19 (Dep't. Health & Human Services, 2001) (hereafter Surgeon General Report).
21. Julian Mack, *The Juvenile Court,* 23 Harv. L. Rev. 104, 120 (1909).
22. The Invention of the Juvenile Court 551 (Frederic L. Faust & Paul J. Brantingham, eds., 1974) (describing the "orthodox" view).
23. Tanenhaus, *The Evolution of Transfer,* at 20–21.
24. Richard E. Redding, *Adult Punishment for Juvenile Offenders: Does It Reduce Crime?* in Handbook of Children, Culture, and Violence 375, 377 (Nancy E. Dowd, Dorothy G. Singer, & Robin Fretwell Wilson, eds., 2006).
25. Richard E. Redding & Barbara Mrozoksi, *Adjudicatory and Dispositional Decision Making in Juvenile Justice,* in Juvenile Delinquency: Prevention, Assessment and Intervention 232, 238, 243 (Kirk Heilbrun, Naomi E. Sevin Goldstein, & Richard E. Redding, eds., 2005); Richard E. Redding & J. C. Howell, *Blended Sentencing in American Juvenile Courts,* in The Changing Borders of Juvenile Justice 151 (Jeffrey Fagan & Franklin E. Zimring, eds., 2000).
26. Elisabeth S. Scott & Laurence Steinberg, *Blaming Youth,* 81 Texas L. Rev. 799, 807–09 (2003).
27. Alfred S. Regnery, *Getting Away with Murder: Why the Juvenile Justice System Needs an Overhaul,* 34 Policy Rev. 65, 66 (2000).
28. Institute of Judicial Administration—American Bar Association, Juvenile Justice Standards, Standards Relating to Juvenile Delinquency and Sanctions xvii–xix (1980).
29. Id. at 152–53.
30. Elizabeth S. Scott & Thomas Grisso, *The Evolution of Adolescence: A Developmental Perspective on Juvenile Justice Reform,* 88 J. Crim. L. & Criminol. 137 (1997); Franklin E. Zimring, *Penal Proportionality for the Young Offender: Notes on Immaturity, Capacity, and Diminished Responsibility,* in Youth on Trial: A Developmental Perspective on Juvenile Justice 267 (Thomas Grisso & Robert G. Schwartz, eds., 2000) (hereafter Youth on Trial). The latter chapter updates arguments from Franklin E. Zimring, Twentieth Century Fund Task Force on Sentencing Policy Toward Young Offenders: Confronting Youth Crime (1978).
31. Richard E. Redding, *Juveniles Transferred to Juvenile Court: Legal Reform Proposals Based on Social Science Research,* 1997 Utah L. Rev. 709, 757 ("About one–third of the states now have determinate or mandatory minimum sentencing laws for juveniles, usually based on the offense and prior record.").
32. Mack, *The Juvenile Court,* at 110 (emphasis added).

33. Institute of Judicial Administration, at 147 (providing that "the purposes of the juvenile delinquency code should be... to forbid conduct that unjustifiably and without excuse inflicts or risks substantial harm to individual or public interests," prevent conviction for "conduct that is without fault or culpability," give fair notice and "recognize the unique physical, psychological, and social features of young persons.").
34. Id. at 160.
35. W. Bennett, J. DiIullio, Jr., & J. Walters, Body Count (1996).
36. *See* Christopher Slobogin, *Treating Kids Right: Deconstructing and Reconstructing the Amenability to Treatment Concept*, 10 J. Contemp. Leg. Issues 299, 332–33 (1999) (finding that transfers purporting to be based on nonamenability to treatment tend to be based instead on the seriousness of the crime and assessments of risk).
37. Idaho Code § 20–501.
38. Va. Code Ann. § 16.1–227(4).
39. Daniel Filler, *The New Rehabilitation*, 91 Iowa L. Rev. 951, 954 (2006) ("Across the nation, in every state, local courts are creating new juvenile tribunals that explicitly seek to. . . rehabilitate juvenile offenders.").
40. Tanenhaus, *The Evolution of Transfer*, at 30.
41. 387 U.S. 1 (1967).
42. Institute of Judicial Administration, at 8 (jury right, rules of evidence); 11 (public trial).
43. *See* Mathews v. Eldridge, 424 U.S. 319 (1976).
44. Barry C. Feld, *A Century of Juvenile Justice: Work in Progress or a Revolution That Failed?* 34 N. Ky. L. Rev. 189, 196 (2007).
45. Id. at 218–21.
46. Id. at 21.
47. Id. at 218.
48. 521 U.S. 346 (1997).
49. Eric S. Janus, *Preventing Sexual Violence: Setting Principled Constitutional Boundaries on Sex offender Commitments*, 72 Ind. L.J. 157, 206 (1996) ("Not one person committed since 1975 has been discharged from a final sex offender commitment.").
50. For a summary of this debate, *see* Edward Rubin, *Just Say "No" to Retribution*, 7 Buff. Crim. L. Rev. 17 (2003).
51. *See* Elizabeth S. Scott & Laurence Steinberg, Rethinking Juvenile Justice: Adolescent Development and the Regulation of Youth Crime 279–81 (2008) ("Our survey suggests that Americans are concerned about youth crime and want to reduce its incidence but are ready to support effective rehabilitative programs as a means of accomplishing that end—and indeed favor this response over imposing more punishment through longer sentences.").
52. E. J. Latessa, *The Challenge of Change: Correctional Programs and Evidence-Based Practices*, 3 Criminol. & Pub. Pol. 547, 549 (2004).

Chapter 2: Juvenile Crime and How to Reduce It

1. Terrie E. Moffitt, *Natural Histories of Delinquency in Cross-National Longitudinal Research on Human Development and Criminal Behavior* 3, 29 (Elmar G. M. Weitekamp & Hans-Jurgen Kerner, eds., 1994).

2. Laurence Steinberg, *Adolescent Development and Juvenile Justice*, 5 Ann. Rev. Clinical Psychol. 459, 466 (2009) ("Dozens of longitudinal studies have shown that the vast majority of adolescents who commit antisocial acts desist from such activity as they mature into adulthood and that only a small percentage—between five and ten percent, according to most studies—become chronic offenders. . . . [M]ost juvenile offenders mature out of crime. . . and. . . will desist whether or not they are caught, arrested, prosecuted or sanctioned."); Terrie Moffitt, *Adolescence-Limited and Life-Course-Persistent Antisocial Behavior: A Developmental Taxonomy*, 100 Psychol. Rev. 674, 675 (1993).

3. *See* Mark R. Fondacaro, *Toward an Ecological Jurisprudence Rooted in Concepts of Justice and Empirical Research*, 69 Univ. Missouri–Kansas City L. Rev. 179, 185 (2000).

4. Lee Ross & Richard E. Nisbett, The Person and the Situation: Perspectives of Social Psychol. (1991).

5. Kurt Lewin, Principles of Topological Psychology (1936).

6. Harry Stack Sullivan, The Interpersonal Theory of Psychiatry (1953).

7. Rudolf H. Moos, *Conceptualizations of Human Environments*, 28 Am. Psychologist 652 (1973).

8. Urie Bronfenbrenner, The Ecology of Human Development: Experiments by Nature and Design (1979)

9. Jennifer L. Woolard, Mark R. Fondacaro, & Christopher Slobogin, *Informing Juvenile Justice Policy: Directions for Behavioral Science Research*, 25 L. & Hum. Behav. 13, 16–17 (2001).

10. The following review of the empirical literature draws heavily from and supplements a previously published book chapter by Mark R. Fondacaro & Lauren G. Fasig, *Judging Juvenile Responsibility: A Social Ecological Perspective*, in Handbook of Children, Culture, and Violence 355–73 (Nancy E. Dowd, Dorothy G. Singer, & Robin Fretwell Wilson, eds., 2006).

11. Laurence Steinberg & Elisabeth Cauffman, *A Developmental Perspective on Jurisdictional Boundary*, in The Changing Borders of Juvenile Justice: Transfers of Adolescents to Adult Court 394 (Jeffrey Fagan & Franklin E. Zimring, eds, 2000) (hereafter Changing Borders).

12. Nuno Ferreira, *Putting the Age of Criminal and Tort Liability into Context: A Dialogue between Law and Psychology*, 16 Int'l J. Children's Rights 29, 35, 36 (2008). *See also* Marie-Anne Suizzo, *The Social-Emotional and Cultural Contexts of Cognitive Development: Neo-Piagetian Perspectives*, 71 Child Dev. 846 (2000); Lawrence Kohlberg, Child Psychology and Child Education—A Cognitive-Developmental View 259 (1987) ("conventional" level of morality is reached between ages 10 and 20).

13. *See also* Daniel Keating, *Cognitive and Brain Development*, in Handbook of Adolescent Psychology (Richard M. Lerner & Laurence Steinberg, eds.) (2d ed., 2004).

14. Elizabeth Cauffman & Laurence Steinberg, *(Im)maturity of Judgment in Adolescence: Why Adolescents Might Be Less Culpable Than Adults*, 18 Beh. Sci. & L. 741, 743–44 (2000).

15. Deanna Kuhn, *Adolescent Thinking*, in Handbook of Adolescent Psychology 152, 182 (Richard M. Lerner & Laurence Steinberg, eds.) (3d ed. 2009) (hereinafter Handbook of Adolescent Psychology, 3d ed.).

16. Judith G. Smetana & Myrian Villalobos, *Social Cognitive Development in Adolescence*, in Handbook of Adolescent Psychology 196 (3d ed.).

17. *See* Laurence Steinberg & Elizabeth Cauffman, *Maturity of Judgment in Adolescence: Psychosocial Factors in Adolescent Decision Making*, 20 Law & Hum. Beh. 249, 260 (1996).
18. Steinberg & Cauffman, *A Developmental Perspective*, at 397. *See also* Kathryn Lynn Modecki, *"It's a Rush": Psychosocial Content of Antisocial Decision Making*, 33 Law & Hum. Beh. 183 (2009) (finding that "all age groups largely took into account the potential legal implications of their decisions" but that adolescents tended to underestimate actual legal consequences more than did college-age students and adults); Kathryn Lynn Modecki, *Addressing Gaps in the Maturity of Judgment Literature: Age Differences and Delinquencies*, 32 Law. & Hum. Beh. 78 (2008).
19. *See* Dana L. Haynie, *Friendship Networks and Delinquency: The Relative Nature of Peer Delinquency*, 18 J. Quantitative Criminology 99, 123 (2002) (describing the significant association between peer behaviors and delinquent involvement by juveniles).
20. *See* Laurence Steinberg et al., *Age Differences in Sensation-Seeking and Impulsivity as Indexed by Behavior and Self-Report: Evidence for a Dual Systems Model*, 44 Dev. Psychol. 1764 (2008) (sensation- seeking increases from age 12 to 15, then steadily declines); Elizabeth S. Scott et al., *Evaluating Adolescent Decision Making in Legal Contexts*, 19 Law & Hum. Beh. 221, 231 (1995) ("Compared to adults, adolescents appear to focus less on protection against losses than on opportunities for gains in making choices[,] seem to discount the future more[,] weigh more heavily the short-term consequences of decisions [and find it harder] to contemplate the meaning of a consequence that will be realized 10 to 15 years in the future, because such a time span is not easily made relevant to adolescent experience.").
21. *See* Laurence Steinberg, Adolescence 88 (6th ed. 2002).
22. *See* Jari-Erik Nurmi, *How Do Adolescents See Their Future? A Review of the Development of Future Orientation and Planning*, 11 Developmental. Rev. 1, 29 (1991); Margo Gardner & Laurence Steinberg, *Peer Influence on Risk Taking, Risk Preference and Risky Decision Making in Adolescence and Adulthood: An Experimental Study*, 41(4) Dev. Psychol. 625, 632 (2005).
23. Steinberg & Cauffman, *Maturity of Judgment in Adolescence*, at 255 (describing research on identity).
24. Pravan Kambam & Christopher Thompson, *The Development of Decision-making Capacities in Children and Adults: Psychological and Neurological Perspectives and Their Implications for Juvenile Defendants*, 27 Beh. Sci. & L. 173, 175 (2009) ("adolescents are particularly susceptible to the potentially deleterious effects of emotions on decision-making."); Reed Larson, Mihaly Csikszentmihalyi, & Ronald Graef, *Mood Variability and the Psychosocial Adjustment of Adolescents*, 9 Youth & Adolescence 469 (1980) (adolescents are subject to more rapid and extreme mood swings than adults).
25. Reed Larso, Mihaly Csikszentmihalyi, & Ronald Graef, *Mood Variability and the Psychosocial Adjustment of Adolescents*, 9 J. Youth & Adol. 9 479 (1980).
26. Kambam & Thompson, *Decision-making Capacities in Children and Adults*, at 187.
27. Daniel Seagrave & Thomas Grisso, *Adolescent Development and the Measurement of Juvenile Psychopathy*, 26 Law & Hum. Beh. 219, 229 (2002).
28. Jay D. Aronson, *Brain Imaging, Culpability and the Juvenile Death Penalty*, 13 Psychol., Pub. Pol. & L., 115, 119 (2007) ("For most of the 20th century, experts

believed that the most important period in human brain development was the first 3 years of a person's life.").

29. Jay N. Giedd et al., *Brain Development During Childhood and Adolescence: A Longitudinal MRI Study,* 2 Nature Neurosci. 861, 862 (1999). *See also* Elizabeth R. Sowell et al., In Vivo *Evidence for Post-Adolescent Brain Maturation in Frontal and Striatal Regions,* 2 Nature Neurosci. 859, 860 (1999) (in longitudinal study of brain development, finding prefrontal cortex loses gray matter only at end of adolescence); Beatriz Luna & John A. Sweeney, *The Emergence of Collaborative Brain Function,* 1021 Annals N.Y. Acad. Sci. 296, 301 (2004).

30. *See generally* Charles Geier & Beatriz Luna, *The Maturation of Incentive Processing and Cognitive Control,* 93 Pharmacol. Biochem. Beh. 212 (2009); American Bar Association, Juvenile Justice Center, Adolescence, Brain Development and Legal Culpability, available at www.abanet.org/crimjust/juvjus/Adolescence.pdf (2004); Jay Giedd et al., *Brain Development During Childhood and Adolescence: A Longitudinal MRI Study,* 2 Nature Neurosci. 861, 861 (1999) (showing net increase in "white matter" between ages 4 and 22 to be 12.4%); Elizabeth R. Sowell et al., In Vivo *Evidence for Post-Adolescent Brain Maturation in Frontal and Striatal Regions,* 2 Nature Neurosci. 859, 860 (1999) (reporting "large group differences" between adults and adolescents in terms of frontal lobe maturation). *See also* Abigail Baird et al., *Functional Magnetic Image Resonance Imaging of Facial Affect Recognition in Children and Adolescents,* 38(2) J. Am. Acad. Child Adol. Psychiat. 195 (1999) (indicating that a small number of functional imaging studies suggest that adolescents tend to employ different brain processes than adults when carrying out identical tasks).

31. *See* B. J. Casey, Sarah Getz, & Adriana Galvan, *The Adolescent Brain,* 28 Dev. Rev. 62, 70 (2008) (hypothesizing that the difference between adolescents on the one hand and pre-teens and adults on the other is an evolutionary response to the need for adolescents to leave the family and find a mate). *See generally* Charles Geier & Beatriz Luna, *The Maturation of Incentive Processing and Cognitive Control,* 93 Pharmacol. Biochem. Beh. 212, 212 (2009) (correlating age with control of behavior); Brian Bower, *Teen Brains on Trial: The Science of Neural Development Tangles with the Juvenile Death Penalty,* 165 Sciences News Online at 3–4, available at www.findarticles.com/p/articles/mi_m1200/is_19_165/ai_n6110300/pg_2?tag=artBody;col1 (2004) (describing brain research suggesting that in order to obtain the same "motivational boost" that adults have to seek rewards, teens need the stimulus from risky behavior).

32. Monique Ernst et al., *Amygdala and Nucleus Accumbens in Responses to Receipt and Omission of Gains in Adults and Adolescents,* 25 NeuroImage 1279, 1289 (2005).

33. Laurence Steinberg, *Adolescent Development and Juvenile Justice,* 5 Ann. Rev. Clinical Psychol. 459, 466 (2009).

34. Adriana Galvan et al., *Earlier Development of the Accumbens Relative to Orbitofrontal Cortex Might Underlie Risk-Taking Behavior in Adolescents,* 26 J. Neuroscience 6885, 6891 (2006).

35. *See* Jennifer White et al., *The Measurement of Impulsivity and Its Relationship to Delinquency,* 103 J. Abnormal Psychol. 192, 202 (1994) (finding "striking" relationship between "behavioral impulsivity" and delinquency, as well as a relationship between "cognitive impulsivity and delinquency, but one which was not independent of IQ").

36. Steinberg and Caufmann caution against drawing "bright line distinctions" based on age alone, and both they and others have found that, while risk preference is highest in mid-adolescence, many individuals both before and after the fourteen- to sixteen-year age range are likely to demonstrate immaturity. *See* Cauffman & Steinberg, *(Im)maturity of Judgment in Adolescence* 757 ("It is important to remember that responsibility, perspective, and temperance—the three components of maturity of judgment studied here—are more predictive of antisocial decision-making than chronological age alone. Indeed, psychosocially mature thirteen-year-olds demonstrate less antisocial decision-making than psychosocially immature adults."); Charles S. Freid & N. Dickon Reppucci, *Criminal Decision Making: The Development of Adolescent Judgment, Criminal Responsibility, and Culpability*, 25 Law & Hum. Beh. 45 (2001).
37. Charles Mathias, Dawn M. Marsh-Richard, & Donald M. Dougherty, *Behavioral Measures of Impulsivity and the Law*, 26 Beh. Sci. & L. 691, 697 (2008).
38. June Arnett, *Reckless Behavior in Adolescence: A Developmental Perspective*, 12 Dev. Rev. 339, 344 (1992).
39. Deborah Gorman-Smith et al., *A Developmental-Ecological Model of the Relation of Family Functioning to Patterns of Delinquency*, 16 J. Quant. Criminol. 169, 170 (2000) ("Family functioning has consistently been among the strongest predictors of risk for delinquent and criminal behavior.").
40. Daniel S. Shaw & Joan I. Vondra, *Infant Attachment Security and Maternal Predictors of Early Behavior Problems: A Longitudinal Study of Low-Income Families*, 23 J. Abnormal Child Psychol. 335 (1995).
41. John Bowlby, A Secure Base: Clinical Implications of Attachment Theory (1988).
42. Id. at 170–71. Gorman-Smith et al., *A Developmental-Ecological Model*, at 187–88 (noting, however, that even children of "exceptionally functioning" families might be at slightly higher risk for minor chronic offending if from poorer neighborhoods). *See generally* Robert D. Laird, et al., *Parents' Monitoring—Relevant Knowledge and Adolescents' Delinquent Behavior: Evidence of Correlated Developmental Changes and Reciprocal Influences*, 74 Child Dev. 752, 765 (2003).
43. *See* Mark R. Fondacaro, M. Dunkle, & M.K. Pathak, *Procedural Justice in Resolving Family Disputes: A Psychosocial Analysis of Individual and Family Functioning in Late Adolescence*, 27 J. Youth & Adol. 101 (1998). *See also* Shelly L. Jackson & Mark R. Fondacaro, *Procedural Justice in Resolving Family Conflict: Implications for Youth Violence Prevention*, 21 L. & Policy 101 (1999).
44. Michael R. Brubacher et al., *Procedural Justice in Resolving Family Disputes: Implications for Childhood Bullying*, 15 Psychol., Pub. Pol. & L. 149 (2009).
45. J. Stuart et al., *Procedural Justice In Family Conflict Resolution and Deviant Peer Group Involvement Among Adolescents: The Mediating Influence of Peer Conflict*, 37 J. Youth & Adol. 674 (2008).
46. Cathy S. Widom & Helen W. Wilson, *How Victims Become Offenders*, in Children as Victims, Witnesses and Offenders: Psychological Science and the Law 255 (Bette L. Bottoms, Cynthia J. Nadjowski, & Gail S. Goodman, eds., 2009) (describing research showing a relationship between violence and both physical abuse and nonphysical abuse); Rolf Loeber et al., *Child Delinquency: Early Intervention and Prevention, Child Delinquency Bulletin*, 5 Juv. Justice & Delinq. Prevention 7, available at www.ncjrs.gov/pdffiles1/ojjdp/186162.pdf (2003).

47. Cathy Spatz Widom, *Does Violence Beget Violence? A Critical Examination of the Literature*, 106 Psychol. Bull. 3, 23 (1989).
48. Anna Stewart et al., *Transitions and Turning Points: Examining the Links Between Child Maltreatment and Juvenile Offending*, 32 Child Abuse & Neglect 51 (2008).
49. Cathy Spatz Widom et al., *An Examination of Pathways from Childhood Victimization to Violence: The Role of Early Aggression and Problematic Alcohol Use*, 21 Violence & Victims 675 (2006).
50. Gayla Margolin & Elana B. Gordis, *The Effects of Family and Community Violence on Children*, 51 Ann. Rev. Psychol. 445, 456 (2000).
51. Veronica M. Herrera & Laura Ann McCloskey, *Gender Differences in the Risk for Delinquency Among Youth Exposed to Family Violence*, 25 Child Abuse & Neglect 1037, 1046 (2001). However, other significant risk factors (e.g., parental psychopathology, substance abuse, parental criminality) were not controlled by Herrera and McCloskey. Id. at 1048.
52. Patrick H. Tolan et al., *Linking Family Violence to Delinquency Across Generations*, 5 Children's Services: Soc. Pol., Res., & Prac. 273 (2002).
53. Benjamin B. Lahey et al., *Psychopathology in the Parents of Children with Conduct Disorder and Hyperactivity*, 27 J. Am. Acad. Child & Adol. Psychiat. 163, 166–67 (1988) ("The present results strongly support previous findings that children with [conduct disorders] are more likely than other clinic-referred children to have both mothers and fathers who qualify for the diagnosis of [antisocial personality disorder] and to have fathers who abuse substances.").
54. Gerald R. Patterson et al., *Predicting Risk for Early Police Arrest*, 8(4) J. Quant. Criminol. 335, 351 (1992) (finding that "social disorganization makes a direct contribution" to arrest rates); Robert J. Sampson & W. Byron Groves, *Community Structure and Crime: Testing Social-Disorganization Theory*, 94 Am. J. Sociol. 774, 781 (1989).
55. Brenda Bryant, *The Neighborhood Walk: A Study of Sources of Support in Middle School Children from the Child's Perspective*, 50 (3 Serial No. 210), Monographs Soc'y Res. Child Dev. 1(1985).
56. Albert J. Reiss, Jr. & David P. Farrington, *Advancing Knowledge About Co-Offending: Results from a Prospective Longitudinal Survey of London Males*, 82 J. Crim. L. & Criminol. 360, 393 (1991) (finding that "the incidence of co-offending decreases with age").
57. J. David Hawkins et al., *Predictors of Youth Violence*, Juvenile Justice Bulletin (2000), available at www.ncjrs.gov/pdffiles1/ojjdp/179065.pdf; Laura V. Scaramella et al., *Evaluation of a Social Contextual Model of Delinquency: A Cross-Cultural Replication*, 73 Child Dev. 175, 189 (2002) (showing a relationship between deviant peer relationships and antisocial behavior in the community, but not in the home); Thomas J. Dishon et al., *Antisocial Boys and Their Friends in Early Adolescence: Relationship Characteristics, Quality, and Interactional Process*, 66 Child Dev. 139 (1995).
58. *See* Margo Gardner & Laurence Steinberg, *Peer Influence on Risk Taking, Risk Preference and Risky Decision Making in Adolescence and Adulthood: An Experimental Study*, 41(4) Dev. Psychol. 625, 632 (2005) (showing strong influence of peer behavior on juvenile antisocial behavior); Thomas J. Berndt, *Developmental Changes in Conformity to Peers and Parents*, 15 Dev. Psychol. 608, 615 (1979) (showing peak peer conformity at grade 9 between grades 3 and 12); Scott et al.,

Evaluating Adolescent Decision-Making, at 230; Jeffrey Fagan, *Contexts of Choice by Adolescents in Criminal Events*, in Youth on Trial, at 371, 373.

59. *See* Franklin E. Zimring, Kids, *Groups and Crime: Some Implications of a Well-Known Secret*, 72 J. Crim. L. & Criminol. 867, 867 (1981) ("The "well-known secret" is this: adolescents commit crimes, as they live their lives, in groups."); Joan McCord & Kevin P. Conway, *Patterns of Juvenile Delinquency and Co-Offending*, in Advances of Criminology Theory, Volume 10: Crime and Social Organization 15 (Elin J. Waring & David Weisburd, eds., 2002).

60. Hawkins et al., *Predictors of Youth Violence.*

61. Berndt, *Developmental Changes*, at 615 ("in both studies conformity to peers on antisocial behavior increased greatly between third and ninth grades, and then declined."); Scaramella et al., *Social-Contextual Model of Delinquency*, at 189.

62. Loeber et al., *Child Delinquency*, at 7–8.

63. Id. at 373.

64. *See* Terrie E. Moffitt, *Adolescence-Limited and Life-Course-Persistent Antisocial Behavior: A Developmental Taxonomy*, 100 Psychol. Rev. 674, 687–88 (1993) (noting that adolescents who want "to prove their maturity" are likely to emulate "life-course-persistents" [criminal perpetrators] because the latter's lifestyle resembles adulthood more than childhood).

65. Devon D. Brewer et al., *Preventing Serious, Violent, and Chronic Juvenile Offending: A Review of Evaluations and Selected Strategies in Childhood, Adolescence, and the Community*, in Sourcebook on Serious, Violent, and Chronic Juvenile Offenders 61 (James C. Howell et al. eds., 1995); Margit Wiesner & M. Windle *Assessing Covariates of Adolescent Delinquency*, 33 J. Youth & Adol. 431 (2004).

66. J. David Hawkins et al., *A Review of Predictors of Youth Violence*, in Serious and Violent Juvenile Offenders: Risk Factors and Successful Interventions 106 (Rolf Loeber & David P. Farrington, eds., 1998).

67. Todd I. Herrenkohl et al., *School and Community Risk Factors and Interventions*, in Child Delinquents: Development, Intervention, and Service Needs 211 (Rolf Loeber & David Farrington, eds., 2001).

68. Allison Ann Payne, *A Multilevel Analysis of the Relationships among Communal School Organization, Student Bonding, and Delinquency*, 45 J. Res. Crime & Delinq. 429 (2008).

69. Gary D. Gottfredson et al., *School Climate Predictors of School Disorder: Results from a National Study of Delinquency Prevention in Schools*, 42 J. Res. Crime & Delinq. 412 (2005); Patricia H. Jenkins, *School Delinquency and the School Social Bond*, 34 J. Res. Crime & Delinq. 337, 340 (1997).

70. John P. Hoffmann & Mikaela J. Dufur, *Family and School Capital Effects on Delinquency: Substitutes or Complements*, 51 Sociol. Perspectives 29 (2008).

71. Richard Cloward & Llyod Ohlin, Delinquency and Opportunity: A Theory of Delinquent Gangs (1961); Clifford Shaw and Henry D. Mccay, Juvenile Delinquency and Urban Areas (1942).

72. Charles R. Tittle & Robert F. Meier, *Specifying the SES/Delinquency Relationship by Social Characteristics of Contexts*, 28 J. Res. Crime & Delinq. 430 (1991); Charles R. Tittle et al., *The Myth of Social Class and Criminality: An Assessment of the Empirical Evidence*, 43 Am. Sociol. Rev. 643 (1978).

73. Robert J. Sampson & John H. Laub, *Urban Poverty and the Family Context of Delinquency: A New Look at Structure and Process in a Classic Study*, 65 Child Dev. 523 (1994).

74. Bradley R. Enter Wright et al., *Reconsidering the Relationship Between SES and Delinquency: Causation but Not Correlation*, 37 Criminol. 175, 188 (1999).
75. Carter Hay et al., *Compounded Risk: The Implications for Delinquency of Coming from a Poor Family that Lives in a Poor Community*, 36 J. Youth & Adol. 593 (2007) (in comparison to those whose parents were employed, those with unemployed parents had an increase in delinquency of .67 standard deviation units when community poverty was set at the mean. When community poverty was elevated at one standard deviation above the mean, juveniles whose parents are unemployed had a 1.69 increase in standard deviation units. When community poverty is at 2 standard deviations above the mean, delinquency increases 2.71 standard deviations for youngsters whose parents are unemployed).
76. Loeber et al., *Child Delinquency*, at 8; Robert J. Sampson et al., *Neighborhoods and Violence Crime: A Multilevel Study of Collective Efficacy*, 277 Science 919, 923 (1997) (social cohesion and trust correlated robustly with reduced violence). *See generally* Tama Leventhal & Jeanne Brooks-Gunn, *The Neighborhoods They Live In: The Effects of Neighborhood Residence on Child and Adolescent Outcomes*, 126 Psychol. Bull. 309 (2000).
77. Donald R. Lynam et al., *The Interaction Between Impulsivity and Neighborhood Context on Offending: The Effects of Impulsivity Are Stronger in Poorer Neighborhoods*, 109(4) J. Abnormal Psychol. 563, 570 (2000).
78. Jeffrey Fagan, *Contexts of Choice by Adolescents in Criminal Events*, in Youth on Trial, at 371, 375.
79. *See* Robert J. Sampson & John H. Laub, Crime in the Making: Pathways and Turning Points Through Life 21 (1993); Neighborhoods and Violent Crime; Delbert S. Elliot et al., *The Effects of Neighborhood Disadvantage on Adolescent Development*, 33 J. Res. Crime & Delinq. 389, 417–18 (1997); Leventhal & Brooks-Gunn, *Neighborhoods They Live In*, at 319–20.
80. Gorman-Smith et al., *A Developmental-Ecological Model*, at 192 (children in "exceptionally functioning" families "are less likely to show any pattern of delinquency and are most protected from (under-represented in) the most serious [neighborhood] patterns.").
81. Beth E. Molnar et al., *Effects of Neighborhood Resources on Aggressive and Delinquent Behaviors Among Urban Youths*, 98 Am. J. Pub. Health 1086 (2008) (emphasis added).
82. Craig A. Anderson et al., *The Influence of Media Violence on Youth*, 4 Psychological Science in the Pub. Int. 81, 81 (2003).
83. Brad J. Bushman, *Moderating Role of Trait Aggressiveness in the Effects of Violent Media on Aggression*, 69 J. Personality & Soc. Psychol. 950, 959 (1995).
84. L. Rowell Huesmann et al., *Longitudinal Relations Between Children's Exposure to TV Violence and Their Aggressive and Violent Behavior in Young Adulthood: 1977–1999*, 39 Dev. Psychol. 201, 215 (2003) ("In this 15-year longitudinal study of 329 youth, we found that children's TV-violence viewing between ages 6 and 9, children's identification with aggressive same-sex TV characters, and children's perceptions that TV violence is realistic were significantly correlated with their adult aggression.").
85. Sampson & Laub, Crime in the Making, at 21 (stating that "changes that strengthen social bonds to society in adulthood will lead to less crime and deviance").
86. *See* Kirk R. Williams & Richard Hawkins, *Perceptual Research on General Deterrence: A Critical Review*, 20 L. & Soc'y Rev. 545, 561–66 (1986).

87. Terrie Moffitt, *The New Look of Behavioural Genetics in Developmental Psychopathology: Gene-Environment Interplay in Antisocial Behaviors*, 131 Psychol. Bull. 533, 535 (2005).
88. Id. at 537.
89. Id. at 544.
90. Id. at 547.
91. Terrie E. Moffitt, *Adolescence-Limited and Life-Course-Persistent Antisocial Behavior: A Developmental Taxonomy*, 100 Psychol. Rev. 674, 687–88 (1993).
92. Id.
93. Jeannette Taylor et al., *Evidence for a Genetic Etiology of Early-Onset Delinquency*, 109 J. Abnormal Psychol. 634, 638 (2000).
94. Isabela Granic & Gerald R. Patterson, *Toward a Comprehensive Model of Antisocial Development: A Dynamic Systems Approach*, Psychol. Rev. 101, 118 (2006).
95. Id. at 119.
96. Id.
97. Gerald Caplan, Principles of Preventive Psychiatry, 29–30 (1964), cited in Kenneth Heller & John Monahan, Psychol. & Community Change, at 120 (1977).
98. Jennifer Woolard et al., *Informing Juvenile Justice Policy: Directions for Behavioral Science Research*, 25 Law & Hum. Beh. 13, 15 (2010).
99. Mark W. Lipsey & Francis T. Cullen, *The Effectiveness of Correctional Rehabilitation: A Review of Systematic Reviews*, 3 Ann. Rev. L & Soc. Sci. 297, 302 (2008). *See also* Richard Redding, *Adult Punishment for Juvenile Offenders: Does It Reduce Crime?* in Handbook, 375, at 389 ("the available evidence, while not definitive, strongly suggests that transferring juveniles to the criminal court increases the recidivism rate"); Donna Bishop et al., *The Transfer of Juveniles to Criminal Court: Does It Make a Difference?* 41 Crime & Delinq. 171, 183 (1996) (finding "transfer actually aggravated short-term recidivism"); Jeffrey Fagan, Aaron Kupchik, & Akiva Liberman, *Be Careful What You Wish For: The Comparative Impacts of Juvenile versus Criminal Court Sanctions on Recidivism Among Adolescent Felony Offenders*, Columbia Law School, Pub. Law Research Paper No. 03–61 (2004) (same).
100. Mark W. Lipsey, *The Primary Factors that Characterize Effective Interventions with Juvenile Offenders: A Meta-Analytic Review*, 4 Victims & Offenders 124 (2009).
101. Lipsey & Cullen, *Effectiveness of Correctional Rehabilitation*, at 302 (emphasis added).
102. Barry Holman & Jason Ziedenberg, *The Dangers of Detention: The Impact of Incarcerating Youth in Detention and Other Secure Facilities*, Washington, D.C.: Justice Policy Institute (2006).
103. Id. at 4. *See* B. B. Benda & C.L. Tollet, *A Study of Recidivism of Serious and Persistent Offenders Among Adolescents*, 27 J. Crim. Just. 111–26 (1999).
104. Barry Holman & Jason Ziedenberg, *The Dangers of Detention: The Impact of Incarcerating Youth in Detention and Other Secure Facilities*, Washington, D.C.: Justice Policy Institute 5 (2006).
105. Id. at 5.
106. Richard G. Wiebush et al., *Implementation of the Intensive Community-Based Aftercare Program, Juvenile Justice Bulletin*, U.S. Department of Justice Office of Justice Programs, Office of Juvenile Justice and Delinquency Prevention (2000).
107. Id. at 6.

108. Amanda Petteruti et al., *The Costs of Confinement: Why Good Juvenile Justice Policies Make Good Fiscal Sense,* Wash., D.C.: Justice Policy Institute (2009).
109. Bart Lubow, *Safely Reducing Reliance on Detention: A Report From the Field,* 67 Corrections Today 66 72 (2005).
110. D. A. Andrews et al., *Does Correctional Treatment Work? A Clinically Relevant and Psychologically Informed Meta-Analysis,* 28 Criminol. 369 (1990); *see also* Mark W. Lipsey, *Juvenile Delinquency Treatment: A Meta-Analytic Inquiry into the Variability of Effects,* in Meta-Analysis for Explanation 83 (Thomas D. Cook et al., eds., 1992).
111. Charles M. Borduin et al., *Multisystemic Treatment of Serious Juvenile Offenders: Long-Term Prevention of Criminality and Violence,* 63 J. Consulting & Clin.Psychol. 569 (1995).
112. Gerald R. Davison et al., Abnormal Psychology, 490–491 (11th ed. 2010).
113. Lawrence S. Wrightsman et al., Psychology and the Legal System, 383 (7th ed. 2011).
114. *See generally* William M. Bolman, *Toward Realizing the Prevention of Mental Illness,* in Progress in Community Mental Health vol. I, 203, 208 (L. Bellack & H. H. Barten, eds. 1969) ("From the standpoint of the community, these distinctions are equivalent to reducing incidence, prevalence and extent of disability respectively.") (summarizing work of Gerald Caplan, Principles of Preventive Psychiatry 16–17, 1964). These concepts are redefined in the juvenile context in Youth Violence: A Report of the Surgeon General 105–14 (Dept Health & Human Services) (2001) (hereinafter Surgeon General Report).
115. Surgeon General Report, at 105.
116. Id., at 111.
117. Id. at 114.
118. *See generally* Moffitt, *Adolescent-Limited and Life-Course- Persistent Antisocial Behavior,* at 676 (contrasting "life-course persistent offenders" with "adolescent-limited offenders").
119. *See* Robert Martinson, *What Works? Questions and Answers About Prison Reform,* 35 Pub. Int. 22 (1974).
120. Center for the Study and Prevention of Violence, University of Colorado–Boulder, *Blueprints for Violence Prevention, available at* www.colorado.edu/cspv/blueprints/(hereinafter *Blueprints*).
121. James F. Alexander & Bruce V. Parsons, *Short-Term Behavioral Intervention with Delinquent Families: Impact on Family Process and Recidivism,* 81 J. Abnormal Psychol. 219 (1973); *Blueprints at http://www.colorado.edu/cspv/blueprints/modelprograms/FFT.html.*
122. *See* James F. Alexander et al., *Family-Based Interventions with Older, At-Risk Youth: From Promise to Proof to Practice,* 21 J. Primary Prevention 185, 193–97 (2000) (describing components of program).
123. *Blueprints* at http://www.colorado.edu/cspv/blueprints/modelprograms/FFT.html.
124. Id.
125. Outcome Evaluation of Washington State's Research-Based Programs for Juvenile Offenders, Washington State Institute for Public Policy (January 2004), available at www.wsipp.wa.gov/rptfiles/04–01–1201–ES.pdf. *See generally* Nancy G. Guerra et al., What Works: Best Practices with Juvenile Offenders, in Treating the Juvenile Offender 79 (Robert D. Hoge et al., eds., 2008).

126. *See Blueprints* at www.colorado.edu/cspv/blueprints/modelprograms/MST.html.
127. Scott W. Henggeler et al., Multisystemic Treatment of Antisocial Behavior in Children and Adolescents (1998).
128. Id.
129. Charles M. Borduin et al., *Multisystemic Treatment of Serious Juvenile Offenders: Long–Term Prevention of Criminality and Violence*, 63 J. Consulting & Clinical Psychol. 569, 573 (1995).
130. Cindy M. Schaeffer & Charles M. Borduin, *Long–Term Follow–Up to a Randomized Clinical Trial of Multisystemic Therapy with Serious and Violent Juvenile Offenders*, 73 J. Consulting & Clinical Psychol. 445, 448 (2005).
131. Scott W. Henggeler et al., *Multisystemic Therapy with Violent and Chronic Juvenile Offenders and Their Families: The Role of Treatment Fidelity in Successful Dissemination*, 65 J. Consulting & Clinical Psychol. 821, 829 (1997).
132. *Blueprints* at www.colorado.edu/cspv/blueprints/modelprograms/MST.html. *See also* MST Website at www.mstservices.com/cost_effectiveness.php.
133. *See Blueprints* at www.colorado.edu/cspv/blueprints/modelprograms/MTFC.html.
134. Patricia Chamberlain & John B. Reid, *Comparison of Two Community Alternatives to Incarceration for Chronic Juvenile Offenders*, 66 J. Consulting & Clinical Psychol. 624, 624–25 (1998).
135. Id at 630.
136. *Blueprints* at www.colorado.edu/cspv/blueprints/modelprograms/MTFC.html.
137. *See Blueprints at* www.colorado.edu/cspv/blueprints/promisingprograms/BPP05.html
138. *See* Nicki R. Crick & Kenneth A. Dodge, *A Review and Reformulation of Social Information–Processing Mechanism's in Children's Social Adjustment*, 117Psychol. Bull. 74 (1994).
139. Id. at 76.
140. Kenneth A. Dodge, *Translational Science in Action: Hostile Attributional Style and the Development of Aggressive Behavior Problems*, 18 Dev. Psychopathology 791–814 (2006); Mark R. Fondacaro & Kenneth Heller, *Attributional Style in Aggressive Adolescent Boys*, 18 J. Abnormal Child Psychol. 75–89 (1990); William Nasby et al., *Attributional Bias Among Aggressive Boys to Interpret Unambiguous Social Stimuli as Displays of Hostility*, 89 J. Abnormal Psychol. 459–468 (1980).
141. Kenneth A. Dodge & Angelia M. Tomlin, *Utilization of Self–Schemas as a Mechanism of Interpretational Bias in Aggressive Children*, 5 Social Cognition 280 (1987); Kenneth A. Dodge & Joseph P. Newman, *Biased Decision–Making Processes in Aggressive Boys*, 90 J. Abnormal Psychol. 375 (1981).
142. Kenneth A. Dodge & Cynthia L. Frame, *Social Cognitive Biases and Deficits in Aggressive Boys*, 53 Child Dev. 620 (1982).
143. Nicki R. Crick & Kenneth A. Dodge, *A Review and Reformulation of Social Information–Processing Mechanism's in Children's Social Adjustment*, 117 Psychol. Bull. 74 (1994).
144. Id.
145. Id.
146. Kenneth A. Dodge, *Translational Science in Action: Hostile Attributional Style and the Development of Aggressive Behavior Problems*, 18 Dev. Psychopathology

791–814 (2006); Laurence Steinberg, *Cognitive and Affective Development in Adolescence*, 9 Trends in Cognitive Sci. 69 (2005).
147. Nancy M. Slough et al., *Preventing Serious Conduct Problems in School–Age Youth: The Fast Track Program*, 15 Cognitive & Beh. Prac. 3 (2008); *Blueprint at* http://www.colorado.edu/cspv/blueprints/promisingprograms/BPP05.html .
148. Moffitt, *Adolescence–Limited and Life–Course–Persistent Antisocial Behavior*; Slough et al., *Preventing Serious Conduct Problems*, at 6.
149. Slough et al., *Preventing Serious Conduct Problems*, at 7.
150. Mark A. Cohen, *The Monetary Value of Saving a High–Risk Youth*, 14 J. Quant. Criminol. 5 (1998).
151. Borduin, *Multisystemic Treatment of Serious Juvenile Offenders*, at 573 (indicating that after four years the recidivism rate for those who successfully completed MST was 22.1% and for those who dropped out of MST was 46.6%); Schaeffer & Bourduin, *Long–Term Followup*, at 448 (indicating that over 13 years recidivism rate for those who completed MST was 50%, compared to 81% for those who did not); Office of Program Policy Analysis and Program Accountability, *Report 09–27*, at 2–3 (May, 2009) (hereafter Office of Program Policy Analysis) (comparing youthful offenders handled through a community–based, family–centered program to youthful offenders with similar criminal history handled through alternative, primary residential programs, and finding that the probability of arrest for the former group was 25% less for any violation, 46% less for any felony, and 48% less for violent felonies).
152. Henggeler et al., Multisystemic Treatment of Antisocial Behavior, at 130; Marsha Swenson & Melanie Duncan, *Multisystemic Therapy: Clinical Outcome and Cost Savings* 1, 2 available at www.mstservices.com/outcomes_1a.pdf. *See also* Office of Program Policy Analysis, at 3 (community–based program saved the state $36.4 million in residential costs and $5.2 million in recommitment and prison costs).
153. For instance, 31 states have MST teams in one or more jurisdictions and other programs have also been popular. *See* MST Services, Licensed Teams by Location, available at http://mstservices.com/licensed_teams_by_location.php.

Chapter 3: The Implications of Science for Juvenile Justice

1. 521 U.S. 346 (1997).
2. Wayne R. LaFave, Criminal Law 244, 246, 382 (4th ed. 2003).
3. Id. at 399.
4. Id. n. 13.
5. Id. at 485–86.
6. *See generally* Juvenile Justice Philosophy: Readings, Cases and Comments 551 (Frederic L. Faust & Paul J. Brantingham, eds., 1974) (explaining the juvenile court's assumption that "children were infinitely malleable, the best possible subjects for the new social sciences to work wonders upon"); Franklin E. Zimring, American Juvenile Justice 35—38 (2005) (discussing the "diversionary" and "interventionist" motivations for juvenile justice).
7. *See* Anna L. Simpson, *Rehabilitation as the Justification of a Separate Juvenile Justice* System, 64 Cal. L. Rev. 984, 984—85 (1976) (arguing children are no more treatable than adults).
8. 422 U.S. 563 (1975).

9. *See* id. at 575.
10. Id.
11. *See* Pierce v. Soc'y of Sisters, 268 U.S. 510 (1925).
12. Id. at 535.
13. In Parham v. J.R., 442 U.S. 584 (1979), the Supreme Court held that even when parents are willing to commit their children, a neutral fact finder must find that the child needs treatment in a hospital. The Court did not specifically decide whether need for treatment is a permissible criterion for commitment. But other courts, in both the adult and juvenile contexts, have rejected that standard to the extent it permits hospitalization on a bare diagnosis. *See*, e.g., State ex rel. Hawks v. Lazaro, 157 W.Va. 417. 438, 202 S.E.2d 109, 123 (1974) (permitting involuntary hospitalization only "when it can be demonstrated that an individual has a self–destructive urge and will be violent towards himself, or alternatively that he is so mentally retarded or mentally ill that by sheer inactivity he will permit himself to die either of starvation or lack of care."); Boggs v. N.Y. City Health & Hosp. Corp, 132 A.D.2d 340, 362, 523 N.Y.S.2d 71, 84 (1987) ("It is well–established in this state that a person may be involuntarily confined for care and treatment, where his or her mental illness manifests itself in neglect or refusal to care for themselves to such an extent that there is presented 'serious Harm' to their own well–being."); Matter of Commitment of N.N., 146 N.J. 112, 679 A2d 1174 (1996) (Commitment of minors under fourteen requires clear and convincing evidence of mental illness, need for inpatient treatment and "danger to the minor herself or to others, which may include the substantial likelihood of significant developmental harm if that treatment is not provided."); Johnson v. Solomon, 484 F.Supp. 278, 287 (D. Md. 1979) (requiring danger to self or others of juveniles).
14. American Bar Ass'n, Standards, Standards Relating to Juvenile Delinquency and Sanctions (1980).
15. Franklin E. Zimring, *Penal Proportionality for the Young Offender: Notes on Immaturity, Capacity, and Diminished Responsibility*, in Youth on Trial: A Developmental Perspective of Juvenile Justice 267–324 (Thomas Grisso & Robert G. Schwartz, eds., 2000) (hereinafter Youth on Trial).
16. Elizabeth S. Scott & Laurence Steinberg, Rethinking Juvenile Justice: Adolescent Development and the Regulation of Youth Crime (2008).
17. 543 U.S. 551, 571 (2005).
18. *Id.* at 568 ("Capital punishment must be limited to those offenders who commit a narrow category of the most serious crimes" and whose extreme culpability makes them "the most deserving of execution.").
19. *See*, e.g., Franklin E. Zimring, Confronting Youth Crime: Report of the Twentieth Century Fund on Sentencing Policy Toward Young Offenders 80–81 (1978) (analogizing the diminished responsibility of adolescents to the "partial responsibility" of people with mental disability who receive "mitigations of punishment").
20. *See* American Psychiatric Association, Diagnostic and Statistical Manual (1994).
21. United States Sentencing Com'n, Guidelines Manual § 5K2.13 (1994).
22. Id. § 5H1.3.
23. Michael L. Perlin & Keri K. Gould, *Rashomon and the Criminal Law: Mental Disability and the Federal Sentencing Guidelines*, 22 Am. J. Crim. L. 431, 447 (1995). *See also, Construction and Application of U.S.S.G. § 5H1.3 Concerning Mental and Emotional Conditions as Grounds for Sentencing Departure*, 34 A.L.R.2d 457 (2009)

(noting rarity of downward departures on disability grounds, especially in cases involving violence).

24. U.S. v. Maldonado–Montalvao, 356 F.2d 65, 74 (1st Cir. 2003).

25. *See*, e.g., United States v. Mata–Vasquez, 111 Fed.Appx 986, 988 (2004) ("four–level" reduction based on IQ of 51 and other impairments reduced sentence by 6 to 12 months); United States v. Cotto, 279 F.2d 64, (E.D. N.Y. 1992) (a "four–level" reduction based on low IQ and drug use reduced sentence from 37 months to 24 months).

26. Note that state and federal courts can and often do have completely different sentencing regimes.

27. Nora V. Demleitner et al., Sentencing Law and Policy: Cases, Statutes and Guidelines 404 (2d ed. 2007) ("At common law those with severe mental impairments could be excused from guilt altogether, but offenders with lesser impairments would usually be subject to the same punishment as mentally sound offenders" while modern statutes require that mental illness "significantly reduced the defendant's culpability for the offense."). *See also* John Q. La Fond & Mary L. Durham, *Cognitive Dissonance: Have Insanity Defense and Civil Commitment Reforms Made a Difference?*, 39 Vill. L. Rev. 71, 102–03 (1994) (noting that offenders found guilty but mentally ill often receive *longer* sentences than those found simply guilty).

28. Christopher Slobogin, Minding Justice: Laws that Deprive People with Mental Disability of Life and Liberty 80–83 (2006) (discussing the type of dysfunction that should form the basis for significant sentence reductions in non-capital cases).

29. 130 S.Ct. at 2034.

30. This prediction is based on the fact that, prior to *Graham*, very few courts were willing to strike down even life *without* parole sentences. State v. Pittman, 647 S.E.2d 144, 163–64 (S.C. 2007); State v. Craig, 944 So.2d 6660, 622 (La.Ct.App. 2006), cert. denied 128 S.Ct. 714 (2007); Comm. v. Wilson, 911 A.2d 942, 946 (Pa. Super Ct. 2006); State v. Rideout, 933 A.2d 706 (Vt. 2007); State v. Eggers, 160 P.3d 1230, 12347–49 (Ariz. App. 2007). *See generally* Hillary J. Massey, *Disposing of Children: The Eighth Amendment and Juvenile Life without Parole after* Roper, 46 B.C. L. Rev. 1083 (2006). But *see* In re Nunez, 173 Cal.App.4th 709, 93 Cal.Rptr.3d 242 (2009) (holding that child of fourteen convicted of a nonviolent kidnapping cannot be sentenced to life without parole).

31. *See*, e.g., Manduley v. Sup.Ct. San Diego Cty., 27 Cal.4th 537 (Cal.Sup.Ct. 2002); State v. Behl, 564 N.W.2d 560 (Minn. 1997).

32. Terry A. Maroney, *The False Promise of Adolescent Brain Science in Juvenile Justice*, 85 Notre Dame L.Rev. 89, 165 (2009). *See also* id. at 127 ("courts tend to view the findings of developmental neuroscience as either irrelevant to the specific determination before them or as insufficiently persuasive as to invalidate schemes for imposition of non-death sentences."). Maroney has since written that *Graham*, which came down after her original article, has not appreciably changed the courts' views on these matters. Terry Maroney, *Adolescent Brain Science After Graham v. Florida*, 86 Notre Dame L. Rev. 353, 388 (2010) (concluding "nothing in *Graham* suggests any meaningful alteration to the normative claims advanced in *False Promise*").

33. Id. at 118–125.

34. State v. Heinemann, 920 A.2d 278, 297 (Conn. 2007).

35. Scott & Steinberg, Rethinking Juvenile Justice, at 131–39.
36. Federal Sentencing Guidelines Manual § 5K2.12 (permitting a reduction in sentence for "coercion and incomplete duress," but "ordinarily" only when the coercion results from a physical threat to person or property).
37. *See*, e.g., United States v. Lopez, 264 F.3d 527, 530–31 (5th Cir. 2001) (trial court willing to depart downward on the basis of duress *and* "extraordinary family responsibilities" from 135 to 108 months).
38. *See* Fed.R.Evid. 404(a)(1) (permitting evidence of character only to show that the person "acted in conformity therewith on a particular occasion" and then only under limited circumstances).
39. The Federal Sentencing Guidelines provide that "prior good works are not ordinarily relevant in determine whether a sentence should be outside the applicable guideline range," U.S. Sentencing Guidelines Manual § 5H1.11, and that "lack of guidance as a youth and similar circumstances indicating a disadvantaged upbringing are not relevant grounds for imposing a sentence outside the applicable guideline range." Id. at § 5H1.12.
40. *See* Scott & Steinberg, Rethinking Juvenile Justice, at 828 n. 119.
41. Scott and Steinberg make a second argument for a separate juvenile court based on research indicating that many youth are not competent to stand trial in adult court. Id. at 149–80. As discussed in Chapter Five, juveniles who are over fourteen probably are competent to stand trial. But if they are not, it is not clear how a retribution-focused juvenile system could try them either.
42. Barry C. Feld, *Juvenile and Criminal Justice Systems' Responses to Juvenile Violence*, 24 Crime & Justice 189, 245 (1998).
43. Scott & Steinberg, Rethinking Juvenile Justice, at 231. *See also* Richard E. Redding, *Adult Punishment for Juvenile Offenders: Does It Reduce Crime?* in Handbook of Children, Culture, and Violence 375, at 389 (Nancy E. Dowd, Dorothy G. Singer, & Robin Fretwell Wilson, eds., 2006) (stating that "punishment that is proportional to the offender's culpability should be at the heart of the justice system" but favoring a wide array of rehabilitative programs).
44. Id. at 147–48.
45. Id. at 181–222.
46. Id. at 244–45 (noting that "treatment-related factors introduce a modest, albeit imperfect, predictive dimension to a regime otherwise committed to basing sanctions of [*sic*] fairness considerations but without unduly compromising proportionality.")
47. Id. at 249.
48. Michael Schumacher & Gwen A. Kurz, The 8% Solution: Preventing Serious, Repeat Juvenile Crime (1999) (exploring the ramifications of a study finding that 8% of first-time juvenile offenders commit roughly 50% of repeat offenses). *See also* David P. Farrington et al., Understanding and Controlling Crime 50–51 (1986) and Marvin E. Wolfgang et al., Delinquency in a Birth Cohort 88 (1972) (reporting research indicating that roughly 5–6% of chronic offenders commit over 50% of juvenile crime).
49. 521 U.S. 346 (1997). Parts of this analysis are drawn from earlier work. *See* Christopher Slobogin et al., *A Prevention Model of Juvenile Justice: The Promise of Kansas v. Hendricks for Children*, 1999 Wis. L. Rev. 185, 192–204.
50. 521 U.S. at 361–62.
51. Stephen J. Schulhofer, *Two Systems of Social Protection: Comments on the Civil-Criminal Distinction, with Particular Reference to Sexually Violent Predator Laws*, 7

J. Contemp. Legal Issues 69, 85 (1996) ("'civil' deprivation of liberty is permissible only as a gap-filler, to solve problems the criminal process cannot address").
52. Eric S. Janus, *Preventing Sexual Violence: Setting Principles Constitutional Boundaries on Sex Offender Commitments*, 72 In. L. J. 157, 212 (1996) ("The principle of criminal interstitiality would allow civil commitment. . . only if the individual's mental disorder rendered him or her unamenable to criminal prosecution.").
53. *See* American Psychiatric Association, Diagnostic & Statistical Manual 340–41 (4th ed. Text–Revised 2000) (placing the "paraphilias" in Axis II, which describes personality disorders, as compared to Axis I, which includes, inter alia, the psychoses).
54. *See* Bruce J. Winick, *Sex Offender Law in the 1990s: A Therapeutic Jurisprudence Analysis*, 4 Psychol., Pub. Pol. & L. 505, 524 (1998) ("People diagnosed with pedophilia do not molest children in the presence of police officers or in other situations presenting a high likelihood of apprehension. Rather, they act with stealth, deception, and premeditation in an effort to avoid detection. This is purposeful, planned, and goal-directed conduct, not spontaneous and uncontrollable action or action that is substantially beyond the individual's ability to avoid.").
55. Id. at 525 (Paraphilias "neither render individuals incompetent to engage in rational decision making nor make them unable to resist their strong desires to molest children or otherwise to act out sexually.").
56. 521 U.S. at 358.
57. 534 U.S. 407, 413 (2002).
58. W. Lawrence Fitch, Sex Offender Commitment in the United States: Legislative and Policy Concerns (Robert Prentky et al., eds., 2003) (only 12% of those committed are diagnosed with a "serious mental illness"; the rest have personality disorders like paraphilia and antisocial personality disorder).
59. 521 U.S. at 368 ("Where the State has 'disavowed any punitive intent'; limited confinement to a small segment of particularly dangerous individuals; provided strict procedural safeguards;... *recommended treatment if such is possible*; and *permitted immediate release upon a showing that the individual is no longer dangerous or mentally impaired*, we cannot say that it acted with punitive intent.") (emphasis added).
60. Id.
61. Scott & Steinberg, Rethinking Juvenile Justice, at 140–41.
62. 543 U.S. at 571. The Court repeated this language in *Graham*, 130 S.Ct. at 2028.
63. 543 U.S. at 571.
64. Elizabeth Scott, *Criminal Responsibility in Adolescence: Lessons from Development Psychology*, in Youth on Trial, at 306.
65. Id. *See also* Rethinking Juvenile Justice, at 132.
66. Scott & Steinberg, Rethinking Juvenile Justice, at 281.
67. *See* Barefoot v. Estelle, 463 U.S. 880 (1983).
68. Robert Martinson, *What Works? Questions and Answers about Prison Reform*, 35 Pub. Int. 22 (1974). According to Francis Allen, Martinson's conclusion that most offender treatment programs had a negligent impact on recidivism reduction had "an immediate and widespread impact." Francis Allen, The Decline of the Rehabilitative Ideal: Penal Policy and Social Purpose 57 (1981).

69. Paul H. Robinson, *Intuitions of Justice: Implications for Criminal Law and Justice Policy*, 81 S.Cal.L.Rev. 1 (2007).
70. Id. at 37–38.
71. *See* Christopher Slobogin, Proving the Unprovable: The Role of Law, Science and Speculation in Adjudicating Culpability and Dangerousness 40–48 (2007) (describing the difficulties associated with ascertaining mental state at the time of the offense).
72. 406 U.S. 715, 738 (1972).
73. 521 U.S. at 368. For further discussion of these three limitations, *see* Slobogin, Minding Justice, at 111–15.
74. Typically juvenile court dispositional jurisdiction ends at age twenty-one, although in some states it extends to age twenty-five. Robert O. Dawson, *Judicial Waiver in Theory and Practice*, in The Changing Borders of Juvenile Justice: Transfers of Adolescents to Adult Court 45, 51 (Jeffrey Fagan & Franklin E. Zimring, eds, 2000) (hereafter Changing Borders).
75. 521 U.S. at 368.
76. *See* Connally v. General Construction Co., 269 U.S. 385, 391 (1926) ("a statute which either forbids or requires the doing of an act in terms so vague that men of common intelligence must necessarily guess at is meaning and differ as to its application, violates the first essential of due process of law.").
77. *See generally* John Calvin Jeffries Jr., Legality, *Vagueness and the Construction of Penal Statutes*, 71 Va. L. Rev. 189 (1985).
78. Kolender v. Lawson, 461 U.S. 352, 358 (1983).
79. *See* John Monahan, The Clinical Prediction of Violent Behavior 71 (1981).
80. Dean J. Champion & G. Larry Mays, Transferring Juveniles to Criminal Courts: Trends and Implications for Criminal Justice 6 (1991).
81. For instance, the Structured Assessment of Violence Risk in Youth (SAVRY) is composed of twenty-four risk factors and six protective factors, none of which focus specifically on running away, truancy, or curfew violations. *See* Randy Borum et al., Manual for the Structured Assessment of Violence Risk in Youth (SAVRY) 40–45 (2007).
82. *Cf.* Chicago v. Morales, 527 U.S. 41 (1999) (striking down ordinance criminalizing failure of a gang member or an associate of a gang member to disperse after a police order to do so).
83. Bordenkircher v. Hayes, 434 U.S. 357, 364 (1978).
84. *See generally* Sara Sun Beale, *You've Come a Long Way Baby: Two Waves of Juvenile Reform as Seen from Jena, Louisiana*, 44 Harv. Civil Rights–Civil Liberties L. Rev. 511 (2009) (describing how the retributive juvenile justice reforms of recent years have shifted power to the prosecutor); Angela J. Davis, Arbitrary Justice: The Power of the American Prosecutor 41 (2007) ("Continuing the same approach to prosecution without consideration of broader notions of fairness will continue to produce the same results—inequitable treatment of victims and defendants in the criminal justice system.").
85. Tate v. State, 864 So.2d 44 (Fla. 2003).
86. *See* Scott & Steinberg, Rethinking Juvenile Justice, at 261–62; Aaron Kupchik, Judging Juveniles: Prosecuting Adolescents in Adult and Juvenile Court 2–5 (2006).
87. 864 So.2d at 48.
88. Kupchik, Judging Juveniles, at 3.

89. *Cf.* Adam J. Kolber, *The Subjective Experience of Punishment*, 109 Colum. L. Rev. 182, 186 (2009) (making this argument).
90. *See generally* H.L.A. Hart, Punishment and Responsibility 28–53, 180–83 (1968).
91. *See*, e.g., Vernon L. Quinsey, *Review of the Washington State Special Commitment Center Program for Sexually Violent Predators*, 15 U. Puget Sound L. Rev. 704, 705–7 (1992).
92. *See* Scott & Steinberg, Rethinking Juvenile Justice, at 279–81 ("Our survey suggests that Americans are concerned about youth crime and want to reduce its incidence but are ready to support effective rehabilitative programs as a means of accomplishing that end—and indeed favor this response over imposing more punishment through longer sentences."); Barry Krisberg & Susan Marchionna, National Council on Crime and Delinquency, *Attitudes of U.S. Voters Toward Youth Crime and the Justice System* (2007), available at www.nccd–crc.org/nccd/pubs/zogby_ feb07.pdf (poll finding that 91% of the respondents believe that future criminal acts by youth can be prevented by rehabilitation and treatment services; 68% do not think that incarcerating youth in adult facilities has a deterrent effect on youth; and 80% believe crime costs will be less in the future if money is spent on rehabilitative and treatment services now); Melissa M. Moon et al., *Is Child Saving Dead? Public Support for Juvenile Rehabilitation*, 46 Crime & Delinquency 38 (2000) (finding that when subjects in Tennessee—not a particularly "liberal" state—were given the choice between spending money to build prisons or to fund prevention-oriented programs, close to 90 percent chose prevention).
93. Paul H. Robinson & John M. Darley, *The Utility of Desert*, 91 Nw. U. L. Rev. 453, 471–77 (1997).
94. Christopher Slobogin, *Is Justice Just Us? Using Social Science to Inform the Criminal Law*, 87 J. Crim. L. & Criminol. 315, 326–27 (1996).
95. This stance is also bolstered by newer "liberal" theories of punishment that treat desert as a necessary but not sufficient condition to punish. As developed by Barbara Hudson, for instance, punishment should usually be justified by some other liberal value beyond desert, such as protecting the public or rehabilitation. Barbara Hudson, Justice in the Risk Society: Challenging and Re-affirming "Justice" in Late Modernity (2003). The individual prevention regime advanced here makes a desert finding necessary, at the adjudication stage, but authorizes intervention only if the requisite degree of risk is present.
96. *See* Fox Butterfield, All God's Children: The Bosket Family and the American Tradition of Violence 226–27 (1997) (describing how public outcry over Bosket's case led to passage of New York's Juvenile Offender Act of 1978).
97. Id.
98. *See* Robert Harlow et al., *The Severity of Intermediate Penal Sanctions: A Psychophysical Scaling Approach for Obtaining Community Perceptions*, 11 J. Quant. Criminol. 72 (1995).
99. *Cf.* Adam J. Kolber, *How to Improve Empirical Desert*, Brooklyn L. Rev. 19–21 (2010) (empirical desert advocates have yet to demonstrate the value of the compliance induced by empirical desert relative to the value of other consequentialist goals).
100. 130 S.Ct. at 2030.
101. Barry Glassner et al., *A Note on the Deterrent Effect of Juvenile v. Adult Jurisdiction*, 31 Social Probs. 31 219, 220–21 (1983) (recounting interviews with

juveniles who said they were less likely to commit crime after age 16, when they could be treated as adults).

102. See generally Paul H. Robinson & John M. Darley, *Does Criminal Law Deter? A Behavioural Science Investigation*, 24 Oxford Leg. Studies 173 (2004).

103. David A. Anderson, *The Deterrence Hypothesis and Picking Pockets at the Pickpocket's Hanging*, 4 Am. L. & Economics Rev. 1, 20–21 (2002).

104. Wanda D. Foglia, *Perceptual Deterrence and the Mediating Effect of Internalized Norms Among Inner-City Teenagers*, 34(4) J. Res.Crime & Delinq. 414, 433–35 (1997) (finding that the threat of formal sanctions "means little to young people from economically depressed urban neighborhoods" and that "peer behavior has the strongest association with law-breaking").

105. Anne Schneider & Laurie Ervin, *Specific Deterrence, Rational Choice, and Decision Heuristics: Applications in Juvenile Justice*, 71 Social Sci. Quart. 585, 598 (1999) ("The results of this study show that juvenile offenders in six different cities did not reduce their propensity to commit crimes as a function of their perception of the certainty or severity of their punishment.").

106. Thomas A. Loughran et al., *Differential Deterrence: Studying Heterogeneity and Changes in Perceptual Deterrence among Serious Youthful Offenders*, 20 Crime & Delinq. 1 (2009).

107. Steve Levitt, *Juvenile Crime and Punishment*, 106(6) J. Political Econ. 1158 (1998).

108. *See also* David S. Lee & Justin McCrary, *The Deterrence Effect of Prison: Dynamic Theory and Evidence*, 34 (Princeton Working Paper No. 550, 2009), available at www.irs.princteon.edu/pubspdgs/550.pdf (finding "small deterrence effects of prison" on juvenile offenders subject to adult court jurisdiction and suggesting that Levitt's methodology conflated deterrence and incapacitation effects).

109. Henry M. Hart Jr., *The Aims of the Criminal Law*, 23 L. & Contemp. Probs. 401, 407–8 (1958).

110. *See*, e.g., Paul H. Robinson, *A Failure of Moral Conviction?* 117 Pub. Int. 40, 44 (1994) (if a preventive approach were adopted, criminal justice might begin to "lose its ability to claim that offenders deserve the sentences they get [which might dilute] its ability to induce personal shame and to instigate social condemnation").

111. *See*, e.g., Tom Tyler, Why People Obey the Law 23–24 (2d ed. 2006); Robert Meir & Weldon Johnson, *Deterrence as Social Control: The Legal and Extralegal Production of Conformity*, 42 Am. Soc. Rev. 292, 302 (1977) (social institutions outweigh criminal law as an influence on conduct).

112. Slobogin, Minding Justice, 163.

113. Id.

114. *See*, e.g., David J. Rothman, Conscience and Convenience: The Asylum and Its Alternatives in Progressive America 159–201 (1980); Wilbert Rideau and Ron Wikberg, Life Sentences 124–47 (1992).

115. Connie Stivers Ireland & JoAnn Prause, *Discretionary Parole Release: Length of Imprisonment, Percent of Sentence Served, and Recidivism*, 28 J. Crime & Justice 27 (2005). *See also* Bert Useem et al., Institute for Social Research, University of New Mexico, Sentencing Matters, but Does Good Time Matter More? 6 (June 1996) (noting that corrections officials have stated that "prisons are safer, more orderly, and more productive when inmates participate in programs").

116. *See*, e.g., Nora V. Demleitner, *Good Conduct Time: How Much and for Whom? The Unprincipled Approach of the Model Penal Code: Sentencing*, 61 U.Fla.L.Rev. 777, 782–84 (2009).

117. *See* John Q. La Fond, *The Costs of Enacting a Sexual Predator Law*, 4 Psychol., Pub. Pol. & L. 468, 500 (1998).
118. Surgeon General Report, at 119–21.
119. *See generally* G.C.N. Hall, *Sexual Offender Recidivism Revisited: A Meta-Analysis of Recent Treatment Studies*, 63 J. Consulting & Clinical Psychol. 802 (1995) (showing modest treatment effects of sex offender treatment programs).
120. Daniel Filler, *The New Rehabilitation*, 91 Iowa L. Rev. 951, 954 (2006) ("Across the nation, in every state, local courts are creating new juvenile tribunals that explicitly seek to treat and rehabilitate juvenile offenders.").
121. Richard E. Redding & J.C. Howell, *Blended Sentencing in American Juvenile Courts*, in Changing Borders, at 146.

Chapter 4: A Preventive Risk-Management Model of Juvenile Justice

1. Mark R. Fondacaro, Denise Stolle, & Brian Wilcox, *Psycholegal Research in Non-judicial Settings: Administrative Law, a New Frontier*. Paper presented at the 1996 Biennial Conference of the American Psychology-Law Society, Hilton Head, South Carolina (1996) (hereinafter Fondacaro et al., *Administrative Law, A New Frontier*).
2. Mark R. Fondacaro, *Toward an Ecological Jurisprudence Rooted in Concepts of Justice and Empirical Research*, 69 UMKC L. Rev. 179, 195 (2000) (discussing specialized domestic violence courts as natural laboratories for basic and applied research on procedural and distributive justice).
3. *See generally* Lois A. Weithorn, *Envisioning Second-Order Change in America's Responses to Troubled and Troublesome Youth*, 33 Hofstra L. Rev. 1305, 1473–505 (2005) (proposing the development of a statewide metasystem that coordinates efforts of youth-serving social institutions, agencies, and programs). *See also* Lois A. Weithorn, *Protecting Children from Exposure to Domestic Violence: The Use and Abuse of Child Maltreatment*, 53 Hastings L. J. 1, 131–52 (2001) (arguing that the coordination among different courts and agencies is essential for an effective response to cases of abuse and neglect under the dependency jurisdiction of the juvenile court).
4. For a review of recent developments in juvenile court jurisdiction, *see* Richard E. Redding & Barbara Mrozoski, *Adjudicatory and Dispositional Decision Making in Juvenile Justice*, in Juvenile Delinquency: Prevention, Assessment, and Intervention (Kirk Heilbrun, Naomi E. Sevin Goldstein, & Richard E. Redding, eds., 2005).
5. *See* Mark R. Fondacaro et al., *Procedural Justice in Resolving Family Disputes: A Psychosocial Analysis of Individual and Family Functioning in Late Adolescence*, 27 J. Youth & Adol. 101, 104 (1998).
6. In re Appeal in Maricopa County, 674 P.2d 841, 845 (Ariz. 1983) (1 1/2 years not long enough to effect rehabilitation); G.B.K. v. State, 376 N.W.2d 385 (Wis. Ct. App. 1985) (expert testimony that juvenile needed a minimum of two years of treatment, and that even more time was probably necessary;because only twenty-six months remained in juvenile court jurisdiction, transfer was justified); In re A.B., 520 A.2d 783 (N.J. Super. Ct. App. Div. 1987); Commonwealth v. Leatherbury, 568 A.2d 1313 (Pa. Super. Ct. 1990); In re T.M., 393 S.E.2d 448 (Ga. Ct. App. 1990); D.E.P. v. State, 727 P.2d 800 (Alaska Ct. App. 1986); Commonwealth v. O'Brien, 673 N.E.2d 552 (Mass. 1996) (distinguishing between "treatment," which refers to any interventions that can help the youth, and

"rehabilitation," which refers only to those interventions that can help the youth by the time juvenile jurisdiction lapses).

7. *Cf.* Michael R. Brubacher et al., *Procedural Justice in Resolving Family Disputes: Implications for Childhood Bullying*, 15 Psychol., Pub. Pol. & L. 149 (2009).

8. *Cf.* Frank R. Ascione, *Animal Abuse and Youth Violence*, Juv. Just. Bull. (2001), available at www.ncjrs.org/html/ojjdp/jjbul2001_9_2/contents.html.

9. Kolender v. Lawson, 461 U.S. 352 (1983).

10. The Model Penal Code recognizes negligence as a basis for liability only in homicide, assault with a deadly weapon, and statutory rape cases. *See* Model Penal Code §§ 210.4; 211.1(b): 213.6(1).

11. *See generally* Wayne R. LaFave, Criminal Law 277–88 (5th ed. 2010) (defining negligence and distinguishing it from recklessness).

12. Leslie Yalof Garfield, A More Principled Approach to Criminalizing Negligence: A Prescription for the Legislature, 65 Tenn. L. Rev. 875 (1998).

13. For a good treatment of a number of different "out-of-system" programs that might accomplish this goal see *Justice for Kids: Keeping Kids Out of the Juvenile Justice System* (Nancy Dowd ed., forthcoming 2011).

14. Terry v. Ohio, 392 U.S. 1 (1967)

15. *See*, e.g., Va. Code § 37.2-814. *Cf.* Gerstein v. Pugh, 420 U.S. 103 (1975) (requiring a probable cause showing to detain an arrestee).

16. Addington v. Texas, 441 U.S. 418 (1979).

17. Fl. Stat. §394.910 (clear and convincing); Texas Code §841.062 (beyond a reasonable doubt).

18. *See*, e.g., Mo.Stat. § 565.030.4(2).

19. In this context, we make no distinction between prisons, jails, "reform schools," and other institutions that restrain freedom on a twenty-four-hour basis. While there are clearly differences in degree among these institutions, they all significantly restrict freedom and separate the person from his or her community. *See generally* J. Herbie DiFonzo, *Deprived of "Fatal Liberty": The Rhetoric of Child Saving and the Reality of Juvenile Incarceration*, 26 U. Tol. L. Rev. 855 (1995).

20. *See*, e.g., Mo.State. §632.480(5) (defining dangerousness as "more likely than not"); Ill. Stat. § 307/5(f) ("substantially probable"); Kan Stat. § 59-29a02(c) ("a propensity to commit acts"); People v. Superior Court (Ghilotti), 44 P.3d 949, 954 (Cal. 2002) ("a serious and well-founded risk" but not necessarily "better than even").

21. John Monahan & David Wexler, *"A Definite Maybe": Proof and Probability in Civil Commitment*, 2 Law & Hum. Beh. 37 (1978).

22. For instance, as one of us has argued in a separate paper, not only the *standard of proof* but the *legal standard* should be proportionate to the degree of intervention, which might mean that while initial intervention would require only clear and convincing proof of a likelihood of violence, long-term intervention would require proof beyond a reasonable doubt of a *substantial* likelihood of violence (e.g., .95 × .75, or a 71% chance of violence). Christopher Slobogin, *Legal Limitations on the Scope of Preventive Detention*, in Dangerous People: Policy, Prediction, and Practice (Bernadette McSherry & Patrick Keyser, eds., 2011).

23. Research on adult offenders suggests that the highest risk groups (which have base rates for recidivism ranging from 35 to 75%) tend to compose between 2 and 8 percent of the samples. *See* Sarah M. Manchak, Jennifer Lynne Skeem, &

Kevin S. Douglas, *Utility of the Revised Level of Service Inventory (LSI-R) in Predicting Recidivism after Long-Term Incarceration*, 32 Law & Hum. Beh. 477 (2008) (high-risk groups, with recidivism rates over 38%, comprised 7.2% of sample); R. Karl Hanson, *What Do We Know About Sex Offender Risk Assessment?* 4 Psychol. Pub. Pol. & L. 50, 64 (1998) (The highest risk group, which comprised 2% of the total sample, had estimated recidivism rates of 50% to 73%.).

24. Estelle v. Smith, 451 U.S. 454, 457 (1981).

25. Id. at 459.

26. Barefoot v. Estelle, 463 U.S. 880 (1983).

27. Id. at 919 ("Doctor Grigson stated that he was not familiar with most of these studies, and that their conclusions were accepted by only a 'small minority group' of psychiatrists—'[i]t's not the American Psychiatric Association that believes that.'").

28. Gary Melton et al., Psychological Evaluations for the Courts: A Handbook for Mental Health Professionals and Lawyers 319–20 (3d ed. 2007).

29. Hugh Aynesworth, *Texas "Dr. Death" Retires after 167 Capital Case Trials*, Washington Times, Dec. 21, 2003, at A2.

30. In *Estelle* the Court excluded Grigson's testimony, but on the ground that he failed to warn either Smith or his attorney that the evaluation results might be used at sentencing. 451 U.S. at 468, 471. In *Barefoot*, the Court specifically affirmed that testimony based on hypothetical questions is permissible as a constitutional matter. 463 U.S. at 905.

31. Much of the following analysis is derived from Christopher Slobogin, Proving the Unprovable: The Role of Law, Science, and Speculation in Adjudicating Culpability and Dangerousness (2007) (hereinafter Proving the Unprovable).

32. Marnie E. Rice et al., *An Evaluation of a Maximum Security Therapeutic Community for Psychopaths and Other Mentally Disordered Offenders*, 16 Law & Hum. Beh. 399 (1992).

33. Vernon Quinsey et al., Violent Offenders: Appraising and Managing Risk 171 (1998).

34. Stephen Hart, Christine Michie, & David J. Cook, *Precision of Actuarial Risk Assessment Instruments: Evaluating the "Margins of Error" of Group v. Individual Predictions of Violence*, 190 Brit. J. Psychiat. 60 (2007).

35. Grant T. Harris, Marnie E. Rice, & Vernon Quinsey, *Shall Evidence-Based Risk Assessment be Abandoned?* 192 Brit. J. Psychiat. 154 (2008).

36. John Monahan et al., Rethinking Risk Assessment: The MacArthur Study of Mental Disorder and Violence 134 (2001).

37. *See* Melton et al., Psychological Evaluations for the Courts 319–20.

38. Fed.R.Evid. 401.

39. Fed.R.Evid. 403.

40. *See* Barefoot v. Estelle, 463 U.S. 880, 931 (Blackmun, J., dissenting); Bruce Ennis & Thomas Litwack, *Psychiatry and the Presumption of Expertise: Flipping Coins in the Courtroom*, 62 Calif. L. Rev. 693, 700–702 (1974).

41. *See* Randy Otto, *On the Ability of Mental Health Professionals to "Predict Dangerousness": A Commentary on Interpretation of the "Dangerousness" Literature*, 18 Law & Psychol. Rev. 43, 63 (1994) (indicating that "recent studies suggest that one out of every two people predicted to be violent would go on to engage in some kind of legally relevant, violent behavior").

42. Fed.R.Evid.401.

43. Slobogin, Proving the Unprovable, at 117.
44. 293 F. 1013, 1014 (D.C. Circ. 1923)
45. 509 U.S. 579, 588–89, 592–94 (1993).
46. *Post-Daubert Standards for Admissibility of Scientific and Other Expert Evidence in State Courts*, 90 American Law Reports, 453, § 2 (2001).
47. *See*, e.g., Daniel W. Shuman & Bruce D. Sales, *The Admissibility of Expert Testimony Based upon Clinical Judgment and Scientific Research*, 4 Psychol., Pub. Pol. & L. 1226, 1250 (1998); David Faust & Jay Ziskin, *The Expert Witness in Psychology and Psychiatry*, 241 Science 31, 33–35 (1988).
48. Elizabeth L. DeCoux, *The Admissibility of Unreliable Expert Testimony Offered by the Prosecution: What's Wrong with Daubert and How to Make It Right*, 2007 Utah L. Rev. 131, 161.
49. Slobogin, Proving the Unprovable, ch. 3.
50. Michael J. Saks, *The Legal and Scientific Evaluation of Forensic Science (Especially Fingerprint Expert Testimony)*, 33 Seton Hall L. Rev. 1167, 1168 (2003) (noting that as long as the fact finder is "informed about the likelihood of error in the opinions, and the court [is] satisfied that the factfinder is capable of properly adjusting the weight to be given to the evidence," such testimony should be admitted under *Daubert*).
51. Daniel A. Krauss & Bruce D. Sales, *The Effects of Clinical and Scientific Testimony on Juror Decision Making in Capital Cases*, 7 Psychol., Pub. Pol. & L. 267, 305 (2003).
52. Daniel A. Krauss et al., *The Effects of Rational and Experiential Information Processing of Expert Testimony in Death Penalty Cases*, 22 Beh. Science & L. 801, 814 (2004).
53. Shari Seidman Diamond et al., *Juror Reactions to Attorneys at Trial*, 87 J. Crim. L. & Criminol. 17, 53–54 & Table 4 (1996).
54. N.Z. Hilton et al., *Communicating Violence Risk Information to Forensic Decision Makers*, 32 Crim. Just. & Beh. 97 (2005).
55. Slobogin, Proving the Unprovable, at 123–24 (comparing impact of clinical testimony in older sex offender commitment cases and death penalty cases, where agreement was over 85%, to impact of actuarial testimony in newer sex offender cases, where agreement rates were much lower).
56. *See* Randy Borum et al., Manual for the Structured Assessment of Violence Risk in Youth (SAVRY) (2007); Leena Augimeri et al., Early Assessment Risk List for Boys: Earl-20b, Version 2 (2001).
57. Robert Hoge & Daniel Andrews, The Youth Level of Service/Case Management Inventory Manual (2006); John F. Edens et al., *Youth Psychopathy and Criminal Recidivism: A Meta-Analysis of the Psychopathy Checklist Measures*, 31 Law & Hum. Beh. 53 (2007); Alicia Leistico & Randy Salekin, Testing the Reliability and Validity of the Risk, Sophistication-Maturity, and Treatment Amenability Inventory (RST-1): An Assessment Tool for Juvenile Offenders, 2 Int'l J. Forensic Men. Health 101 (2003).
58. Lorraine Johnstone, *Assessing Violence Risk in Children: Implications for Dangerous Offender Provisions*, in Dangerous People: Policy, Prediction, and Practice (Bernadette McSherry & Patrick Keyser, eds., 2011).
59. Delbert Elliott, David S. Huizinga, & B.J. Morse, *Self-reported Violent Offending: A Descriptive Analysis of Juvenile Offenders and Their Offending Careers*, 1 J. Interpersonal Violence, 472 (1986).

60. Randy Borum, *Assessing Violence Risk in Youth*, in Principles and Practice of Child and Adolescent Forensic Mental Health 192 (Elliza P. Benedek, Peter Ash, & Charles L. Scott, eds., 2006).
61. Dante Cicchetti & Fred A. Rogosch, *A Developmental Psychopathology Perspective on Adolescence*, 70 J. Consulting & Clinical Psychol. 6 (2002).
62. *See*, e.g., Fed.R.Evid 404(a)(1).
63. Michelson v. United States, 335 U.S. 469, 476 (1948).
64. *See*, e.g., Fed.R.Evid. 404(a)(1).
65. Slobogin, Proving the Unprovable 116.
66. *See* Eric Fritsch & Craig Hemmens, *Juvenile Waiver in the United States 1979-1995: A Comparison and Analysis of State Waiver Statutes*, Juv. & Fam. Ct. J., Summer 1995, at 17, 24–31 tbls.1, 2.
67. 521 U.S. at 365–66.
68. Id. at 366.
69. *See* Bruce J. Winick, *Sex Offender Law in the 1990s: A Therapeutic Jurisprudence Analysis*, 4 Psychol., Pub. Pol. & L. 505, 531 (1998).
70. 521 U.S. at 366.
71. *See* Christopher Slobogin, *Treating Kids Right: Deconstructing and Reconstructing the Amenability to Treatment Concept*, 10 J. Contemp. Leg. Issues299, 312–13 (1999).
72. 383 U.S. 541, 566–67 (1966).
73. By 1987, thirty–nine states had adopted all or a majority of the *Kent* criteria. *See* Beth Wilbourn, Note, *Waiver of Juvenile Court Jurisdiction: National Trends and the Inadequacy of the Texas Response*, 23 Am. J. Crim. L. 633, 639 (1996). *See also* Royce S. Buckingham, *The Erosion of Juvenile Court Judge Discretion in the Transfer Decision Nationwide and in Oregon*, 29 Willamette L. Rev. 689, 694 (1993).
74. State v. Garza, 492 N.W.2d 32, 44 (Neb. 1992) ("Rehabilitation has traditionally played a key role in the treatment of young offenders. . . . Nevertheless, the concept of deterrence and the need to balance individual justice with the needs of society. . . also have a place in the juvenile justice system."); In re S.K., a Minor Child, 587 N.W.2d 740, 742–43 (S.D. 1999) (to transfer, judge need only find the juvenile is nonamenable or a threat to public safety); State v. Duncan, 250 N.W.2d 189, 194 (Minn. 1977); Commonwealth v. Waters, 483 A.2d 855, 858 (Pa. Super. Ct. 1984) (same). *But see* A Juvenile v. Commonwealth, 347 N.E.2d 677, 685 (Mass. 1976) (error to transfer solely because of dangerousness).
75. For instance, in Green v. State, 916 S.W.2d 756, 759 (Ark. 1996), the court stated, "The seriousness of an offense, when coupled with the employment of violence, is a sufficient basis for. . . trying a juvenile as an adult." *See also* State v. Campbell, 598 N.E.2d 1244, 1247 (Ohio Ct. App. 1991) (despite favorable testimony regarding amenability, waiver appropriate in light of defendant's age—sixteen—and charge of killing victim with a baseball bat); In re D.F.B. 433 N.W.2d 79 (Minn. 1988) (age plus serious offense permits waiver); Cole v. State, 913 S.W.2d 779, 783 (Ark. 1996) ("The extreme seriousness of the crimes charged. . . alone [was] clear and convincing evidence which supported the circuit court's decision" to retain adult court jurisdiction).

76. *See*, e.g., Miss. Code Ann. § 43–21–157(5)(1972 & Supp. 1993) (stating that the "seriousness of the offense" and "danger to the public" should be considered in determining whether there are "reasonable prospects of rehabilitation"); State v. Campbell, 598 N.E.2d 1244, 1247 (Ohio Ct. App. 1991) ("In determining a juvenile's amenability to rehabilitation, a juvenile court may consider the nature and seriousness of the alleged criminal act."). *See also* Hicks v. Superior Ct., 43 Cal. Rptr. 2d 269 (Ct. App. 1995); State ex rel. Lyles, No. JN90–0922, 1994 WL 811742 (Del. Fam. Ct. 1994); P.H. v. State, 504 P.2d 837, 842 (Alaska 1972).
77. *See*, e.g., In re K.J.K., 357 N.W.2d 117, 119–120 (Minn. Ct. App. 1984) (transfer held permissible after a brief listing of record); In re T.M., 393 S.E.2d 448, 449 (Ga. Ct. App. 1990) (same); Armer v. State, 773 P.2d 757 (Okla. Crim. App. 1989) (despite evidence of rehabilitative potential, transfer was permissible where rape had been forceful and violent and where juvenile had had prior contacts with juvenile system, some involving inappropriate sexual and violent behavior); MMT v. Dist. Ct., 637 P.2d 876 (Okla. Crim. App. 1981); D.R.D. v. State, 767 P.2d 207, 211 (Alaska Ct. App. 1989) (noting that "dangerousness is the converse of amenability to rehabilitation" and that a person can be "dangerous" simply because of "repeated criminality.").
78. M.L.S. v. State, 805 P.2d 665 (Okla. Crim. App. 1991).
79. *See* State v. Harris, 494 N.W.2d 619, 625 (S.D. 1993) ("Neither the statute nor our decisions have required the court to find that the juvenile unsuccessfully exhausted the resources of this state's juvenile justice rehabilitation programs prior to transferring proceedings to adult court."); Commonwealth v. Berry, 648 N.E.2d 732 (Mass. 1995) (past treatment of juvenile was a failure because juvenile "had been hospitalized with a diagnosis of conduct disorder [and] drug abuse [and]... had been enrolled in a drug rehabilitation program" yet had reverted to his former antisocial behavior after treatment); People v. Lyons, 513 N.W.2d 170 (Mich. Ct. App. 1994) (describing in brief several failed treatment attempts, most of them aborted by the juvenile's escape); C.H. v. State, 252 S.E.2d 22, 23 (Ga. Ct. App. 1979) (listing treatment failures). For an example of a good effort to evaluate past treatment attempts, *see* J.A.G. v. Guerrero, 552 N.W.2d 317, 321–22 (N.D. 1996).
80. *See* Kirk Heilbrun et al. *A National Survey of U.S. Statutes on Juvenile Transfer: Implications for Policy and Practice*, 15 Beh. Sci. & L. 125, 128–43 (1997) (indicating that at least five states use this type of language); *see also* Kan. Stat. Ann. § 38–1636(e)(6) (1993 & Supp. 1997); State v. Buelow, 587 A.2d 948, 953 (Vt. 1990) (indicating that "maturity of the individual" is a relevant factor).
81. *See* Lawrence Winner et al., *The Transfer of Juveniles to Criminal Court: Does It Make a Difference?* 43 Crime & Delinq. 557 (1997) (a comparison of 2,800 youths transferred to adult court and a same-sized sample identified higher short-term and long-term recidivism rates among the transferred youths); Jeffrey Fagan, *The Comparative Advantages of Juvenile Versus Criminal Court Sanction on Recidivism Among Adolescent Felony Offenders,* 18 Law & Policy 77, 94–95 (2000) (concluding that recidivism rate for juveniles prosecuted for robbery in criminal court is twice that of those tried in juvenile court, regardless of sentence type or severity).
82. Jeffrey A. Fagan, *This Will Hurt Me More Than It Hurts You: Social and Legal Consequences of Criminalizing Delinquency*, 16 Notre Dame J. Law, Ethics & Public Policy28 (2002). *See also* Randi Hjalmarsson, *Juvenile Jails: A Path to the Straight and Narrow or to Hardened Criminality?*, 52 J. L. & Economics, 779 (2009)

(juveniles incarcerated in juvenile facilities have lower propensities to commit crime than those transferred to adult court).

83. Franklin E. Zimring & Jeffry Fagan, *Transfer Policy and Law Reform*, in The Changing Borders of Juvenile Justice: Transfer of Adolescents to the Criminal Court 407, 410 (Franklin E. Zimring & Jeffry Fagan, eds., 2000).

84. Heilbrun et al., *A National Survey*, at 128–43 (listing over 25 states that use *Kent's* language). See also Ind. Code Ann. § 31–6–2–1.5 (Michie 1997) (the court must determine that the juvenile is beyond rehabilitation under the juvenile justice system); R.C. § 2151.26(A) (c)(i) (requiring the court to find that the juvenile "is not amenable to care or rehabilitation. . . in any facility designed for the care, supervision, and rehabilitation of delinquent children").

85. State v. Simpson, 836 S.W.2d 75 (Mo. Ct. App. 1992).

86. In re R.M., 648 S.W.2d 406 (Tex. Ct. App. 1983). *See also* Commonwealth v. Cessna, 537 A.2d 834 (Pa. 1988) (juvenile did not show that there was a juvenile facility that would accept him).

87. Stanford v. Commonwealth, 734 S.W.2d 781, 792 (Ky. 1987).

88. *See*, e.g., Dillard v. State, 623 P.2d 1294 (Idaho 1981) (transfer permissible because contract with California to provide juvenile treatment had expired and there were no placement contracts with other states); P.K.M. v. State, 780 P.2d 395, 399 (Alaska Ct. App. 1989) (no obligation to look beyond state borders).

89. In justifying its decision, the majority emphasized that *Hendricks* was placed in a unit segregated from the general prison population and received some treatment. *See* 521 U.S. 346, 367–68.

90. 531 U.S. 250, 265 (2001).

91. This theory was first proposed by Roy G. Spece, in *Preserving the Right to Treatment: A Critical Assessment and Constructive Development of Constitutional Right to Treatment Theories*, 20 Ariz. L. Rev. 1, 33–46 (1978). It derives from the Supreme Court's First Amendment cases holding that state interference with the freedoms of speech and press must be carried out in the least drastic manner possible. *See*, e.g., Shelton v. Tucker, 364 U.S. 479, 488 (1960). Surely, liberty is a more fundamental interest than speech and press.

92. 457 U.S. 307 (1982).

93. *See* 457 U.S. at 319 (holding "respondent's liberty interests require the State to provide minimally adequate or reasonable training to ensure. . . freedom from undue restraint").

94. Eric S. Janus and Wayne A. Logan, *Substantive Due Process and the Involuntary Confinement of Sexually Violent Predators*, 35 Conn. L. Rev. 319 (2003).

95. Id. at 357.

96. Id. at 376–77.

97. In Haziel v. United States, 404 F.2d 1275, 1280 (D.C. Cir. 1968). *See also* Welfare of C. v. State, 225 N.W.2d 245 (Minn. 1975) (remanding for a determination as to whether, if no treatment program for the juvenile was available, it was feasible to put together such a program and, if so, why the Department had failed to do so).

98. Id.

99. See, e.g., Morgan v. Sproat, 432 F. Supp. 1130 (S.D. Miss. 1977); Pena v. N.Y. State Div. for Youth, 419 F. Supp. 203 (S.D.N.Y. 1976); Inmates of Boys' Training Sch. v. Affleck, 346 F. Supp. 1354 (D.R.I. 1972); Morales v. Turman, 364 F. Supp. 166 (E.D. Tex. 1973).

100. *See*, e.g., Lane v. Jones, 257 S.E.2d 525, 526–27 (Ga. 1979); State v. Martin, 530 N.W.2d 420 (Wis. Ct. App. 1995) (same). *See also* State v. A.L. 638 A.2d 814, 818 (N.J. Super. Ct. App. Div. 1994) ("Since statutes governing transfer from juvenile court do not involve a fundamental right or suspect classification, they survive challenges based on due process or equal protection grounds if they are not arbitrary and bear a rational relationship to a legitimate state interest."); Cox v. United States, 473 F.2d 334, 337 (4th Cir.), cert. denied, 414 U.S. 869 (1973) (same); *cf.* Marshall v. United States, 414 U.S. 417, 428 (1974) (upholding exclusion of addicts with two or more felony convictions from discretionary rehabilitation under Narcotic Addict Rehabilitation Act of 1966 because reasonable for Congress to conclude that defendants with prior felonies would be less treatable).

101. *See* Christopher Slobogin, Ralph Reisner, & Arti Rai, Law & the Mental Health System: Civil and Criminal Aspects 1131–88 (5th ed. 2009) (recounting the impact of the right to treatment litigation beginning with Wyatt v. Stickney and other litigation pushing for community alternatives to hospitalization).

102. *See*, e.g., Va. Code Ann. § 16.1–278.8(3) (Michie 1995). A number of experimental programs have encountered difficulties enrolling parents of high-risk youth. Karol L. Kumpfer & Charles W. Turner, *The Social Ecology Model of Adolescent Substance Abuse: Implications for Prevention*, 25 Int'l J. Addictions 435 (1990–91).

103. At common law, parents were not liable for the torts of their children. Today in virtually every state they may be liable for the wilful and wanton acts of their children, but not for negligent acts. Samuel M. Davis et al., Children in the Legal System 108 (2d ed. 1997).

104. Kirk Heilbrun, *Prediction Versus Management Models Relevant to Risk Assessment: The Importance of Legal Decision-Making Context*, 21 L. & Hum. Beh. 347 (1997); Donald A. Andrews & James Bonta, The Psychology of Criminal Conduct (4th ed., 2006).

105. Heilbrun, *Prediction Versus Management Models*; Andrews & Bonta, The Psychology of Criminal Conduct.

106. Nancy G. Guerra et al., *What Works: Best Practices with Juvenile Offenders*, in Treating the Juvenile Offender 79–102 (Robert D. Hoge et al., eds., 2008).

107. Peter Henry Rossi et al., Evaluation: A Systematic Approach (7th ed. 2004).

108. *See* Mark R. Fondacaro & Lauren G. Fasig, *Judging Juvenile Responsibility: A Social Ecological Perspective*, in Handbook of Children, Culture, and Violence 355–73 (Nancy E. Dowd, Dorothy G. Singer, & Robin Fretwell Wilson, eds., 2006).

109. Christopher Slobogin & Mark Fondacaro, *Rethinking Deprivations of Liberty: Possible Contributions from Therapeutic and Ecological Jurisprudence*, 18 Beh. Sciences & L. 499–516 (2000).

110. For one description of this distinction, *see* Kirk Heilbrun, *Prediction Versus Management Models Relevant to Risk Assessment.*

111. *See generally* Rosalind E.H. Catchpole and Heather M. Gretton, *The Predictive Validity of Risk Assessment with Violent Young Offenders: A 1-Year Examination of Criminal Outcome,* 30 Crim. Just. & Beh. 688 (2003).

112. *See generally* John Monahan et al., Rethinking Risk Assessment: The MacArthur Study of Mental Disorder and Violence 163 (2001) (showing a correlation of .12 between race and violence).

113. Terence P. Thornberry, *Sentencing Disparities in the Juvenile Justice System*, 70 J. Crim. L. & Criminology 164 (1979).
114. For instance, given their social and economic status in society, black youths may become "more deeply embedded in and dependent upon the gangs and the illicit economy that flourish in their neighborhoods," which might suggest particular kinds of interventions. Delbert S. Elliot, *Serious Violent Offenders: Onset, Developmental Course, and Termination*, 32 Criminology 1, 19 (1994).
115. Barry Krisberg & James F. Austin, Reinventing Juvenile Justice 129–30 (1993) ("Lack of ethnic balance and Anglo–American dominance of high–level juvenile justice jobs contribute to the overrepresentation of certain minority groups in secure juvenile justice facilities… . Minority youth being processed in the juvenile justice system, as well as their parents, do not always understand how the system works."). *Cf.* Sandra T. Azar & Corina L. Benjet, *A Cognitive Perspective on Ethnicity, Race, and Termination of Parental Rights*, 18 Law & Hum. Beh. 249 (1994) (detailing ways in which cultural differences might affect interviewers' ability to discover relevant information about abuse and neglect).
116. *See* Christopher Slobogin, Mark R. Fondacaro, & Jennifer Woolard, *A Prevention Model of Juvenile Justice: The Promise of Kansas v. Hendricks for Children*, 1999 Wis. L. Rev.185 (1999).
117. Astrid Birgden, *Therapeutic Jurisprudence and Offender Rights: A Normative Stance is Required*, 78 Rev. Jur. U.P.R. 53 (2009) (outlining a means of balancing community and offender interests).
118. *See generally*, Punishing Juveniles: Principle and Critique (Ido Weijers & Antony Duff, eds., 2002) (book-length treatment of the advantages and disadvantages of applying restorative justice to the juvenile justice system).
119. *See* Fondacaro et al., *Administrative Law, A New Frontier* (arguing that administrative rather than judicial approaches are better suited for implementing forward-looking policy objectives that draw on social and behavioral science as a guide).
120. Elizabeth S. Scott & Laurence Steinberg, Rethinking Juvenile Justice: Adolescence Development and the Regulation of Youth Crime 261–62 (2008).
121. *See* David A. Harris, *The Criminal Defense Lawyer in the Juvenile Justice System*, 26 U. Tol. L. Rev. 751, 756–61 (1995), from which this case is taken. Even in a technically rehabilitation-oriented system, Charles was sentenced to training camp at the time recounted in the excerpt and eventually ended up in an adult detention center.
122. Franklin E. Zimring, Twentieth Century Fund Task Force on Sentencing Policy Toward Young Offenders: Confronting Youth Crime (1978).
123. Id. at 84.
124. Id. at 89.
125. Id.
126. Id. at 90.
127. Id. at 97.
128. Department of Health & Human Services, Youth Violence: A Report of the Surgeon General 48 (2001) (describing study conducted by D.S. Elliot, D. Huizinga, & S. Menard, Multiple Problem Youth: Delinquency, Substance Use, and Mental Health Problems (1989)).
129. Id. (describing study by P.E. Tracy & K. Kempf-Leonard, Continuity and Discontinuity in Criminal Careers (1996)).

Chapter 5: The Procedural Implications of Social Science Research

1. *See*, e.g., Harling v. United States, 295 F.2d 161, 164 (D.C. Cir. 1961); Juvenile Delinquency, Hearings before the Subcommittee to Investigate Juvenile Delinquency of the Senate Committee on the Judiciary, 86th Cong., 1st Sess. (1959-1960); Joel F. Handler, *The Juvenile Court and the Adversary System: Problems of Function and Form*, 1965 Wis. L. Rev. 7, 7 (1965).
2. Kent v. United States, 383 U.S. 541, 556 (1966).
3. *See*, e.g., Gary B. Melton, *Taking Gault Seriously: Toward a New Juvenile Court*, 68 Nebraska Law Review 146, 167 (1989); Martin R. Gardner, *Punitive Juvenile Justice: Some Observations on a Recent Trend*, 10 Int'l J. L. & Psychiat. 129, 147 (1987); Irene M. Rosenberg, *The Constitutional Rights of Children Charged with Crime: Proposal for a Return to the Not So Distant Past*, 27 UCLA L. Rev. 656, 720–21 (1980).
4. Janet E. Ainsworth, *Re-imagining Childhood and Reconstructing the Legal Order: The Case for Abolishing the Juvenile Court*, 69 N. C. L. Rev. 1083, 1120 (1991); Barry C. Feld, *Abolish the Juvenile Court: Youthfulness, Criminal Responsibility and Sentencing Policy*, 88 J. Crim. L. & Criminol. 68, 97 (1998).
5. Samuel M. Davis et al., Children in the Legal System 745 (1997).
6. Julian Mack, *The Juvenile Court*, 23 Harv. L. Rev. 104, 120 (1909).
7. Gideon v. Wainwright, 372 U.S. 335, 342 (1963).
8. Pointer v. Texas, 380 U.S. 400, 403 (1965) (Sixth Amendment right to confront and cross-examine witnesses); Malloy v. Hogan, 378 U.S. 1, 6 (1964) (Fifth Amendment privilege against self-incrimination).
9. 383 U.S. 541 (1966).
10. 387 U.S. 1 (1967).
11. 397 U.S. 358 (1970).
12. Of course, there is also *Breed v. Jones*, which applied the Double Jeopardy Clause to juvenile delinquency proceedings, with Chief Justice Burger himself writing that "it is simply too late in the day to conclude. . . that a juvenile is not put in jeopardy at a [delinquency] proceeding." 421 U.S. 519, 529 (1975). However, this decision is not "procedural" in the sense we are using that term, since it does not have to do with the adjudication process. Furthermore, within three years of *Breed* the Court upheld a state procedure that allowed prosecutors in juvenile court to appeal referee decisions acquitting a child of delinquency charges, a decision that significantly undermines the thrust of *Breed.* Swisher v. Brady, 438 U.S. 204 (1978).
13. 383 U.S. 541, 556 (1966).
14. Id. at 561–62.
15. 387 U.S. 1, 21 (1967).
16. Id. at 72.
17. 397 U.S. at 366.
18. Id. at 375 (Harlan, J., concurring).
19. Id. at 376 (Burger, C.J., dissenting).
20. 403 U.S. 528 (1971).
21. Id. at 533–34 (quoting Kent v. United States, 383 U.S. 541, 562 (1966)). The Court continued: "The Court has insisted that these successive decisions do not spell the doom of the juvenile court system or even deprive it of its 'informality,

flexibility, or speed.'" Id. at 534 (quoting In re Winship, 397 U.S. 358, 366 (1970)).
22. Id. at 543.
23. Id. at 543, 545, 550.
24. Id. at 547.
25. Indeed, a number of articles, mostly by students, declare that *Gault* was based on the Sixth Amendment. *See*, e.g., David T. Huang, *"Less Unequal Footing": State Courts'* Per Se *Rules for Juvenile Waivers During Interrogations and the Case for Their Implementation*, 86 Cornell L. Rev. 437, 445 (2001).
26. Henry J. Friendly, *Some Kind of Hearing*, 123 U. Pa. L. Rev. 1267, 1316 (1975).
27. 397 U.S. 254 (1970).
28. 424 U.S. 319 (1976).
29. *See* William F. Fox, Jr., Understanding Administrative Law 142, 144 (1997).
30. Londoner v. City of Denver, 210 U.S. 373, 386 (1908).
31. 341 U.S. 123, 162–63 (1951) (Frankfurter, J., concurring).
32. 397 U.S. at 264.
33. Id. at 266–67.
34. Id. at 267–71.
35. This phrase was first used by Judge Friendly and has been adopted by a number of commentators. *See* Jerry L. Mashaw, Due Process in the Administrative State 8–9 (1985).
36. Richard J. Pierce, *The Due Process Counterrevolution of the 1990s?*, 96 Colum. L. Rev. 1973, 1980 (1996).
37. 424 U.S. at 335.
38. Id. at 340–41; 343–44; 348.
39. *See generally* Jerry L. Mashaw, *The Supreme Court's Due Process Calculus for Administrative Adjudication in Mathews v. Eldridge: Three Factors in Search of a Theory of Value*, 44 U. Chicago L. Rev. 28 (1976).
40. 419 U.S. 565 (1975).
41. Id. at 582–83.
42. Parham v. J.R., 442 U.S. 584 (1979).
43. Id. at 605–6.
44. Id. at 609.
45. Id. at 613.
46. 442 U.S. at 606–7.
47. Although the average length of civil commitment has shortened considerably in the past decade, perhaps 25 percent of those committed stay in the hospital for over four years. *See* Christopher Slobogin, Arti Rai, & Ralph Reisner, Law and the Mental Health System: Civil and Criminal Aspects 852 (5th ed. 2009).
48. The majority in *Parham* did recognize that juveniles who are committed are entitled to periodic review, 442 U.S. at 617, and Justice Brennan argued that such review should be more adversarial in nature. Id. at 633–34 (Brennan, J., concurring in part and dissenting in part). However, the majority refused to address this issue in any greater detail, stating simply "we have no basis for determining whether the review procedures of the various hospitals are adequate to provide the process called for or what process might be required if a child contests his confinement by requesting a release." Id. at 617. Thus, as it stands, the staff physician procedure that is adequate for initial admission may be adequate for periodic review.

49. *See* John Thibaut et al., *Procedural Justice as Fairness*, 26 Stanford L. Rev. 1271, 1289 (1974).
50. John Thibaut & Laurens Walker, Procedural Justice: A Psychological Analysis (1975).
51. *See* E. Allan Lind & Tom R. Tyler, The Social Psychology of Procedural Justice 3 (1988).
52. Id. at 3–4.
53. *See,* e.g., Thibaut & Walker, Procedural Justice, at 80 (reporting a study finding that adversary representation produced "greater satisfaction of the involved parties with the judgment, quite independently of both the favorableness of the judgment and the participants' beliefs concerning the issue under adjudication").
54. Lind & Tyler, Social Psychology, at 26.
55. Thibaut & Walker, Procedural Justice, at 67.
56. John Thibaut & Laurens Walker, A Theory of Procedure, 66 Calif. L. Rev. 541, 546 (1978).
57. Id. at 547. *See generally*, Thibaut & Walker, Procedural Justice, at 118.
58. Thibaut & Walker, Procedural Justice, ch. 8 (finding respondents in four countries—the United States, France, West Germany, and Great Britain—all preferred the adversarial process to the inquisitorial process).
59. John Thibaut et al., *Adversary Presentation and Bias in Legal Decisionmaking*, 86 Harv. L. Rev. 386, 388 (1972).
60. For a summary of the criticism of Thibaut and Walker's use of "pure" adversarial and inquisitorial models, *see* Blair H. Sheppard, *Justice Is No Simple Matter: Case for Elaborating Our Model of Procedural Fairness*, 49 J. Personality & Social Psychol. 953, 953–55 (1985).
61. Rebecca A. Anderson & Amy L. Otto, *Perceptions of Fairness in the Justice System: A Cross-Cultural Comparison*, 31 Social Behavior & Personality 557 (2003); Kwok Leung, *Cross-Cultural Study of Procedural Fairness and Disputing Behavior*, 53 J. Personality & Social Psychol. 898, 903 (1987).
62. Lind & Tyler, Social Psychology, at 117.
63. Sheppard, Justice Is No Simple Matter, at 956–57.
64. *See* Lind & Tyler, Social Psychology, at 87.
65. Norman Poythress et al., *Procedural Preferences, Perceptions of Fairness and Compliance with Outcomes: A Study of Alternatives to the Standard Adversary Trial Procedure*, 18 Law & Hum. Beh. 361 (1994).
66. Id. at 373.
67. Id. at 375.
68. Donna Shestowsky, *Procedural Preferences in Alternative Dispute Resolution: A Close, Modern Look at an Old Idea*, 10 Psychol., Pub. Pol. & L. 211 (2004).
69. Id. at 240.
70. Tom R. Tyler, *Procedural Justice Research*, 1 Soc. Just. Res. 41, 45 (1987) ("Often,... litigants' conceptions of fair process differ from the need to have a formal trial and can be accommodated in informal dispute resolution settings."); William Austin et al., *Effect of Mode of Adjudication, Presence of Defense Counsel, and Favorability of Verdict on Observers' Evaluation of a Criminal Trial*, 11 J. Applied Social Psychol. 281, 297 (1981).
71. The scenario in Shestowsky's study involved damage to an $800 bicycle, while Poythress's hypothetical involved a psychiatric malpractice suit, posed to mental

health professionals, and Sheppard questioned undergraduates and airport passengers. However, other studies producing similar results have been more closely related to the criminal setting. *See* Leung, *Cross-Cultural Study* (using a reckless driving scenario resulting in physical injury in a study finding no strong preference for adversarial over mediation procedures); Austin et al., *Effect of Mode of Adjudication* (survey of criminal defendants finding dissatisfaction with adversarial process when outcome is unfavorable).

72. Barton Poulson, *A Third Voice: A Review of Empirical Research on the Psychological Outcomes of Restorative Justice*, 2003 Utah L. Rev. 167, 179–80 table 1.

73. Id. at 181–93 tables 2, 3, 4, 6, and 9.

74. Id. at 179–93 tables 1–9. Many of the studies described in this meta-analysis involved random assignment. Id. at 169–70. In some, however, parties chose mediation or refused it; the former group therefore may have been predisposed to see mediation as beneficial.

75. Lind & Tyler, Social Psychology, at 19.

76. Thibaut & Walker, Procedural Justice, at 547.

77. Id. at 556.

78. Id. at 41–53; *see also* John Thibaut et al., *Adversary Presentation*, at 397.

79. Thibaut & Walker, Procedural Justice, at 41–53.

80. Lind & Tyler, Social Psychology, at 114.

81. Thibaut & Walker, Procedural Justice, at 28–40.

82. Blair H. Sheppard & Neil Vidmar, *Adversary Pretrial Procedures and Testimonial Evidence: Effects of Lawyer's Role and Machiavellianism*, 39 J. Personality & Social Psychol. 320, 322 (1980).

83. Id. at 329.

84. Neil Vidmar & N.M. Laird, *Adversary Social Roles: Their Effects on Witnesses' Communication of Evidence and the Assessment of Adjudicators*, 44 J. Personality & Social Psychol. 888 (1983). This study did not involve a witness testifying for the other side, which might have reduced the biasing effect.

85. Richard A. Rosen, *Disciplinary Sanctions Against Prosecutors for Brady Violations: A Paper Tiger*, 65 N. C. L. Rev. 693, 697–703, 720–30 (1987) (cataloguing scores of instances in which prosecutors failed to turn over exculpatory evidence but only nine cases in which discipline was considered and only two which resulted in serious sanction).

86. *See* Harold J. Rothwax, Guilty: The Collapse of Criminal Justice 141 (1996) ("Given the probability that the defendant is guilty, the defense attorney knows that the defendant will win only if counsel is successful in preventing the truth from being disclosed—or, failing that, misleading the jury once it is disclosed. So, when the defendant is guilty, the defense attorney's role is to prevent, distort, and mislead." (emphasis omitted)).

87. Mirjan Damaska, *Presentation of Evidence and Factfinding Precision*, 123 U. Pa. L. Rev. 1083, 1093–94 n.22 (1975).

88. Id. at 1088–89 (In a nonadversary system, "the parties are not supposed to try to affect, let alone to prepare, the witnesses' testimony at trial. 'Coaching' witnesses comes dangerously close to various criminal offenses of interfering with the administration of justice.").

89. Geoffrey C. Hazard, Jr. et al., The Law and Ethics of Lawyering 469 (2d ed. 1994) (citing studies showing that 90–95% of all civil and criminal cases are settled rather than tried).

90. *See generally* Mirjan Damaska, *Evidentiary Barriers to Conviction and Two Models of Criminal Procedure: A Comparative Study*, 121 U. Pa. L. Rev. 506, 582 (1973) ("An official inquiry must. . . disregard possible interparty arrangements, and pursue the search for the real truth.").

91. Gerald E. Lynch, *Screening Versus Plea Bargaining: Exactly What Are We Trading Off?*, 55 Stanford L. Rev. 1399, 1404 (2003) ("The defining characteristic of the existing 'plea bargaining' system is that it is an informal, administrative, inquisitorial process of adjudication, internal to the prosecutor's office—in absolute distinction from a model of adversarial determination of fact and law before a neutral judicial decision maker.").

92. *See* Stephanos Bibas, *Brady v. Maryland: From Adversarial Gamesmanship Toward the Search for Innocence?* in Criminal Procedure Stories 146 (Carol Steiker ed., 2006).

93. Gary B. Melton et al., Psychological Evaluations for the Courts: A Handbook for Mental Health Professionals and Lawyers 480 (3d ed. 2007).

94. *See* Jeffrey Fagan & Tom R. Tyler, *Legal Socialization of Children and Adolescents*, 18 Soc. Just. Res. 217, 217 (2005).

95. In re L.M. 186 P.3d 164, 170 (Kan. 2008).

96. Godinez v. Moran, 509 U.S. 389 (1993).

97. Richard J. Bonnie, *The Competence of Criminal Defendants*, 10 Beh. Sci. & L. 291 (1992).

98. For a summary, *see* N. Dickon Repucci et al., *Challenging Juvenile Transfer: Faulty Assumptions and Misguided Policies*, in Children as Victims, Witnesses and Offenders 295, 299–304 (Bette L. Bottoms and Cynthia Nadjowski, eds., 2009) (hereinafter Children as Victims, Witnesses and Offenders). *See* also Elizabeth S. Scott & Thomas Grisso, *Developmental Incompetence, Due Process, and Juvenile Justice Policy*, 83 N.C. L. Rev. 793, 797 (2005); Allison Redlich et al., *The Police Interrogation of Children and Adolescents*, in Interrogations, Confessions, and Entrapment 107 (G. Daniel Lassiter, ed., 2004).

99. *See*, e.g., Wheeler v. United States, 159 U.S. 523 (1895).

100. Faretta v. California, 422 U.S. 806 (1975).

101. Currently most states permit juveniles to waive counsel, while others prohibit it or limit it substantially. Ellen Marrus, *Best Interests Equals Zealous Advocacy: A Not So Radical View of Holistic Representation for Children Accused of Crime*, 62 Md. L. Rev. 288, 316–17 (2003).

102. Griffin v. California, 380 U.S. 609 (1965), held that the right to silence is unconstitutionally burdened by prosecutorial or judicial comment on the defendant's failure to take the stand.

103. Allision D. Redlich and Saul M. Kassin, *Police Interrogation and False Confessions: The Inherent Risk of Youth*, in Children as Victims, Witnesses and Offenders, at 275–94.

104. *See* Redlich & Kassin, *Police Interrogation* (summarizing studies).

105. Jessica R. Meyer & N. Dickon Repucci, *Police Practices and Perceptions Regarding Juvenile Interrogation and Interrogative Suggestibility*, 25 Beh. Sci. & L. 1 (2007).

106. Indeed, the Supreme Court has strongly suggested that the Miranda warnings are not required by the due process clause, but only by the Fifth Amendment. *See* Dickerson v. United States, 530 U.S. 428 (2000).

107. H. Richard Uviller, *The Tilted Playing Field: Is Criminal Justice Unfair?* 201–2 (1999); *Richard A. Posner, An Economic Approach to the Law of Evidence*, 51 Stanford L. Rev. 1477, 1527 (1999).

108. 478 U.S. 364 (1986).
109. *Self-Incrimination Rights Conflicts with Treatment, Home Release Programs*, 4 Correctional Law Reporter 1 (1992); *see also* Stephanos Bibas & Richard A. Bierschback, *Integrating Remorse and Apology into Criminal Procedure*, 114 Yale L. J. 85, 148 (2004).
110. *See* Christopher Slobogin, *An Empirically-Based of American and European Regulatory Approaches to Police Investigation*, 22 Michigan J. Int'l L. 423, 442–44 (2001).
111. The Honorable Anthony J. Sciolino, *The Changing Role of the Family Court Judge: New Ways of Stemming the Tide*, 3 Cardozo Public Law, Policy & Ethics J. 395, 400 (2005).
112. *Cf.* Lind & Tyler, Social Psychology, at 114 (countering Thibaut & Walker's argument that the adversarial process enhances distributive justice through helping "disadvantaged" litigants by noting that the "disadvantage" is often simply a "paucity of evidence," not social or economic disadvantage).
113. 5 John Henry Wigmore, Evidence in Trials at Common Law § 1376 (3d ed. 1940)..
114. *See* Roger C. Park, *Adversarial Influences on the Interrogation of Trial Witnesses*, in Adversarial v. Inquisitorial Justice: Psychological Perspectives on Criminal Justice Systems 131, 145–63, 166 (Peter J. van Koppen & Steven D. Penrod eds., 2004).
115. Margaret C. Stevenson et al., *Understanding Adult Perceptions of Juvenile Offenders, in* Children as Victims, Witnesses and Offenders, at 349–368. *See generally*, Dan Simon, *Criminal Trials: What Are They Good For?* 64 Vand. L. Rev. 1 (2011) (describing courtroom decisionmaking distortion due to racial prejudice, judgments of demeanor and the decision maker's cognitive process).
116. Melinda G. Schmidt et al., *Effectivness of Participation as a Defendant: The Attorney-Juvenile Client Relationship*, 21 Beh. Sci. & L. 175, 192 (2003).
117. Paul Holland, Developing Effective (and Reflective) Practitioners in Problem-Solving Courts (2009).
118. Melton et al., Psychological Evaluations for the Courts, at 480 (footnote omitted).
119. William Ayers, A Kind and Just Parent 29 (1997) (describing the Cook County Juvenile Court, where at any given moment 1500 to 2000 cases are pending and the average time given to any case is 12 minutes, with the typical judge making one hundred decisions a day).
120. Emily Buss, *Rethinking the Connection Between Developmental Science and Juvenile Justice*, 76 U. Chi L. Rev. 493, 512 (2009).
121. Id. at 511.
122. 424 U.S. at 322.
123. Allison R. Shiff & David B. Wexler, *Teen Court: A Therapeutic Jurisprudence Perspective*, in Law in a Therapeutic Key: Developments in Therapeutic Jurisprudence 287, 290–95 (David B. Wexler & Bruce J. Winick eds., 1996).
124. Gwen Robinson and Joanna Shapland, *Reducing Recidivism: A Task for Restorative Justice?*, 48 British J. Criminol. 337 (2008); John Braithwaite, *Restorative Justice: Assessing Optimistic and Pessimistic Accounts*, in 25 Crime and Justice: A Review of Research 20–28 (Michael Tonry ed., 1999).
125. *See generally*, Tamar R. Birckhead, *Toward a Theory of Procedural Justice for Juveniles*, 57 Buffalo L. Rev. 1447, 1449 (2009) (discussing judicial adoption of this theory).

126. The quid pro quo theory has routinely been advanced as a rationale for the informal process provided in juvenile court and in civil commitment proceedings. *See* Morgan v. Sproat, 432 F.Supp. 1130, 1136 (S.D.Miss.1977) (collecting cases).

Chapter 6: The Future of (Juvenile) Justice

1. Another such area is enforcement of child support laws. *See* Mark R. Fondacaro & Dennis P. Stolle, *Revoking Motor Vehicle and Professional Licenses for Purposes of Child Support Enforcement: Constitutional Challenges and Policy Implications*, 5 Cornell J. Law & Pub. Policy 355 (1996).
2. Mark R. Fondacaro, Dennis P. Stolle, & Brian L. Wilcox, *Psycholegal Research in Non-Judicial Settings: Administrative Law, a New Frontier.* Paper Presented at the Biennial Meeting of the American Psychology- Law Society (1996).
3. *See* Michael C. Dorf & Charles F. Sabel, *Drug Treatment Courts and Emergent Experimentalist Government*, 53 Vand. L. Rev. 831 (2000).
4. *See generally*, Rachel Barkow, *The Court of Life and Death: The Two Tracks of Constitutional Sentencing Law and the Case for Uniformity*, 107 Mich. L.Rev. 1145 (2009).
5. Gottfredson and Hirsch argue that almost all crime, adult and juvenile, is impulsive, an observation that might form the jurisprudential basis for a preventive regime in the adult context. Michael R. Gottfredson & Travis Hirschi, A General Theory of Crime 108-09(1990) ("The level of self-control, or criminality, distinguishes offenders from nonoffenders, and the degree of its presence or absence can be established before (and after) criminal acts have been committed.").
6. *See* Jeremy Travis et al., From Prison to Home: The Dimensions and Consequences of Prisoner Reentry 5 (2001), available at www.urban.org/UploadedPDF/from_prison_to_home.pdf.
7. Jennifer Woolard et al., *Informing Juvenile Justice Policy: Directions for Behavioral Science Research*, 25 Law & Hum. Beh. 13, 15 (2001).

Index

CPSIA information can be obtained
at www.ICGtesting.com
Printed in the USA
BVHW042156280520
580533BV00007B/41

9 780199 778355